SEEKING BIPARTISANSHIP

Seeking Bipartisanship

MY LIFE IN POLITICS

Ray LaHood
with Frank H. Mackaman

**Cambria Politics, Institutions, and
Public Policy in America (PIPPA) Series**
Editors: Scott A. Frisch and Sean Q. Kelly

CAMBRIA
PRESS

Amherst, New York

Requests for permission should be directed to:
permissions@cambriapress.com, or mailed to:
Cambria Press
University Corporate Centre, 100 Corporate Parkway, Suite 128
Amherst, New York 14226, U.S.A.

Cover image of DOT portrait of Ray LaHood, reproduced with
permission from the Department of Transportation and Simmie Knox.

Library of Congress Cataloging-in-Publication Data

LaHood, Ray, 1945-

Seeking bipartisanship : my life in politics /
Ray LaHood ; with Frank H. Mackaman.

pages cm. -- (Cambria politics, institutions, and public policy in america series)

Includes bibliographical references.

ISBN 978-1-60497-905-3 (alk. paper)

1. LaHood, Ray, 1945- 2. United States. Congress. House--Biography.
3. Cabinet officers--United States--Biography. 4. United States--
Politics and government--1989- I. Mackaman, Frank H. II. Title.

E901.1.L35A3 2015

352.2'93092--dc23

[B]

2015024709

TABLE OF CONTENTS

List of Figures

INTRODUCTION

THE CALL

Midmorning on Wednesday, December 17, 2008, my Blackberry rang at my home in Peoria. Rahm Emanuel, Barack Obama's chief of staff–designate, asked, "Ray, will you take Transportation?"

"Absolutely," I replied without hesitation. I was thrilled. I had already decided to accept a Cabinet post in the Obama administration, even without knowing which one. His would be a historic presidency. No need to think about it for 24 hours. No reason to equivocate.

So began the last chapter of my public life, a career spent mostly in Congress but capped now by service to the new president.

Of course, that phone call did not come out of thin air. Seven weeks earlier, on October 28, 2008, the Wednesday before the presidential election, Rahm had called me: "Obama wants me to be his White House chief of staff."

"Don't you think you ought to wait for the election next Tuesday before you start planning your next job?" I kidded.

He asked for my reaction, and I told him it was a terrible idea. "You have a young family. You will work 16-hour days. You'll miss your kids growing up." I reminded him that he had planned a career in the House of Representatives that could lead right to Speaker. Why give that up? I knew my advice was not what my friend wanted to hear.

Without replying, Rahm hung up.

The Thursday following the election, I called the chief-of-staff-to-be to congratulate him. He told me the Obama team was thinking about the Cabinet and wondered where my retirement planning stood. Taking the hint, I told him I would have "some interest" in serving in the new administration. At that point, I played my cards close to the vest, not wanting to appear too eager. I was testing Rahm's temperature to see how serious the president-elect's team was about me. I had my answer immediately.

"What would you be interested in?" Rahm asked.

"I certainly would be qualified for Agriculture."

If he had said to me, "I don't think this is in the cards," I would have traveled a different path. But he didn't. His interest was genuine.

Rahm warned, "Don't say anything to anybody; don't tell anybody; don't talk to the press; don't talk to anybody—I have to run this by our little group." I assumed the little group consisted of David Axelrod, Robert Gibbs, David Plouffe, Joe Biden, Valerie Jarrett, and the president-elect.

I broke my pledge of secrecy only with my wife, Kathy. She knew about my earlier conversation with Rahm, and we spent a good deal of time discussing the prospect of remaining in Washington. We had kept a home in Peoria and hoped to spend more time there with our children and grandchildren. In many respects, we had never really left central Illinois. Despite spending 30 years in the capital city, for example, I had never gotten a haircut there—Pam Springer cuts my hair in Peoria. But Kathy and I agreed that if the right offer came, I had to accept.

Rahm called me three days later to report, "Everyone has signed off on it."

What did that mean?

"It means that everyone agrees you would be a good candidate for the Cabinet." Again, Rahm told me to keep the conversation absolutely confidential. Over the next few days, the transition team began to name other Cabinet nominees publicly—Hillary Clinton at State, Robert Gates continuing at Defense, Timothy Geithner at Treasury, Arne Duncan at Education, and so on. I exchanged a couple of e-mails with Rahm. "Everything is fine," he reassured me. "Everything is on track."

For the next three weeks, I occupied myself by closing down my congressional and campaign offices and handing off my job to Aaron Schock, the Republican who easily won the race to replace me in the House. I had no other plans. I had decided to wait until January, when my tour of duty in the House officially ended, to think about new opportunities. Now even that could wait. The prospect of continuing in government service, especially from the vantage point of the executive branch after so many years in Congress, and working for a new president— it was all so intriguing. I was content to let the appointment process play out.

In the first week of December, one of Rahm's assistants called me: "President-elect Obama would like to meet with you in Chicago on Friday, December 12, at 4:45."

I phoned Rahm. "What's going on?"

"You're going to have an interview."

"Do you know what it's for?"

"It's for Obama to decide if he wants to offer you a Cabinet post."

That was the extent of it. Rahm asked no questions, did not probe my thinking, and provided no details. Would there be 50 people in the room? Just the president-elect and me? How long would it last? How should

I prepare? I had no idea. All this struck me as a pretty casual approach to filling out an administration.

People on the outside, and I counted myself among them before going through the process, believe that a Cabinet appointment follows a series of well-defined and carefully conducted phases that involve detailed questionnaires, several interviews, much background research, a comprehensive assessment of a candidate's strengths and weaknesses, and a thoughtful analysis of the politics of an appointment. In other words, a businesslike, protracted process.

Here I was headed to an interview with the next president, and none of that had taken place. Why not? In hindsight, I think I sailed through because Obama and Emanuel knew me well enough to judge my character. We were all members of the Illinois congressional delegation, we had worked together on projects to benefit our state, and Rahm and I had dined together often and hosted bipartisan dinners for our House colleagues. The two of them knew me as well as they knew any member of Congress.

On the appointed Friday, I left a Rotary Club of Peoria meeting early, picked up Kathy, and drove to Chicago. We arrived at the Union League Club at 3:30 p.m. Kathy went shopping while I relaxed before leaving at 4:30 for the John C. Kluczynski Federal Building. I headed up in the elevator to the transition team's suite of offices. A young woman greeted me and directed me to a very small room. After a few minutes, a door opened and Obama walked in. He gave me his customary handshake and hug. I congratulated him on a great campaign, and we went back to another office. He said, "What do you think you're interested in?"

"I'm a respected Republican. If you're looking for someone bipartisan, no one can fit the bill better than I can. I know people on both sides of the aisle."

He repeated his question, and I replied, "Agriculture."

We talked about that for a little bit, and I reminded him of my six years on the Agriculture Committee. He said, "I need to think about this."

I knew he was conflicted, that an appointment to his Cabinet wasn't a done deal. He asked whether I would consider anything else, and I mentioned DOT (Department of Transportation), my service on the House Committee on Transportation and Infrastructure, and our working together on a big highway project in Pekin, in my congressional district.

The president-elect repeated that he needed to think about it. After 40 minutes, I left. Obama did not offer me a job. Rahm was sitting in a small office nearby with five phones in his ear. I did not bother him. Kathy and I drove back to Peoria.

At 9:00 Saturday morning, I sent Rahm an e-mail: "I have my fingers crossed. MANY THANKS for your friendship and help!"[1] Rahm replied that afternoon: "Your [sic] the best. Down to you and one other. Each of you bring [sic] a different set of skills."[2]

Who was the second candidate? I tried to track that down at the time and now believe the president-elect thought seriously about offering DOT to Ron Kirk, the former Dallas mayor who had lost a bid for the U.S. Senate as a Democrat. But his identity then was a mystery to me.

I called Rahm two days later, Monday, December 15, for an update. Obama still had me under consideration, he reported. "Would you take something lower than a Cabinet post?"

I said no. Without a Cabinet appointment, I intended to return to the private sector.

The press reported the selection of Tom Vilsack as secretary of agriculture on Tuesday, December 16. I admit that this came as startling news to me. Rahm did not alert me to the selection even though I had expressed my preference for Agriculture. I assumed, however, that because of yesterday's conversation with him that I was still under consideration for another Cabinet post.

The next day, Rahm made it official by offering me Transportation. Thirty minutes later Mike Froman, an adviser to what was known as the

Obama-Biden Transition Project, phoned. He told me I was in "vetting," that we would do a quick vet now, and if all went well, we would set a time for the formal announcement. Again, not a single follow-up question. A transition team staff member sent me an e-mail explaining the vetting process at 10:15 a.m.[3] CNN broke the story at 5:30 p.m. Eastern time.

After the FBI had completed an expedited background check, Rahm called to schedule the president-elect's announcement for Friday, December 19. I asked Rahm what he wanted me to do for the announcement, and he said "show up" at the Drake Hotel, write your own statement, and run it by us. Still a surprisingly relaxed approach to a Cabinet appointment, I thought. Thankfully, Margaret Buford, a transition team staff member, followed up with the details.

Mike Dorning, a reporter with the *Chicago Tribune*'s Washington bureau, called me on Thursday, the 18th, to confirm rumors he had picked up from Democratic and Republican officials that I was Obama's choice for DOT. I refused to confirm the speculation, as did the Obama transition team. Dorning filed the story anyway, noting that "the credentials he brings are based more on his political experience than background specific to the subject."[4]

Late Thursday afternoon, four of us hopped in the car for the trip north: me, Kathy, our son Darin, and Tim Butler, my press aide. During the two-and-a-half-hour trip to Chicago, we hammered out a statement, revising it on the fly. I read it to Rahm over the phone, and he made a couple of tweaks.

That evening, I spent three or four hours with Sam Skinner. Sam had called with an offer to give me a sense of what the job would be like. We had known each other for a long time. Sam had held a number of government positions and practiced law in Chicago. More to the point as far as I was concerned, Sam had served as secretary of transportation and White House chief of staff in George H. W. Bush's administration. My session with Skinner was the first and only in-depth conversation I had with anyone about the nature of the job.

Friday, we arrived at the Drake Hotel's Walton Room early, before the scheduled 12:15 start of the afternoon's events. Eventually, three other nominees and their families and guests joined us. Rahm arrived a few minutes later, followed by David Axelrod, one of Obama's closest political advisers, and then the president-elect. After exchanging small talk, the guests were escorted to the Grand Ballroom while Rahm, Axelrod, and a press aide reviewed with us what they called "the run of show" for the press conference to follow—who was going to speak, in what order, for how long, and what questions to expect. This briefing session lasted from about 12:30 to 1:00 p.m. The president-elect and his people then asked us to leave while they held a private meeting.

At 1:15 p.m., we all moved to the Grand Ballroom, where the president-elect began his press conference:

> Whenever I've been asked how I measure the strength of the American economy, my answer is simple: jobs and wages. I know we will be headed in the right direction again when we are creating jobs instead of losing them, and when Americans are gaining ground in terms of their incomes instead of treading water or falling behind. In recent weeks, I've announced members of my economic team who will help us make progress in these areas.
>
> Today, I'm announcing several other appointees who will play an integral role in our efforts to turn our economy around: Congresswoman Hilda Solis as Secretary of Labor; former Congressman Ray LaHood as Secretary of Transportation; Karen Mills as Administrator of the Small Business Administration; and Mayor Ron Kirk as United States Trade Representative. Together with the appointees I've already announced, these leaders will help craft a 21st Century Economic Recovery Plan, with the goal of creating two and a half million new jobs and strengthening our economy for the future.

Obama spoke briefly about each of us in turn. When he came to me, he said, "When I began this appointment process, I said I was committed to finding the best person for the job, regardless of party," before concluding,

"Ray's appointment reflects that bipartisan spirit—a spirit we need to reclaim in this country to make progress for the American people."[5]

Hilda Solis followed the president-elect and introduced me. We each had two minutes to speak. Working from the script we had prepared on the trip to Chicago the day before, I thanked the president-elect and immediately spoke the only words Rahm had added to our text: "President-elect Obama and I share the same philosophy on infrastructure. His agenda for the Department of Transportation is my agenda." The challenge ahead, I said, was "to rebuild America, to reclaim our leadership in infrastructure development." Most important, I emphasized the importance of bipartisanship:

> I have often said that once the election is over, we must put aside our partisan labels and work together for the good of the American people. That is exactly the approach President-Elect Obama will take as President and it is exactly the approach I will take as Secretary of Transportation.

After thanking Kathy and our family, I finished by introducing Ron Kirk. The president-elect took a few questions and ended the press conference at about 2:00 p.m.[6]

I spent the rest of December preparing for my confirmation hearings.

My nomination surprised many of my Washington friends and probably a good many more Democrats. When the *Washington Post* had identified candidates for the post in late November 2008, I was not among them.[7] The paper had named four likely contenders, all well qualified. Mortimer Downey, deputy secretary of transportation under Bill Clinton from 1993 to 2001, headed the list. Jane Garvey, Federal Aviation Administration chief from 1997 into 2002, including the period of the September 11 attacks, was singled out, too. President Obama could have selected Steve Heminger, executive director of San Francisco Bay area's Metropolitan Transportation Commission. Nancy Pelosi had appointed Heminger to the National Surface Transportation Policy and Revenue Study Commission—

it never hurts for a new president to have a friend in the Speaker of the U.S. House of Representatives. Finally, James L. Oberstar, congressman from Minnesota's 8th district since 1975 and chair of the House Transportation and Infrastructure Committee, with whom I had served, possessed a nearly encyclopedic knowledge of the federal transportation program.

An impressive list. As I later told a reporter, "I don't think they picked me because they thought I'd be that great a transportation person."[8]

To understand why a newly elected Democratic president selected a relatively unknown, recently retired Republican member of the House of Representatives—to make sense of it, I have to go back to the beginning.

NOTES

1. RL to Emanuel, e-mail, December 13, 2008, RLP-Memoir, f. Introduction.
2. Emanuel to RL, e-mail, December 13, 2008, RLP-Memoir, f. Introduction.
3. Kate Shaw to RL, December 17, 2008, RLP-DOT, f. Confirmation (1).
4. Mike Dorning, "Obama Reportedly Picking LaHood for Transportation Chief," chicagotribune.com, December 18, 2008, RLP-Memoir, f. Introduction.
5. Barack Obama, "Remarks in Chicago Announcing Nominations for the Departments of Labor, Transportation, United States Trade Representative, and Small Business Administration," December 19, 2008, *PPP*, RLP-Memoir, f. Joining the Cabinet.
6. Margaret Buford to RL, e-mail, December 18, 2008, RLP-Memoir, f. Introduction; RL, "Department of Transportation Secretary-Designate Announcement," December 19, 2008, RLP-Memoir, f. DOT. Appointment to Cabinet.
7. "In Transition: Transportation Secretary," *Washington Post*, November 25, 2008, RLP-Memoir, f. Introduction.
8. John D. Schultz, "Man on the Move," *Logistics Management*, November 2011, RLP-Memoir, f. DOT. Leading DOT.

SEEKING BIPARTISANSHIP

CHAPTER 1

TOWARD A CAREER IN PUBLIC SERVICE

We never talked about politics at home. Back in those days, I would not have known who a city councilman was, or even the mayor. Politics never played a role in our lives. Never. Not for one second.
—Ray LaHood

PEORIA, ILLINOIS: MY HOMETOWN

I was not born into politics. My father, Ed, owned a working-class restaurant and bar, Sam LaHood's Tavern on Southwest Jefferson Street in Peoria. Dad, who did not graduate from high school, spent his life working 12 hours a day, seven days a week. The hardest-working guy I have ever known, he taught me the value of education, of hard work, of taking responsibility for what you do. But Dad had no interest in politics.

My mother, Mary, worked in the restaurant alongside Dad. She had three sons to contend with, too—Mike (the oldest), Steve (the youngest), and me. We were a deeply religious family with strong ties to St. Bernard Roman Catholic parish. We socialized within our extended family—dozens of cousins, uncles, and aunts. My grandparents came from the village of Aitou, as did many of the other 5,000 Lebanese who settled in central Illinois. My family lived in a close-knit, working-class neighborhood on Peoria's East Bluff. No one had much money. Our lives revolved around family, friends, and church—not politics.

I think my parents probably were Democrats, but I never asked them. I believe they voted, but I never asked them. Nothing in my childhood hinted at a future career in public service—not my upbringing, not my education, not my family's activities. Many folks assume that a member of Congress must come from a political family. This was not the case for me.

My hometown has become famous as a representation of the average American city. On the Vaudeville circuit, it was said that if an act succeeded here, it would work anywhere. The question *Will it play in Peoria?* became a metaphor for whether or not something appealed to the American mainstream public. Today, companies use Peoria as a test market for new products, services, even public policy polling. My politics reflected those of my constituents in central Illinois—solid, midwestern, mainstream.

When I was born on December 6, 1945, just four months to the day after the U.S. Air Force had dropped the atomic bomb on Hiroshima, Japan, Peoria resembled many other small midwestern cities preparing for the postwar world. Because of its proximity to river transportation on the Illinois River and access to corn for grain alcohol, Peoria had become one of the largest manufacturers of liquor in the United States early in the 20th century. Many of the mansions that remain on High Street and Moss Avenue are a direct result of the Peoria whiskey baron era. That was not my side of town.

Growing up, I worked a series of jobs, as most kids in my neighborhood did. Besides helping in my dad's restaurant, I worked as an outdoor carhop and in a grocery store. I attended St. Bernard's Grade School and Spalding Institute, graduating in 1963. My modest earnings paid for the $125 annual high school tuition.

THE VALUE OF EDUCATION

I did not really want to go to college, but Dad pushed me to get an education. Several classmates decided to enroll at Canton Community College (CCC, now Spoon River College), located about 30 miles from home. When I entered CCC in the fall of 1963, the college occupied just four rooms in the back of Canton High School. Because we shared that space, many of our classes began at 7:00 a.m., others not until 4:00 in the afternoon. During the week, I lived with a family in town, going home on weekends to work in the Jewel/SuperValu grocery store.[1] Undecided about a career, I took general education courses during my two years at CCC. I left in 1965 without a degree.

Bradley University saved me. Founded in 1897, it is a private, independent university located in Peoria, only a couple of miles from my home. It offered programs in the liberal and fine arts, the sciences, business administration, and education, among others. Beginning in 1965, I entered what I call the "slow learner program," majoring in education. I attended night classes and taught during the day, first at St. Joseph School in Pekin and then at Holy Family School in Peoria. In those years, a school could hire someone who did not have a teaching certificate as long as he or she was enrolled in a program leading to an education degree, as I was. No great shakes as a student, I took biology three times, flunked twice, and dropped it the third time. Finally, a charitable professor, Dr. Kolb, discovered a general science course that fulfilled the graduation requirement. He awarded me an undeserved C to get me through.

I had better luck finding my future wife. In January 1967, a snowstorm blanketed Peoria, keeping many students from traveling home for the weekend. Bradley's St. Joseph Newman Center, a campus ministry program of the Catholic Diocese of Peoria, sponsored an event that attracted many students waylaid by the storm—Kathleen Dunk, from Villa Park, Illinois, among them. Kathy majored in accounting and, like me, worked her way through school. We dated steadily and, still students, were married on November 10, 1967.

In 1970, a local issue prompted my first foray into politics. When Peoria tried to impose a city utility tax, I ran as a Republican for precinct committeeman pledging to support the tax. I won. Entering that race did not signal a commitment to a career in politics, however. Frankly, I did not spend a great deal of time thinking about the future—getting by day to day posed enough challenges. It was clear to me, however, that the Republican Party best reflected my thinking on the issues at the time, although I confess that I had admired John Kennedy as president.

Finally, in December 1971, six years after first enrolling, I graduated from Bradley with a bachelor of science degree in education and sociology. Even now, I count graduation day as one of the most joyous of my life. Although I had prepared myself for a teaching career, my practical experience in the classroom eventually led me in a different direction. After graduation, I joined the faculty at Oak Grove West near Bartonville, just outside Peoria. Teaching government to young people during the Vietnam War years ignited my interest in public service and politics. It seemed to me that I could make a bigger difference in politics than in teaching.

THE LURE OF PUBLIC SERVICE

In 1972, at age 26, I was named the first director of the Rock Island County Youth Service Bureau, a delinquency-prevention program with headquarters in Moline, in the western part of the state. Kathy and I packed up our two kids for the move. Two years later, I left the Youth Service Bureau to join the Bi-State Metropolitan Commission as the chief planner for social services. I stayed there for three years, working primarily on law-enforcement issues with local and county governments, with schools, and with police departments and the juvenile court to raise funds for social service programs. I made two runs for a seat on the United Township High School Board of Education in 1975 and 1976. I lost the first race by 183 votes, the second by 44.[2] Not an auspicious start in politics.

My philosophy of government evolved during those five years. I came to believe, and I still do, that government can be helpful, that government can solve problems, that Democrats and Republicans can work together. This seemed like common sense at the time; only later did I discover how unpopular that view would prove to be.

In 1977, I received a call from Congressman Tom Railsback, a Republican from Moline, who was looking for a district administrative assistant. As he recalled, "Ray came in and had this shaggy hair. But he was very articulate, very positive. After meeting with him for 15 or 20 minutes, I thought, 'this guy is great.' So I brought him into congressional politics and service."[3]

Railsback had won the first of eight terms in the U.S. House of Representatives in 1967 after having served two terms in the Illinois General Assembly. A moderate Republican, he served on the Judiciary Committee in the mid-1970s as the second-ranking Republican. When the committee conducted the impeachment inquiry into Richard Nixon in 1974, Railsback joined the "fragile coalition," a group of four Republicans and three conservative Democrats who drafted two of the articles of impeachment against the president. The congressman was one of just six Republicans to support at least one article. There is some irony here—I began my congressional service, albeit as a staffer, with a member who played an important part in one presidential impeachment; I later presided in the House during the impeachment of another president.

Illinois lost two districts after the 1980 census, forcing Railsback to run in the newly configured 17th in March 1982. A considerably more conservative Republican, Kenneth G. McMillan, defeated my boss in a very close primary. Democrat Lane Evans beat McMillan in November.

When Tom lost the primary, I was out of a job after five years. Luckily, I received an appointment in May 1982 to the Illinois House of Representatives to replace Ben Polk, who had fallen ill and resigned. In November, I ran for a seat on my own but lost to Bob DeJaegher, a popular Democrat. At that point in my career, I had run for four positions and lost three times—not exactly an encouraging track record.

In January 1983, I went to work for Congressman Robert H. Michel as his district administrative assistant, and our family moved back to Peoria. Bob hired me because he had almost lost his reelection bid in 1982, winning only 51 percent of the vote, the narrowest margin ever, before or since. As Republican leader in the House, Bob had carried the water for President Ronald Reagan's legislative program during the president's first term. People back in the district increasingly viewed Bob as out of touch with his constituents, and frankly, Bob had not emphasized constituent service. He hired me and former Illinois state representative Craig Findley, who worked out of the Jacksonville office, to reestablish himself in the district. I traveled all over, representing Bob at every community event imaginable. I also involved Bob more deeply in local activities. In 1990, I became his chief of staff, traveling between Washington and Peoria.

As we settled down in Peoria, I made time for community service, partly to represent Bob but primarily because I knew the value of a prosperous, forward-looking community. I served as president of the Notre Dame High School Board in Peoria and on the advisory board of Children's Hospital of Illinois. I was active in the Peoria Area Retarded Citizens, the Bradley University National Alumni Board, the Peoria Area Chamber of Commerce Board of Directors, the Economic Development Council Board of Directors, the ITOO Society,[4] and the Downtown Rotary Club. Naturally, these connections helped me later in my own congressional career, but that was the farthest thing from my mind in the 1980s— after all, I had just lost three elections in a row. Kathy and I had four children to raise, too.

The job of congressional staffer was rewarding in its own right; I had no plans to do otherwise. I expected that my boss would serve in the House at least as long as Ronald Reagan was president, so through 1988. When George H. W. Bush succeeded Reagan in 1989, I knew that Bob would continue because he enjoyed such a special relationship with the new president. I came to realize, however, that if I did my job in a way that reflected Bob Michel in style and values and showed that he did care about the district, my work would endear me to people who would then see me as his likely successor.

When Bill Clinton defeated Bush in 1992, I could tell that Bob's enthusiasm for the job faltered. The fun left him. Although Clinton treated Bob decently, Bob knew that serving in the Republican minority with a Democratic president to boot meant he would not call the shots. "Do I really have the same zest for the job that I once had? No," he told a reporter.[5]

Challenges to Bob's style of leadership from the Republican ranks took a toll, too. It was widely believed that Newt Gingrich, the minority whip, would challenge Bob for the top Republican leadership slot in the House following the 1994 elections. In stark contrast to Bob, Gingrich practiced slash-and-burn politics. He had been central to our party's efforts to exploit the House bank and post office scandals in the early 1990s, when he took every opportunity to blame such problems on Democrats' "corrupt, one-party" rule over the preceding 40 years. The whip's approach, at least implicitly, and often more overtly, contradicted my boss's more accommodating style. Bob admitted that facing a battle against Gingrich for the party's leadership discouraged him.[6]

During this time, Bob and I began to talk about his retiring and my replacing him. Bob wanted to announce his decision early enough to give me time to put together an organization. Kathy and I talked about the prospects once I could tell that Bob was growing weary. She raised no objections at all. She knew me well enough to see that I had made up my mind. Kathy has always been supportive; however, she has not been what some might call a "political" wife in the sense of having political ambitions for me. Kathy does not enjoy politics. I remember early on inviting her to walk in a parade in Morton. She hated it. I never asked her again! Kathy was more than willing to help me if I asked, but she did not covet the role. Unlike some spouses, she did not attend campaign-strategy meetings or interfere with campaign or office operations. Kathy had a career of her own, too. A certified public accountant, she was an assistant vice president at Peoria's largest bank when I ran for Congress.

Bob Michel announced his intention to retire on October 4, 1993. He might have continued had President Bush won reelection the year before, but Bob had put in 38 years in the House, eight years as a congressional staffer to his predecessor, and three years in the army—almost 50 years of public service. He was 70 years old. "That ought to be enough," he told the press. "I think it's a good time to hang it up." He predicted that Republicans would gain seats in 1994, but not enough to win the majority—he missed his bet on that one. He announced early in order to give his party in the House time to plan "an orderly transition from my Leadership to whomever." He closed with these words:

> I'd like to feel that as I prepare to leave the Congress, I've lived up to my parents [sic] high ethical standard and that I'll be remembered by my constituents for representing them faithfully and well, and that nationally I will be judged as having contributed significantly to the deliberations of the House and served the institution of Congress with honor and in an exemplary fashion.[7]

I consider myself a graduate of the Robert H. Michel School of Applied Political Arts and Sciences. His classrooms were his office, the floor of the House, its committee rooms, and the farms and towns of the 18th district. Everywhere he went, he taught his staff by his example what it means to be a great public servant. Bob taught us that the House floor should be a forum for reasoned debate among colleagues equal in dignity. He had inherited an old-fashioned Peoria work ethic from his beloved parents. He went to the House every day to do the work of the people, not to engage in ideological melodramas or political vendettas.

Bob taught me the difference between war and politics. Bob knew warfare firsthand from his days as a combat infantryman in World War II. While still in his early 20s, he had fought his way across France, Belgium, and Germany. He was wounded by machine-gun fire and received two Bronze Stars for gallantry. Because he knew war, Bob never used macho phrases like *warfare* and *take no prisoners* when discussing politics. He knew that the rhetoric we often use shapes the political actions we take.

I owe Bob Michel an enormous debt of gratitude.

THAT FIRST CAMPAIGN, 1994

I announced for the seat on October 5, 1993, the day after Bob's disclosure, traveling to three cities in the district. I stressed four major issues facing voters in central Illinois: jobs and economic development, health care reform, promotion of agriculture and agribusiness, and responsible stewardship of our natural resources. On October 7, *Roll Call*, the Capitol Hill newspaper, called me the heir apparent to Bob's seat.[8] I had inherited Bob's entire campaign apparatus, including the services of his campaign manager for the past 10 years, Mary Alice Erickson.

Naturally, I knew the district like the back of my hand. It stretched 100 miles in length and covered almost 6,200 square miles (about 11 percent of the state). The 1990 census pegged the population at 571,580. Redistricting had altered the boundaries somewhat, taking away the western counties that extended to the Mississippi River and adding territory to the north and east. As a result, the 18th was the only district in the state that contained no part of the Chicago metropolitan area and yet did not border on another state. It was Illinois's true heartland district.[9]

Overall, the 18th district was considered safely Republican. The last Democrat to hold the seat had lost his reelection bid in 1916. Abraham Lincoln and Everett McKinley Dirksen had represented the same district in their time. My party held sway in the mostly small towns and farmlands that made up much of the 14-county district. Nearly all the rural counties gave both George H. W. Bush and Michel better than 60 percent of the vote in 1992. Half the voters lived in the two counties surrounding my home base of Peoria, however, and Democrats made up a sizeable portion of those voters. President Bush did not break 40 percent in either county in 1992, and Bob Michel ran below his district average in each. Based on that contest and on President's Bush's dismal reelection showing locally, I knew that Democrats would field a strong candidate.

The general election posed the second hurdle, however. First, I had to survive a Republican primary, which would take place on March 15, 1994. Other Republicans reportedly interested in challenging me included ex-state representative Judy Koehler, ex-state senator Roger Sommer, state representative David Leitch, and ex-state representative Craig Findley—the same Craig Findley Bob Michel had hired in 1983 to run his Jacksonville office.

It was tough to juggle campaigning and continuing as Bob's chief of staff. My opponents and the press tried to make an issue of my staying on the federal payroll, but I followed the regulations scrupulously. In reality, I could not afford to quit. All of our kids were students: Darin, 25, at John Marshall Law School; Amy, 23, at Rush Medical College in Chicago; Sam, 18, an undergraduate at St. Norbert College in Green Bay; and Sara, 16, at Peoria Notre Dame High School.

As the primary neared, I took a leave of absence from my job in February. I won the primary relatively easily, with 33,956 votes (50 percent) to Judy Koehler's 26,809 (40 percent) and Dennis Higgins's 6,959 (10 percent). I rejoined Michel's staff the next day, March 16. On September 2, 1994, I stepped down from my staff position to campaign full time for Bob's seat.

Doug Stephens, 42, won the Democratic primary. Like me, Stephens had been born and raised in Peoria and still lived there—in fact, he had grown up in my working-class neighborhood. His father, Don, drove a truck and also served as the business representative for Teamsters Local 627. Doug had attended Spalding Institute, as I had. He and his wife, Sherry, had four children and attended Holy Family Catholic Church, as did my family. In 1982, when he was 31 and politically unheralded, Stephens won the Democratic primary and faced off against Bob Michel, nearly upsetting him in a recession-torn environment. He tried again in 1988 but could only hold Bob to 55 percent of the vote. Stephens made his mark in Peoria and became a millionaire trying workers' compensation cases, which resulted in strong ties to organized labor. He owned three small businesses, too.

Aside from the fact that I was a Republican and Stephens a Democrat, we shared a similar background and political philosophies befitting two men raised in Peoria. We both opposed abortion and favored welfare reform. We both opposed President Clinton's health care plan. We both endorsed an amendment to the Constitution that would require Congress to balance the federal budget. The only major thing we disagreed about was the recently enacted crime bill, which he supported and I opposed.

The election was not so much about issues, then, or ideology, as much as it was about who was better suited for the job. Stephens portrayed himself as a small businessman who had created jobs in the private sector. Hoping to exploit voter dissatisfaction with Congress, he depicted me as a Washington insider, a semi-incumbent.

I did not try to downplay my Washington ties. I thought my experience counted for something. No one would have to teach me how to introduce a bill, I argued. If someone came to me with a problem, I knew which buttons to push to solve it. I also touted my civic involvement, something Stephens sorely lacked.

Democrats counted on heavy support from United Auto Workers members on strike against Caterpillar (CAT), the largest employer in the district and the world headquarters of which was in Peoria. CAT employed 18,000 people in plants across the district. The 6,500 who were not working a full eight-hour day in the fall of 1994 held the potential to elect a Democrat. Stephens tried to make the case that the local congressman should intercede to get both parties to the bargaining table. I, in contrast, did not think that politicians could settle the strike.

According to an independent poll conducted a week before the election, I held a comfortable lead over Stephens, drawing 49 percent of likely voters to his 28 percent, with 23 percent undecided. I led in every region of the 14-county district. Only the strike against Caterpillar kept the race that close—of the respondents who said they were on strike, 53 percent supported my opponent, and 24 percent backed me. With regard to Stephens's charge that I was a Washington insider, 37 percent saw my experience as a plus, 28 percent as a liability, and 35 percent held no opinion. With regard to his so-called business background, 67 percent saw that as a benefit, 10 percent as a liability, and 23 percent were undecided. I held a huge advantage in campaign funds. As of September 30, 1994, I had raised $572,416 and spent $519,653; Stephens had raised $303,342 and spent $299,173.

Both of us brought in big guns to campaign for us. Al Gore appeared for Stephens. Dick Cheney and Newt Gingrich visited Peoria for me. Ironically, in light of what would happen after I won the House seat, Gingrich told the Peoria press, "I literally do not know that there's any candidate in the country who knows the House better or has more personal friends on both sides of the aisle."[10]

I won with 60 percent of the vote in November. Most analysts chalked the win up to the fiscally conservative policies I supported. I favored slashing the number of congressional staff by half, supported a balanced budget amendment, and opposed the "pork" provisions in a recently passed crime bill, which my opponent supported. Differences over issues undoubtedly figured into the outcome, but not as much as most believed. I won in a Republican year with a larger campaign war chest than my opponent, with higher name recognition because of my work with Bob Michel, with an unpopular Democrat in the White House, and defending a Republican seat against a two-time loser. My victory marked the day Republicans won control of the House for the first time in four decades.

"The torch has been passed," I told the 700 campaign workers who joined me and my family election night at the Countryside Banquet, my brother Mike's business, in Washington, Illinois. "There will be an opportunity for a new generation. My win has been very humbling and I'm just very excited to have the opportunity to represent my area in Washington."[11]

NOTES

1. Lisa Young, "Freshman Congressman Once a Freshman Here," *Spoon River College Anthology* (Winter 1995), RLP-Peoria-TBS, f. LaHood Profile Articles and RLP-Memoir, f. Toward a Career in Public Service.
2. RLP-Campaign, f. LaHood, United Township High School Board of Education Campaign.
3. Edward Felker, "Q-C 'Apprentice' Goes to Congress," *Dispatch and the Rock Island Argus*, March 19, 1995, RLP-Memoir, f. Toward a Career in Public Service.
4. The Itoo Society was established in 1914 to create and maintain unity among the Aitou community in Peoria, to maintain strong ties to the families remaining in Aitou, and to provide for the general welfare of both the Aitou community in Peoria and the citizens of the village of Aitou, Lebanon.
5. Timothy J. Burger and Jim O'Connell, "Michel Quits," *Roll Call*, October 7, 1993, RHMIF, f. Biographical.
6. Burger and O'Connell, "Michel Quits."
7. Press release, October 4, 1993, RHMIF, f. Biographical.
8. Burger and O'Connell, "Michel Quits."
9. Phil Duncan, "Michel Aide Has Edge for GOP Nomination," *CQ*, October 9, 1993, 2672–2673, RLP-Campaign, f. FORL 1994.
10. Stephen Witmer, "Gingrich Offers His Views on Politics," *Peoria Journal Star*, August 25, 1994, RLP-Campaign, f. FORL 1994.
11. Paul A. Driscoll, "LaHood Retains Michel's Congressional Seat for Republicans," *Decatur Herald and Review*, November 9, 1994, RLP-Campaign, f. FORL 1994.

CHAPTER 2

THE GINGRICH REVOLUTION
AND MY FIRST TERM

I was sworn in as the congressman from Illinois's 18th congressional district on January 3, 1995. The transition from staffer to congressman went smoothly for me. After more than 17 years working for Tom Railsback and Bob Michel, I knew the importance of hiring talented, ambitious, experienced staff. Mary Alice Erickson, who had run my campaign and Bob Michel's campaigns and who knew the district well, became my top staffer in the district office. I sat down with each of Bob's key staff members in Washington, too. Diane Liesman accepted my offer to continue to head the Washington, DC, office located in the Rayburn House Office Building. Joan Mitchell and Paul Vinovich also stayed on in key positions there.

For the next 14 years, the House of Representatives served as my window on history. Never seriously challenged for reelection, I served in the Republican majority for all but the last of my seven terms. Although my career did not produce the legacy of an Everett Dirksen or a Bob Michel, both of whom had held my seat in the House, three historic events marked my service: (1) Republicans winning control of the House,

(2) the impeachment of President Bill Clinton, and (3) the terrorist attacks of September 11, 2001.

Over this period, even dating back to my years with Railsback, a troubling underlying trend emerged that set the stage for virtually all things congressional—the decline in civility and bipartisanship in the House. Attempting to counter that trend became the single most important effort of my career.

REPUBLICANS SEIZE CONTROL OF THE HOUSE

Democrats suffered a rout in the 1994 congressional elections. Republicans took 52 seats from them, gaining control of the House for the first time in 40 years. The tide swept out Speaker of the House Thomas Foley (D-WA), only the third such defeat in history for a sitting Speaker. Almost 37 million people voted Republican, about nine million more than in 1990. It was the biggest midterm-to-midterm increase in votes for one party in American history.[1]

No one was more surprised than I. *Shocked* might be a better word. In leadership meetings over the years, sitting with Bob Michel, I had listened to Gingrich predict victory so many times that I ignored his predictions in 1994. Gingrich thought the Contract with America was our party's road to the majority; I thought it was a gimmick. I was delighted to be in the majority, of course, but my enthusiasm was tempered by the prospect of a House led by Newt Gingrich, someone I knew all too well.

Speaker-to-be Gingrich had come to the House in 1978 after losing two bids to represent his Atlanta constituents. Ironically, given what would happen later, Bob Michel had received an evaluation of candidate Gingrich in 1974, noting:

> Dr. Gingrich has had considerable experience in previous congressional and statewide races in Georgia. Because of this, he should be able to put together a good campaign team. I was very much impressed with him as an individual; however, as a candidate I

would rate him as fair at this time, but with a little coaching I think he could become a good candidate. It appeared to me that he was not as aggressive or forceful as he should be to make a good candidate. He spoke in a very low voice, barely audible[;] perhaps he would need some training for political speaking.[2]

Twenty years wrought a new Newt Gingrich. Unlike the tradition of legislative leadership set by Democrats Sam Rayburn (TX), John McCormack (MA), Tip O'Neill (MA), Jim Wright (TX), and Tom Foley, or their Republicans counterparts, including Gerald Ford (MI) and Bob Michel, Gingrich shunned the role of insider. He did not revere the institution or work to create a network of friendships across the aisle in order to pass legislation. He took a defiant approach, lambasting Congress, the way it functioned, its leaders (including Republicans), and Democrats in general. He held dear only two objectives: to win and then to rule.

I had witnessed Gingrich's run-ins with Michel firsthand. The rivalry began when Newt organized the Conservative Opportunity Society (COS) in 1983, assembling a group of members who shared his conservative and confrontational beliefs. To harass Democrats, the COS used special orders on the House floor to level their charges and to boost their public visibility. Gingrich also used ethics charges, most notably against Speaker Jim Wright, to grandstand. Bob Michel resented Newt's trashing of the institution and tried without success to moderate COS's tone and tactics. Gingrich augmented his influence when he took the chair of GOPAC, a political action committee, in 1986. From that post, Gingrich traveled exhaustively to recruit and indoctrinate Republican candidates for House seats. As he once explained, "You would capture seventy or eighty percent of the incoming freshmen class every two years and at some point you would have transformed the whole structure."[3] GOPAC gave Gingrich the means to seize control of the Republican Party in the House.

Gingrich made no secret of his growing disenchantment with Bob Michel's style of leadership, which Newt viewed as too soft, too accommodating vis-à-vis the Democratic majority. "There are two ways to rise," Gingrich famously said. "One is to figure out the current system and figure out how you fit into it. The other is to figure out the system that ought to be, and as you change the current system into the system that ought to be, at some point it becomes more practical for you to be a leader than for somebody who grew out of the old order."[4]

He was able to put together a coalition of disaffected colleagues who elected him Republican whip in 1989 over Bob's candidate, Ed Madigan (IL), by two votes. The next year Michel joined Democrats to support President George H. W. Bush's budget deal with Democrats—a deal that included higher taxes. Gingrich opposed it. The result was an unexpected and stunning legislative defeat for the president in early October. The upstart Republican whip led 105 Republicans to vote against the budget deal; Michel's forces produced only 71 votes in favor. The final agreement passed with the help of Democrats, but the episode further burnished Gingrich's leadership credentials.

President Bush's reelection defeat in 1992 spelled the beginning of the end for my boss. Republicans picked up nine seats in the House. The freshman class, largely indebted to Gingrich and GOPAC for its success, numbered 47. When the party met to elect its leadership, Gingrich allies won every seat except Bob's. Gingrich and Republican Conference Chairman Dick Armey (TX) muscled my boss aside, telling him he had one more term in office before the new generation planned to push him out. It fell to me to relay the message to Bob. Even as evidence of his colleagues' restiveness mounted, Bob thought he would win in 1994 if push came to shove. I had my doubts.

More than a year before the 1994 midterm elections, however, Bob announced his plans to retire. For the next week, he held countless interviews, and although he refrained from criticizing Gingrich directly, he made no bones about his discontent with the widespread Congress-bashing that had become a mantra for Newt and his crowd. Moving quickly to squelch competition, Gingrich held a press conference a week later to report that 106 of the 175 House Republicans had pledged to support him as our party's next leader.

Gingrich approached the 1994 congressional elections with single-mindedly determination. He campaigned in 125 congressional districts, spreading his message of reform. He pledged to change the character of the country, reversing what he called the "Great Society, counterculture, McGovernick" legacy handed down by the Democrats.[5] His goal: to "redirect the fate of the human race."[6]

Despite my personal distaste for him, I could not ignore Gingrich's popularity or the value he offered to a Republican running for a first term. I swallowed hard and invited him to campaign for me in my district. We used his appearance to raise money—a lot of money. The campaign banked over $100,000 in a single event, funds we desperately needed to pay for television in the closing months of the campaign. His appearance also confirmed to doubters that I was conservative enough to have Newt's support. I needed those voters if I was to win. Inviting him served another purpose, as well. I knew that Gingrich would be our party's leader in the next Congress, whether as minority leader or, unimaginable at that point, Speaker. I had to improve our relationship if I hoped to have influence in the House. After all, I had not signed the Contract with America. Gingrich delivered, too, and not just by raising money. He spoke enthusiastically about my connections in Washington, my knowledge of House rules and procedures, and my reputation for friendships on both sides of the aisle. As I was to learn, his actions spoke louder than his words.

Following the election, Gingrich moved to cement his control over the party. We opened our party conference on December 5. After dispensing with the formality of endorsing Newt for the speakership, we elected Dick Armey as majority leader. I thought it was wrong that Armey went unchallenged. But he and his staff had put together the Contract with America, and Gingrich owed him—that was his reward. Tom DeLay, also from Texas, won the most heated contest, a three-way race for majority whip.

It was difficult then for me to separate my personal feelings about the new Speaker, based on my time with Bob Michel, from the opportunities our party, now in the majority, faced. I was equally concerned about the platform on which we Republicans had achieved the majority—Newt's Contract with America.

THE CONTRACT WITH AMERICA

Several weeks before the November 1994 election, I had received a Contract with America survey from the Republican leadership. In an effort to determine the priority of issues for Republican House members and candidates, the survey sought our assessment of the "desirability and political feasibility" of more than 60 potential legislative initiatives, which we were to rate on a five-point support scale. Here is the rank order I assigned to a dozen issue areas in terms of "the emphasis we as a [Republican] Conference should invest in each":

1. Real Congressional Reform
2. Common Sense Health Care Reforms
3. Welfare Reform
4. Strengthening Our National Defense and Foreign Policy
5. Job and Wage Growth Measures
6. Easing the Regulatory Burden
7. Senior Citizen Fairness
8. Enhancing Personal Safety
9. Cut Spending Now
10. Pro-Family Tax Reforms
11. Parental and Local Empowerment
12. Common Sense Legal Reforms[7]

Within each of these general subject areas, the survey listed several specific legislative proposals. For my top-rated goal, "Real Congressional Reform," the survey suggested these: set term limits for members, apply all laws to Congress, cut the number of committees and congressional staff, initiate a comprehensive audit of the House's books, pass a sunshine rule to end closed-door committee hearings, ban ghost (proxy) voting in committees, rotate committee chairships, use honest budget numbers (no baseline budgeting), and give voters the right to advisory initiatives and referenda. The survey closed by asking whether we considered ourselves "very conservative," "fairly conservative" (which I marked), "moderate," or "liberal."[8]

On September 27, 1994, six weeks before the November 8 election, approximately 350 House Republican members and candidates unveiled the Contract with America in a made-for-TV event staged on the Capitol lawn. The meat of the contract spelled out 10 pieces of legislation proposed for the new Congress.[9] Their titles illustrate the breadth of Gingrich's ambition:

> The Fiscal Responsibility Act
> The Taking Back Our Streets Act
> The Personal Responsibility Act
> The Family Reinforcement Act
> The American Dream Restoration Act
> The National Security Restoration Act
> The Senior Citizens Fairness Act
> The Job Creation and Wage Enhancement Act
> The Common Sense Legal Reform Act
> The Citizen Legislature Act

The purpose of the contract could not have been clearer. Gingrich intended it as a high-profile national platform on which all Republican candidates could run and from which we could attack the Democrats. He promised that it would chart our course for the first 100 days in the 104th Congress.

According to the Heritage Foundation, which helped to develop the contract behind the scenes, the items in the contract had been carefully selected to address issues of fundamental policy importance but that also were "doable." Its authors claimed that only proposals favored by 60 percent of the American people had made the cut. No hot-button social issues, such as abortion and school prayer, were allowed because of the political risk of pitting Republican against Republican, not to mention alienating Democrats and independents.[10] Smart politics on their part.

I did not join those gathered on the Capitol lawn in late September. I did not sign the contract. Back in Illinois, I campaigned by hammering home the need to reduce the deficit. Tax cuts, in contrast, represented the contract's crown jewel. I could not support both. People were astounded by my decision to pass on the contract. To my critics within the party I simply replied, "I was not elected by anyone in Washington." On September 27, I issued a press release announcing a Contract with the Citizens of the 18th District, in which I pledged to support reforms in congressional procedures and to endorse a principled Republican approach to health care, welfare, and tax reform.[11]

Politically, Gingrich's contract found a receptive audience in the fall elections. Voters expressed their disappointment both with Congress and with the lackluster leadership provided by Bill Clinton in the White House. The Clinton campaign in 1992 had encouraged people to expect great change in domestic policies. Moreover, that Democrats controlled both branches of the Congress along with the White House seemed to create the means for change. But Democrats' failure to reform public policy in any consequential way in 1993 and 1994 paved the way for Republican victories in November 1994.[12]

I admit that Gingrich deserves high marks for his use of the Contract with America. He arranged to have it published in *TV Guide* a few weeks before the election so that it could be torn out in a single page and kept by people to make sure we lived up to it. He achieved his objective of putting the contract's provisions front and center in the national political debate. But I disagreed with those who thought the contract won the day for us. I gave more credit to voters' profound disappointment with President Clinton's failure to live up to expectations.

I also worried that the contract created the wrong legislative environment. It was all about change and criticism. Past accomplishments counted for nothing. Personal relationships built up over the years between Democrats and Republicans constituted weakness, not strength. Gingrich showed no inclination to consult, compromise, or collaborate. Domination, not accommodation, would rule the day. The new Speaker's approach had achieved a majority for our party in the House, but would it yield either long-term political success or effective public policy? I was skeptical.

STRANGER IN MY OWN CLASS

That decision—refusing to sign the Contract with America—shaped my congressional career more than any other decision I made. Only three Republicans declined to sign, and I was one of them, the only nonincumbent.[13] It left me an odd man out in my own party. It closed the door to any leadership position in the House.

I learned quickly the cost of apostasy. In early December 1994, I wrote letters to every member of the leadership and to every member of the Republican Steering Committee, each with a handwritten postscript, requesting assignment to the Appropriations Committee:

> As Bob Michel's Chief of Staff, I became very familiar with the appropriations process because of his twenty-five year assignment to that committee. With the current view of the leadership, and the nation as a whole, that we must make tough decisions to cut government spending, I am not only willing to participate aggressively in this process, but I am experienced in making recommendations for these types of actions. We must keep our pledges to scale back, and it is important to my own re-election to be able to point to specific savings that the Congress has achieved through careful scrutiny of how the taxpayer's money is being spent.[14]

Freshmen Republicans who had a say in committee assignments argued, however, that anyone who had opposed the Contract with America was unfit for such a plum post. I was refused. All of my class had run on the idea that we had to reform Congress, change Congress, turn Congress upside down. Many of the younger members saw me as a remnant of a defeatist Republican mentality that sought compromise rather than confrontation with Democrats. They saw no value in my experience and seemed to believe that I lacked the zeal for reform.

I do not regret the decision, however—not for a minute. It set me apart as an independent member beholden to no one. The terms of the contract did not reflect the wishes of most of my constituents. They did not elect me to turn the House upside down. They elected me to solve problems.

Something equally important was at play, too. I knew the real Newt Gingrich, the real Dick Armey, the real Tom DeLay. I had watched these guys elbow their way up the ladder. I had seen them in every leadership meeting when I was Bob Michel's chief of staff. For them it was not about the Republican Party—it was about them. They could hold a grudge relentlessly. I never bought into their style and tactics.

There is no question I paid a price. DeLay, for example, never forgave me for voting against him when he ran for whip. He called me after the December 5 party conference to chew me out. When I sought a seat on the advisory group to the National Republican Campaign Committee, Bill Paxon (R-NY), who chaired the NRCC, told me that "higher powers intervened" during the selection. I said, "What the hell does that mean?" He told me that because I had not signed the contract, the party did not believe I was conservative enough. The higher powers could have been only DeLay or Gingrich.

I am the case study for how leaders punish wayward members. Another example: we held a series of votes on the contract's various planks during the first days of the 104th Congress. When we got to tax cuts, one of the last items, I voted no because I had campaigned on the promise to reduce the debt before passing any more tax cuts. Immediately after the vote, I was pulled from presiding over the House for several weeks. I went to Gingrich's staff and asked, "What's going on here?" and was told that I had voted against the crown jewel of the Speaker's plan.

I believed then, and still do, that I was qualified for party leadership and deserved consideration. In 1995 I had more seniority and more knowledge about House operations than any of the 86 freshmen (73 Republicans and 13 Democrats). I knew every member of the House. After years of advising Michel on strategy and policy as a staff member and attending every single meeting in which our leaders plotted strategy, I knew how things worked. After I was elected, however, the leaders never invited me to any of those meetings. I was just one of the troops.

SET ASIDE DIFFERENCES TO MAKE A DIFFERENCE

Lacking seniority and on the outs with my leadership, I knew I was not going to be effective in introducing bills, passing bills, or getting my name on bills even though we held the majority. That left service to my district. Back home a problem was not a Republican or Democratic problem—it was a community problem. I thrived on the ability to get people together around the table in Peoria to solve a puzzle—a much different strategy from the ones my colleagues in Washington pursued. I could use my new position as a member of Congress, which carried a lot of weight with people, to work things out.

My friendship with George Shadid reflected my approach to politics and public service: "Set aside differences to make a difference." George, a Democrat, represented Peoria in the Illinois Senate during much of my time in the U.S. House. I had known him for 30 years. We were once neighbors, and George's sons had babysat my kids. We shared a Lebanese heritage. We attended each other's fundraisers. We marched together in Peoria's annual Santa parade. We met for coffee hundreds of times. He was a member of the Central Illinois Six, a bipartisan group of Illinois General Assembly members who met with me regularly to discuss community issues. I did not think of George as representing a Democratic point of view; I saw him as a friend. And we worked together on scores of joint projects ranging from building roads to setting up community health centers.

Every member, of course, works for his or her constituents. Otherwise, they wouldn't last long in Washington. I placed more emphasis on that role than most, however, because of my unique situation. The role, which I sometimes called "mayor of the district," came naturally, too, because of my staff work for Tom Railsback and Bob Michel.

My second responsibility, of course, was to vote: to be there for the votes, and to vote the way I had promised to vote when I campaigned. I consider myself to be a progressive, conservative Republican. On social issues, I am conservative. I had a 100 percent voting record with the National Rifle Association and with right-to-life groups. I did not equivocate on those issues. On others, I tried to be progressive. To take an example from late in my House days, I voted for the $70 billion auto-industry bailout because the government had to step in—almost all the conservative Republicans voted against it. I have consistently believed that there is a constructive role for government in people's lives.

To help constituents and to vote—there is nothing earthshaking in those two roles. To have settled for them would have meant an ordinary, if meaningful, time in Congress. I was blocked from leadership in the House Republican Party and without much influence on the legislative side; however, another door opened—presiding over the House. Here my experience counted for something.

I did not know it in the beginning, of course, but my willingness to preside at every opportunity, especially during contentious debates, set me apart from my colleagues. I occupied the chair, for example, during the debate over the ban on partial-birth abortions and a Medicare overhaul. As a result, I gained the influence and respect that were denied me by more traditional paths. By the time Democrats retook the majority following the 2006 elections, I had presided over the House more frequently than any other member since 1995. Even during those periods when I opposed the Republican leadership on bills or political strategy, they knew I would rule confidently, decisively—both key attributes in maintaining order during complicated, highly charged debate.

Presiding did not confer the same power and authority as chairing a committee or winning a leadership post, but it was a very high-profile opportunity. Did I make a calculated decision to seek influence by presiding? Did I seize the opportunity for a larger political purpose? Sometimes I wish I were that clever. But at first I did not know that I would be very skilled at the task, so I approached presiding cautiously. Only with experience did I figure out that I was good at it. Other people recognized it, too. It was my style, the way I approached presiding— that it was a privilege, not a burden, not a routine chore. I grew into the role. I did not see it as a means to an end. Two unintended consequences resulted. First, presiding gave me the kind of position and profile that very few other members enjoyed. Second, it put me at the center of the action during the Clinton impeachment proceedings.

THE FIRST TERM ENDS

As my first year in the House drew to a close, I had to decide whether to run for reelection. Fifty years old and I had not left much of a mark on Congress. I had not spent time trying to make a name for myself by holding press conferences, seeking publicity, or pushing through boatloads of legislation. The only bill I had passed was a resolution naming the Lincoln, Illinois, post office in honor of the late Edward Madigan, a former congressman and secretary of agriculture.

My 99.7 percent voting record, pressing the button 883 times out of a possible 885, stood me in good stead with constituents.[15] Judging strictly by the numbers, I looked like a typical House Republican, siding with Gingrich 91.8 percent of the time. My support score matched the average for House Republicans and was only half a percentage point below the average for GOP first-termers.[16] I had voted with my party to overhaul welfare and health programs for the poor and the elderly; to limit punitive damages in product liability cases; to cut spending in most nondefense domestic programs; to oppose sending U.S. troops to Bosnia; and to seek constitutional amendments to require balanced federal budgets, to ban flag desecration, and to limit the number of terms a person could serve in Congress. I also supported telecommunications deregulation, Environmental Protection Agency (EPA) funding cuts, a bill to bar new listings on the endangered species list, changes in the Clean Water Act, and a measure to allow nonunion workplace advisory groups. All these votes reflected majority opinion in central Illinois.

Yet I had opposed the Republican leadership on several occasions, too. Firmly convinced that most people back home wanted the money saved from spending cuts to be used to reduce the deficit, not to cut taxes, I was one of 11 Republicans voting against a tax-relief package worth $189 billion over five years (the so-called crown jewel of the Contract with America). I continued to object to the leadership's approach to fiscal policy in October 1995 during the debate on the massive budget-reconciliation bill, which was the centerpiece of the Republican agenda to cut taxes, reduce the size of the federal government, and balance the budget. That bill, with $245 billion in tax cuts, passed the House 227–203; I was one of just 10 Republicans voting no.[17]

I had opposed other Republican-sponsored legislation, including reductions in funding for the Public Broadcasting System and limits to EPA enforcement of air and water regulations. On those matters and others, I stood apart from the party. But I must have done something right during my first term. The nationally respected *Congressional Quarterly* named me one of 11 "freshmen to watch." More important, my constituents returned me to office in 1996. I won the general election with 59 percent of the vote. That first reelection campaign is the toughest. Having survived it, I won each subsequent election handily.

NOTES

1. Daniel J. Balz and Ronald Brownstein, *Storming the Gates: Protest Politics and the Republican Revival* (Boston: Little, Brown & Co., 1996), 55.
2. Candidate interview, October 19, 1973, RHMP, Campaigns and Elections Series, Box 36, f. NRCC. Recruiting Committee. Southern Region.
3. Balz and Brownstein, *Storming the Gates*, 142–143.
4. Ibid., 115.
5. Maureen Dowd, "G.O.P.'s Rising Star Pledges to Right Wrongs of the Left," *NYT*, November 10, 1994, RLP-Memoir, f. Republican Party's Fortunes.
6. Katherine Q. Seeyle, "With Fiery Words, Gingrich Builds His Kingdom," *NYT*, October 27, 1994, RLP-Memoir, f. Republican Party's Fortunes.
7. "GOP 'Contract with America' Survey," RLP-Campaign, f. Candidate Questionnaires. "Contract with America."
8. "GOP 'Contract with America' Survey."
9. See appendix A for the terms of the contract.
10. Jeffrey B. Gayner, "The Contract with America: Implementing New Ideas in the U.S.," October 12, 1995, Heritage Foundation Lecture #549, http://www.heritage.org/research/politicalphilosophy/hl549.cfm.
11. News release, September 27, 1994, RLP-Campaign, f. FORL 1994.
12. Gayner, "Contract with America."
13. Lincoln Diaz-Balart and Ileana Ros-Lehtinen, both from Florida, did not sign the contract.
14. RL to many, December 7, 1994, RLP-DC-S, Republican Leadership, f. Republican Steering Committee.
15. I had happily chosen to attend our daughter Sara's high school graduation and missed two sure-to-pass votes on measures to restrict foreign aid.
16. Bob Estell, "LaHood Comfortable on Capitol," *State Journal-Register*, February 4, 1996, RLP-Memoir, f. Republican Party's Fortunes.
17. Philip D. Duncan and Christine C. Lawrence, *Congressional Quarterly's Politics in America 1998: The 105th Congress* (Washington, DC: Congressional Quarterly, 1997), 494–496.

CHAPTER 3

REPUBLICANS UNRAVEL

THE SPEAKER'S DAYS ARE NUMBERED

As my second term in the House began in 1997, an unfolding drama in the Republican leadership ranks threatened to heighten partisanship within the chamber and to wreak havoc within our party.

The beginning of the end to Newt Gingrich's career in the House can be pinned to any number of episodes. In my mind, his demise began, ironically, when Democrats decided to level ethics charges against him, in effect turning the tables on him. The allegations stemmed from a course called Renewing American Civilization, one that Gingrich created and taught between 1993 and 1995 at two small Georgia colleges. An ethics inquiry discovered that then congressman Gingrich had financed his course through donations solicited by tax-exempt groups. This subterfuge allowed supporters to make undisclosed contributions and to claim tax write-offs.

For two years, a House ethics subcommittee conducted a highly charged, partisan investigation of Gingrich. Finally, the subcommittee alleged that Gingrich had failed "to take appropriate steps to insure [sic] that the activities" he undertook were legal.[1] In a carefully crafted 500-word response on December 21, 1996, the Speaker admitted to improper conduct. "I have brought down on the people's house a controversy which could weaken the faith people have in the Government," the Speaker said.[2]

Although Gingrich's admission cleared the air of one charge against him, the Democrats had brought 73 others, not a small contribution to the increasingly poisonous atmosphere in the House.[3] The cumulative effect also cast doubt upon his ability to remain Speaker when the new Congress convened in January. The threat to Gingrich was real. There were 227 Republicans, 207 Democrats, and one independent entitled to vote. If all Democrats and the one independent voted for minority leader Dick Gephardt (D-MO), just 20 Republicans withholding support from Gingrich would throw the election to Gephardt.

Most of my colleagues knew the risk. Peter King (R-NY) and Chris Shays (R-CT), hoping to head off the embarrassment of seeing the Speaker unseated, tried in November to force him to resign until the ethics charges were resolved.[4] But Gingrich and his supporters worked the phones around the clock to rally support. They succeeded by defusing the King-Shays rebellion quickly. "On a scale of 1 to 10, I think it's a 10 that Newt will be re-elected," Shays said in late December. After receiving a call from the Speaker, King echoed Shays. "Politically, I still have difficulties with Newt, and I am not going to be invited to any of his New Year's parties," he said. "But I think it is wrong to deny the guy another term based on what the Ethics Committee has turned up."[5]

I did not jump to Newt's defense quite as quickly as King and Shays. As late as January 2, 1997, I was among 27 Republicans still uncommitted to Gingrich. As part of the effort to hold the ranks together, the leadership reassured us "undecideds" that Gingrich's offenses merited only a reprimand, not censure, which, under party rules, would have denied him a leadership position.[6] Majority Leader Armey offered another rationale in a conference call to 100 of us. His message: Democrats were trying to win the House through a perversion of the ethics process because they could not win it at the polls.[7] The next day, January 3, I signed a Dear

Colleague letter in which 10 of us announced our support for Gingrich's reelection as Speaker. "After reviewing all the available facts," we wrote, "we agree with Porter Goss and Steve Schiff, the two members [of the investigating committee] with the most intimate and detailed knowledge of the situation: we know of no reason why Newt Gingrich would be ineligible to be Speaker."[8]

On January 7, Gingrich retained the speakership over Gephardt, 216 to 205. Six Republicans voted "present," and four voted for other Republicans. I voted with the majority. Later that month, the House formally reprimanded Gingrich, 395–28, and assessed a $300,000 fine for ethics violations. I sided with the 196 Republicans who voted in favor of the reprimand, not with the 28 who listened to Tom DeLay's plea for leniency. In an interview with *Chicago Tribune* reporter Mike Dorning, I said that Gingrich had tested party loyalty "to the limit" and that any further embarrassments "would be very problematic for him in our [party] conference."[9]

The entire controversy surrounding the Speaker's ethical lapses and his fitness to serve left a bad taste in my mouth. His behavior confirmed my experience with him over the years as someone who played fast and loose with the rules, who let his ego or ambition or hubris overrule his obvious intelligence, who contented himself with the big picture at the expense of attention to detail, who polarized rather than united. His actions, reciprocated by Democrats, created an unwelcoming and unproductive atmosphere in the House of Representatives.

The Republican Conference grew increasingly restive as doubts grew about the Speaker's ability to lead. In March 1997, Gingrich, who had been negotiating with President Clinton about a balanced-budget deal, announced to the press that House Republicans would agree to postpone their tax cuts temporarily to achieve a budget agreement with Clinton. The pronouncement outraged conservatives, including House majority leader Dick Armey, who saw it as a betrayal of a core Republican commitment. Armey said he would never support a budget deal without tax cuts.[10]

As dissatisfaction grew, about two dozen Republicans began meeting in secret to discuss Gingrich's fate. Although Gingrich succeeded in striking a deal with the White House to balance the budget in May, he ran into trouble again during work on a supplemental appropriations bill to provide relief for flood-ravaged states in the Midwest and Upper Plains in June. Armey and his cohorts decided to attach favored riders to the bill in the belief that Clinton would not veto the politically popular measure. They outsmarted themselves. Clinton did veto the bill, and we Republicans took the hit. For his part, Gingrich ordered the bill stripped of the riders, but he did so without consulting Armey. Although the House passed the revised bill on June 12, all of Gingrich's top lieutenants—Armey, majority whip Tom DeLay, and GOP Conference chair John Boehner (R-OH)—voted against it.[11]

THE PLOT FAILS

By now the leadership was in shambles. On June 17, GOP rebels met to consider Gingrich's ouster; Armey refused to defend the Speaker at a press conference later. On July 9, Republican leaders, without Gingrich, met privately—sources quoted Armey as having "Newt fatigue," that he was not willing to "clean up another one of Newt's messes." The next day, at 11:00 a.m., Tom DeLay met with about 20 conservative dissidents to hear their complaints about Gingrich. Although I did not attend these meetings, apparently DeLay urged quick action to replace Gingrich with Bill Paxon (R-NY), chair of the GOP Leadership Council, by passing a motion to declare the Speaker's chair vacant. The press caught wind of the effort to replace Gingrich on July 16, prompting Paxon to resign from the leadership the next day.[12] "Obviously we have a fractured leadership team," I told the *Washington Post*.[13]

I had first heard of the plot at a meeting of sophomore Republicans on the 16th. I immediately sided with Gingrich, a move that surprised some. "He's the guy that has probably done more for the party and the House of Representatives than anyone else," I told the *Chicago Sun-*

Times.[14] I remembered how the constant plotting against Bob Michel had undermined him and compromised our party's unity. We abhorred the way these guys cavorted in the background against our boss. "I think it's very distressing when you have our elected leaders trying to carve one another up, and there seems to be a great deal of disunity," I explained to a reporter back home. "It is not good for [House Republicans] to have our leaders carping at one another and trying to gut one another."[15] As much as I questioned Gingrich's ethical judgments, I disliked Armey and DeLay's tactics more.

To help resolve the matter, I led an effort to hold a special meeting of the Republican Conference to hear from Armey, DeLay, and Boehner.[16] I called Boehner and told him that if he didn't call the meeting, I would circulate a letter among the rank and file and collect enough signatures to force it. All three leaders and the Speaker opposed me. DeLay and Armey sent their lieutenants onto the House floor to dissuade members from signing the petition. But I got the 50 signatures necessary under our party's rules to force a meeting of the conference. "I'm not a vengeful person," I said in one interview. "The point is these people are the highest elected leaders of our conference and they need to be held accountable. They carried out some indiscretions and they were trying to duck it."[17] "I think it's extraordinary when we are preached to on a regular basis about team work and working together and cooperating," I said to another reporter, "and then you see our elected leaders out to get the speaker and out to try to bring him down. I think it's nonsense, and I think most people think it's very bizarre behavior and they need to account for it."[18] In the end, Gingrich short-circuited the process, agreed to call for a conference, and asked me to call off the petition drive, which I did.

The three-hour, closed-door meeting began at 8:00 p.m., Wednesday, July 23, in a packed meeting room in the Capitol basement. "I strongly encourage every Republican member to participate in this dialog," Gingrich had told Reuters News Service earlier in the day. "Let me emphasize: I will not allow another chapter to be written in this tiresome and overwrought saga. This discussion will be the end of the story."[19] Conference vice chair Jennifer Dunn (R-WA) presided. The Speaker began the meeting by quoting the biblical epistle to the Romans: "Bless those who persecute you; bless them and do not curse them."[20]

Each of the accused leaders of the abortive coup—Armey, DeLay, and Boehner—spoke for about 10 minutes. They apologized to Gingrich and the rest of us for participating in discussions about ousting the Speaker. DeLay confessed that he would have sided with the dissidents to remove Gingrich but then said his actions were a mistake in judgment brought on by fatigue. He said, "If you want a head, you've got one, and it's mine."[21] After he finished, he received a long round of applause. Others spoke that evening, including two of the dissidents. The spirit was positive, with no name-calling or demands for resignations. Instead, we approved a resolution pledging the party "to unite with its leadership to continue its work" and declaring that our differences would "not prevent us from carrying out our common agenda."[22] United, we left the meeting to face a horde of reporters.

At the conclusion of this unhappy episode, however, many of us thought that Gingrich had been betrayed. As we adjourned, I told the press that Gingrich had emerged stronger than ever. "He's the most popular leader now," I explained. "He's the only one who has been able to stay above the fray."[23] I appreciated the irony that I had helped save Gingrich. Newt wrote to me a few days later to say, "Your heartfelt views are very helpful for all of us as we put the past couple of weeks behind us."[24]

I could not forgive Armey and DeLay, however. As I told a reporter in my district, "I'm not surprised by their behavior because they reacted like this when they were in the leadership when Michel was leader. They were always conniving about something."[25]

Republican Leadership Races, 1998

Others shared my disaffection with the faction-ridden party leadership as we headed into the November 1998 congressional elections. Stories began to circulate in the press about how this member or that intended to run for leadership posts in the new Congress.[26] I knew I could not mount my own bid for a leadership post, so I decided to back two challengers: Bob Livingston (R-LA) to replace Gingrich, and Steve Largent (R-OK) to unseat Dick Armey, the majority leader. I believed that both could reverse the party's diminishing fortunes.

Livingston, an attorney, had lost his first race for a House seat, but in a special election in August 1977, he became the first Republican to represent New Orleans in Congress since Reconstruction. In 1978, he won a full term and was reelected 11 times, the last nine unopposed. Although well known in Louisiana, Livingston was a relatively low-key member of Congress for his first 18 years in Washington. Early in his career he managed, however, to land a coveted spot on the Appropriations Committee, on which I also served. Livingston instantly became one of the most powerful members of Congress when Republicans took the majority. He impressed me, and I became one of a handful of Republicans who met regularly to promote him to a leadership position, probably majority leader—all this before Speaker Gingrich landed in hot water. I was looking for new leadership, and I thought Bob was the right guy. Early in 1998, Livingston announced that he would seek the speakership whenever Gingrich stepped aside. Despite Gingrich's troubles, no one knew when that would be.

I also decided to support Steve Largent's campaign to defeat majority leader Dick Armey. Largent was more conservative than I, but a progressive or moderate did not stand a chance, so I supported Steve as the best bet to knock off Armey. Most people knew Largent as the Pro Football Hall of Fame receiver for the Seattle Seahawks, where he had played 14 years. Following his retirement, he moved to Tulsa, Oklahoma. In 1994, the governor appointed Largent to the 103rd Congress to fill a vacancy.

He was elected in his own right to the 104th Congress in 1994. Like that of many in our freshmen class, Largent's voting record was very conservative. He was one of the "true believers" in that class, devoting most of his time to issues important to conservative Christians.

Largent impressed me, though, for several reasons. He distinguished himself in our conference as someone who had the vision, confidence, and courage to challenge the status quo. The climate of the upcoming 106th Congress required a new dynamic. Our current leaders contented themselves with an unfocused, business-as-usual operating style that had produced successive declines in our Republican majority. Although conservative, Largent promoted a Reaganesque style, putting his confidence in the American people to manage their own affairs if government would let them. He had paid his dues to the party, too, raising hundreds of thousands of dollars for Republicans all across the country before he ever became involved in the leadership race. He was a consensus builder. In Washington, he shared an apartment with two Democrats. There's nothing like the after-hours give and take of personal conversation for learning to understand how the other person thinks and how to build bridges.[27]

The November 1998 midterm election results roiled the leadership race. Four years after confounding the experts and winning control of the House for the first time in 40 years, we Republicans suffered a shellacking. Democrats won a net gain of five seats in the House, marking the first time since 1934 that the party controlling the White House had gained seats in the House in a midterm election. Gingrich was right to say that Republicans had won the third consecutive election for the first time since the Great Depression, but his days were numbered. It did not help that he had predicted a net Republican gain of 24 votes—some of us wondered whether he saw the same voters we did.

On Friday morning, November 6, three days after the election, Bob Livingston announced his intention to challenge Gingrich for the speakership. "Revolutionizing takes some talent, many talents," said Livingston.

"My friend Newt Gingrich brought those talents to bear and put the Republicans in the majority. Day-to-day governing takes others. I believe I have those talents." As Speaker, Livingston said, he would do a better job than Gingrich at "making sure that the trains run on time" and "assessing, setting, and articulating a practical agenda."[28] Livingston also pledged to support what he described as the hallmarks of Republican philosophy: smaller government, fewer taxes, safer communities, a stronger defense, and the best-quality education for our children.[29] I would have counseled Bob to include reducing the deficit as a higher priority than cutting taxes, but that plea had fallen on deaf ears in our party for years. I applauded his focus on running the House more smoothly.

Gingrich did not yield to Livingston without a fight. "Last Tuesday's elections were a tremendous disappointment to the Speaker and every other Republican," the Speaker's spokesperson said. "The question is not whether something went wrong, but how best to fix it. As architect of the Republican majority, Speaker Gingrich is determined to correct the mistakes of the past and implement a positive, issue-oriented legislative agenda."[30]

Gingrich could do little to stop defectors, however, as more Republicans stepped forward to back Livingston publicly. Matt Salmon (R-AZ) predicted that at least seven Republican members of the House would not vote to reelect Gingrich as Speaker. "There may be as many as 30 or 40," he said on NBC's *Today* show. "Four years ago we won the Super Bowl [the 1994 Republican triumph]," Salmon said. "We haven't had a winning season since. We've got to change coaches or we'll lose our franchise."[31] Bob Barr (R-GA) joined the chorus, accusing the national leadership of the Republican Party of having "some serious problems in terms of defining and delivering a consistent message." Barr, whose Georgia district was next to Gingrich's, said that he didn't think "the current team" would remain in place—"nor should it."

Largent went public with his challenge to Armey on Friday morning, as well. "On November 3rd the Republican party hit an iceberg. And I think the question that is before our conference today is whether we retain the crew of the Titanic," he told the press. Delivering a scathing criticism of the current GOP leadership, Largent said,

> We've had a leadership vacuum for four years in Washington, D.C., that has basically been blown about by the winds of public opinion polls and focus groups as opposed to relying upon a standard and principle ... that define the Republican party. That has been the reason we've had conflict within our own conference.[32]

On CNN's *Larry King Live* that night, Largent said, "What the Republican Party needs so desperately is not retreads, not old has-beens, but the new fresh ideas, fresh faces, and I'm excited."[33]

In his campaign to retain his post, Armey sent a damage-control letter to Republican members outlining the issues to his way of thinking. I received a fax version at 4:30 p.m., Friday afternoon. Armey said he had spoken to more than 130 members since the election and had come up with six areas of focus. He called on us "to rekindle the spirit of the Contract with America," claiming responsibility for pulling it together in 1994. We must, he wrote, "craft a clear, powerful Agenda 2000" centered on cutting taxes, reforming Social Security, reforming education, and rebuilding our defenses. In addition, he stressed the importance of "getting our work done on time" so that the White House and the Senate could not control the action. He counseled closer cooperation with Republican governors, more vigorous efforts to communicate our message, and more attention to maintaining alliances. "We need to learn how to work with our coalitions to win and then win again, not just have intramural fights," he said.[34]

To cap off one of the most eventful days in terms of our party's leadership, Gingrich gave up the fight and decided to retire from the speakership and from the House. In the second of two conference calls to Republicans, Gingrich blamed House conservatives for his downfall. He had brought them to power; then they turned on him. He called them cannibals who had blackmailed him into quitting.[35] The press reported that Gingrich had made the choice when told that as many as 30 Republicans would refuse to vote for him as Speaker when the new Congress convened. Rumor had it that prospective Republican presidential candidates in 2000 also warned that Gingrich would drag them down if he stayed.

Amidst all this turmoil in our party, I received a letter from Minority Leader Gephardt asking me, and I presume many others, to "put aside partisanship in favor of progress." "I want to create a coalition for change—of like-minded Democrats and Republicans who care about doing what's right for our nation," he wrote. I agreed with his closing sentiment: "Voters are sick and tired of Congressional inertia on the real-life challenges that face our country, and they demand action."[36] The trouble was that we Republicans had no leadership at the moment.

Over the next 10 days, our members positioned themselves for the leadership elections to be held on November 18. My files contain letters and statements from more than 80 colleagues either announcing their interest in a leadership post or lobbying on behalf of their preferred candidate. That doesn't count the endless stream of telephone calls and hallway conversations. For those 10 days, however, I focused my attention on Steve Largent's campaign. Gingrich's resignation had cleared the way for Livingston, so he did not need my help. Chris Cox (R-CT), Bill Archer (R-TX), and Jim Talent (R-MO) thought about challenging for the speakership, but Bob had the race sewn up within a couple of days.

The race for majority leader became a three-person affair: Armey, Largent, and Jennifer Dunn (R-WA). On November 9, Largent made public his campaign steering committee. Joining me were John Shadegg (R-AZ), Michael Forbes (R-NY), Sue Myrick (R-NC), John Doolittle (R-CA), Steve Chabot (R-OH), Nathan Deal (R-GA), and Zach Wamp (R-TN).[37]

The next day, Jennifer Dunn announced her candidacy in a Dear Colleague letter. She asked for support "as a Member who will serve as a fresh face for the Party, delivering a clear message that will build broad support for our vision from all Americans. We need to clarify our message and show our renewed commitment to our basic principles," she declared before concluding:

> Even though our successes have been many, at times our message has failed to resonate. We must make the most of our opportunities to define who we are and where we stand. We are at a critical time. We can drive the debate, and without compromising our principles, successfully move our nation forward on the right track. Or we can miss opportunities and squander our Republican Majority. In many ways our choices are clear—we can lead, follow or simply get in our own way.[38]

Dunn represented the eighth congressional district in Washington State, covering most of the eastern edge of metropolitan Seattle. She was the first woman to lead the Washington State Republican Party, serving as its chair for 12 years starting in 1981. After her election to Congress in 1992, she became the first freshman woman to win a place on the House Republican leadership team and was given a seat on the prestigious Ways and Means Committee. In 1998, she was the highest-ranking woman in the House Republican Conference, serving as vice chair. Dunn's voting record was generally conservative on economic and foreign policy issues and more moderate on cultural issues.[39]

It was difficult to assess the impact of Dunn's announcement. Although her pro-choice stance threatened to hurt her chances, Dunn offered herself as an alternative to Armey's failed leadership and to Largent's inexperience. Armey's people claimed they had 100 of the 112 votes needed to prevail, but I doubt that Dunn would have entered the race if she'd felt Armey had it locked up. The conventional wisdom held Dunn to be a greater threat to Armey than Largent was. Complicating the situation was the tension between Livingston and Armey—they had clashed several times over the years. Both Livingston and DeLay, either of whom could have quashed a challenge to Armey, refused to back the majority leader.

I signed a Dear Colleague letter on November 11 promoting Largent. I praised Steve's strengths: his ability to communicate, that he represented a new generation of leadership, his open-mindedness, and his commitment to a family-friendly legislative schedule, among others. To rebut the charge that Steve lacked experience, I reminded my colleagues that no Republican had been able to claim experience running the floor when we achieved the majority four years earlier. I felt that if we had a strong agenda that set the course and provided guidance for our leaders, they would make things happen. "Steve Largent may be untested as a congressional leader, but he *is* tested as a leader in the athletic world as an NFL Hall of Famer," I wrote, "and he exhibits the potential to lead and to articulate our goals and accomplishments."[40] As the leadership elections approached, dozens of other members composed similar letters. Of course, the Armey and Dunn camps circulated letters of their own.

In hindsight, Dunn and Largent and even Armey, to a degree, ran on the same platform: better communication, an improved image, renewed fidelity to core principles, and leadership in a new direction—all of which confirmed how much the GOP had unraveled.

Our strategy to elect Largent conceded that Armey would tally the most votes on the first ballot. We believed, however, that he would fall short of the 112 votes necessary to win outright. If we could get to a second ballot, we hoped for the support of the anyone-but-Armey people. On Friday, November 13, Largent's staff delivered a preliminary count. Despite the spin circulating on the Hill that Largent was stuck in third place, our numbers showed him with 63 votes to Armey's 61 and Dunn's 23, with 76 undecided. Each of us on the steering committee received a list of reporters and pundits and their phone numbers to work our own spin.[41]

Monday brought a new development. Tom Ewing (R-IL) and Mike Castle (R-DE) announced that they would place Denny Hastert's name in nomination for majority leader, making it a four-person race. A member of the Illinois delegation and a friend, Denny was deputy whip to DeLay and had achieved success in managing health care and antidrug legislation.

Castle wrote the members of the Tuesday Group, an informal caucus of about 40 moderate Republicans to which I belonged, that Largent and Dunn risked splitting the anti-Armey vote and that Hastert had a better chance of uniting the reformers.[42] Admittedly, Hastert was a very popular figure; everyone liked him. Largent was probably too conservative for the Tuesday Group. If I had known of Denny's interest earlier, I would have backed him. At that late hour, however, I had to stick with Largent.

Two days later, November 18, our conference met to elect the leadership for the 106th Congress. The voting took place by secret ballot behind closed doors in the ornate caucus room of the Cannon Office Building. Livingston was nominated as the Republican candidate for Speaker without opposition, effectively making him Speaker-elect come January.

Next came the vote for majority leader. I rose to nominate Steve Largent. "Being an effective Majority Leader requires leadership, organization, communication, and trust," I began. I repeated the arguments I had been making for the past two weeks. But to no avail.[43]

It took Dick Armey three ballots to defeat Largent, Dunn, and Hastert. On the first ballot, he had 100 votes; Largent, 58; Dunn, 45; and Hastert, 18. On the second ballot, Armey lost one vote to win 99; Largent had 73, and Dunn had 49. On the final ballot, Armey received 127 to Largent's 95.[44] Once Hastert and Dunn were eliminated, we had hoped to attract the moderates. They did not like Armey, but they apparently felt that Steve was too inflexible or too inexperienced, leaving them with no choice but to support the incumbent. If we had been able to consolidate the opposition to Armey behind Largent on either the first or second ballot, my candidate would have prevailed. It was not to be. As Largent told the press, "Steve Largent has been too slow and too small his whole life, and this is just one more occasion."[45] Needless to say, my role did not endear me to the majority leader.

The third-ranking House Republican, Tom DeLay of Texas, ran unopposed for another term as majority whip. But the party's yearning for a new, softer image cost Ohio's John Boehner his leadership post. I supported Boehner, but he was upended by J. C. Watts of Oklahoma for chair of the GOP Conference by a vote of 121 to 93. The winds of change also removed John Linder of Georgia as chair of the National Republican Congressional Committee. He lost to Tom Davis (R-VA), whom I supported, 77 to 130. Chris Cox was reelected chair of the Policy Committee.

In his appearance before the press, Speaker-designate Livingston pronounced Republicans as united, adding: "We're all going to have to work together," a formidable task that will entail "reaching out to Democrats." He continued: "We want the American people to know that they are going to get good, clean, honest, efficient government from us. We muffed our message a little bit in the last elections. We may have slipped, but we haven't fallen."[46]

By the end of the day, November 18, we had selected our leadership for the Congress to be seated in January 1999. We had put the contests behind us. I welcomed the change Bob Livingston promised for Republicans. He had already signaled a sincere willingness to build a relationship with Dick Gephardt, something Gingrich never did. Bob's brand of conservatism was more pragmatic, more in the Bob Michel mode than Gingrich's had been. Whereas Newt had to be the center of attention and relied on his facility for expressing "vision," Livingston lacked Gingrich's ego—no illusions of grandeur. If he also lacked Gingrich's intellect, Bob at least had avoided the ethical scandals that doomed Newt's speakership.

Or so I thought. On December 19, just hours before the House had scheduled votes on the impeachment of President Clinton, Bob Livingston announced he was resigning from the House following the disclosure of his extramarital affairs. I was astounded—and blindsided. Despite what I thought was a personal friendship with Bob, I had no prior knowledge of his decision.

Now what? Tom DeLay had been tipped off by Livingston and began immediately containing the damage. With the impeachment at hand, he realized that yet another leadership controversy could taint the proceedings. Much to my surprise, DeLay overcame his own ambition for the top job, perhaps realizing that his hard-charging style was ill suited to such a turbulent time for the party. Neither could Armey pursue the speakership. He knew he would lose, and he knew that DeLay would block it in any case. DeLay settled on Denny Hastert and began rounding up votes.

I knew Hastert well. When Denny was first elected to the House in 1986, Bob Michel had taken him under his wing. Bob marked Hastert as an up-and-comer during House consideration of the Clinton health care plan. When the White House asked Bob for a contact, Bob assigned Hastert the role. That was a clear signal that Denny had a promising future. Over time, DeLay saw promise in the Illinoisan, too, and took him on as his chief deputy in the party's whip organization. In that role, Denny bridged the divide between the GOP moderates and conservatives. He earned respect from the party's ideological, generational, and geographical factions.

His chief handicap was the unknown, both in terms of what he faced and in that he was largely invisible. Denny had no strong support base of his own. He did not campaign for the office. He lacked public visibility. Even I, close a friend though I was, had no idea what his agenda for leadership and the party would be. Denny was a pragmatist, not an ideologue.

On the first day of the 106th Congress, Dennis J. Hastert, age 57, was elected Speaker. "Solutions to problems cannot be found in a pool of bitterness," he said. "They can be found in an environment in which we trust one another's word." "Let's bury the hatchet," Democratic leader Dick Gephardt responded, as he handed the gavel to the new Speaker.

Promises, promises.

Notes

1. Adam Clymer, "Panel Concludes Gingrich Violated Rules on Ethics," *NYT*, December 22, 1996, RLP-Memoir, f. Republican Party's Fortunes.
2. "Statement Issued by Speaker Gingrich," *NYT*, December 22, 1996, RLP-Memoir, f. Republican Party's Fortunes.
3. Fax transmittal, "Facts about the Speaker's Ethics Case," December 30, 1996, RLP-DC-S, Republican Leadership, f. Gingrich.
4. Jerry Gray, "Gingrich Weathering His Ethics Storm," *NYT*, December 24, 1996, RLP-Memoir, f. Republican Party's Fortunes.
5. Ibid.
6. Adam Clymer, "Gingrich Strains to Retain His Hold on the House," *NYT*, January 3, 1997, RLP-Memoir, f. Gingrich Resignation.
7. "House GOP Is Said to Be United on Keeping Gingrich as Speaker," *NYT*, January 4, 1997, RLP-Memoir, f. Republican Party's Fortunes.
8. Dear Colleague, January 3, 1997, RLP-DC-S, Republican Leadership, f. Gingrich.
9. Mark Dorning, "House Hands Gingrich His Punishment," *Chicago Tribune*, January 22, 1997, RLP-DC-S, Republican Leadership, f. Gingrich.
10. CQ, *Congress and the Nation*, vol. 10, 1997–2001 (Washington DC: CQ Press, 2002), 762–763.
11. Ibid.
12. Sandy Hume, "GOP Leaders Seek to Avoid Purge," *The Hill*, July 23, 1997, RLP-Peoria-TBS, f. House Politics (1).
13. John Yang, "Paxon Quits House GOP Leadership," *Washington Post*, July 18, 1997, RLP-Peoria-TBS, f. House Politics (1).
14. Basil Talbott, "Gingrich Foes in Hot Water," *Chicago Sun-Times*, July 22, 1997, RLP-Peoria-TBS, f. House Politics (1).
15. Adriana Colindres, "LaHood Questions GOP Leaders' Apparent Feud," *Peoria Journal Star*, July 19, 1997, RLP-Peoria-TBS, f. House Politics (1).
16. RL and others, "We, the undersigned members of the Republican Conference," July 22, 1997, RLP-DC-S, Republican Leadership, f. Gingrich.
17. Dori Meinert, "LaHood Satisfied with GOP Meeting," *The State Journal-Register*, July 25, 1997, RLP-Peoria-TBS, f. House Politics (1).
18. "Gingrich Tries to Calm His Colleagues," *AllPolitics*, July 22, 1997, RLP-Peoria-TBS, f. House Politics (1).

19. Jackie Frank, "Gingrich Asks Republicans to End Internal Strife," Reuters, July 23, 1997, RLP-Peoria-TBS, f. House Politics (1).
20. Laurie Kellman and Nancy Roman, "Gingrich Lets Rebels Keep Leadership Posts," *Washington Times*, July 24, 1997, RLP-Peoria-TBS, f. House Politics (1).
21. Ibid.
22. John Yang, "House Republicans Close Rank," *Washington Post*, July 24, 1997, RLP-Peoria-TBS, f. House Politics (1).
23. Kellman and Roman, "Gingrich Lets Rebels Keep Posts."
24. Gingrich to RL, July 30, 1997, RLP-Peoria-TBS, f. House Politics (1).
25. Dori Meinert, "Hastert Might Be in Line," *State Journal-Register*, July 22, 1997, RLP-Peoria-TBS, f. House Politics (1).
26. Tony Blankley, "Grand Old Party Crack-Up," *Between the Lines*, April 29, 1998, RLP-Peoria-TBS, f. House Politics (2).
27. "Steve Largent Can Be a Strong, Effective Majority Leader," n.d., RLP-DC-S, Republican Leadership, f. Leadership Races, 1998 (1).
28. "Gingrich Calls It Quits," *AllPolitics*, November 6, 1998, RLP-Memoir, f. Republican Party's Fortunes.
29. "Statement by U.S. Representative Bob Livingston," November 6, 1998, RLP-DC-S, Republican Leadership, f. Leadership Races, 1998 (1).
30. "Martin Statement on Livingston Challenge," November 6, 1998, RLP-DC-S, Republican Leadership, f. Leadership Races, 1998 (1).
31. "Gingrich Calls It Quits."
32. "Gingrich Calls It Quits."
33. Alison Mitchell, "Without Focus on Gingrich, Rivalries Engulf the G.O.P., *NYT*, November 8, 1998, RLP-Memoir, f. Republican Party's Fortunes.
34. Armey to RL, November 6, 1998, RLP-DC-S, Republican Leadership, f. Leadership Races, 1998 (1).
35. Katharine Q. Seeyle, "Facing a Revolt, Gingrich Won't Run for Speaker," *NYT*, November 7, 1998, RLP-Memoir, f. Republican Party's Fortunes.
36. Gephardt to RL, November 6, 1998, RLP-DC-S, Republican Leadership, f. Leadership Races, 1998 (1).
37. Press release, "Largent Welcomes Dunn Candidacy," November 9, 1998, RLP-DC-S, Republican Leadership, f. Leadership Races, 1998 (1).
38. Dunn to Dear Republican Colleague, November 10, 1998, RLP-DC-S, Republican Leadership, f. Leadership Races, 1998 (1).
39. Editorial reprinted in Doc Hastings to Dear Colleague, November 10, 1998, RLP-DC-S, Republican Leadership, f. Leadership Races, 1998 (1).

40. RL to Dear Colleague, November 11, 1998, RLP-DC-S, Republican Leadership, f. Leadership Races, 1998 (2).
41. Joan Mitchell to Diane Liesman (e-mail), November 13, 1998, RLP-DC-S, Republican Leadership, f. Leadership Races, 1998 (2).
42. Castle to Dear Tuesday Group Colleagues, November 16, 1998, RLP-DC-S, Republican Leadership, f. Leadership Races, 1998 (2).
43. Reading copy of the remarks, November 18, 1998, RLP-DC-S, Republican Leadership, f. Leadership Races, 1998 (2).
44. Handwritten tallies, November 18, 1998, RLP-DC-S, Republican Leadership, f. Leadership Races, 1998 (3).
45. Katharine Q. Seeyle, "Mix of Old and New Is to Lead House G.O.P.," *NYT*, November 19, 1998, RLP-Memoir, f. Republican Party's Fortunes.
46. Seeyle, "Mix of Old and New."

Chapter 4

Civility in Retreat

Congress does not need to be—indeed should not be—a contest to see who can shout the loudest or who can throw the most accusations at the other party. We should rationally attempt to address, discuss, and solve problems on behalf of the citizens we represent.

—Ray LaHood, 1998[1]

Vanishing Comity in the House

By 1996, my second year in Congress, the image of the House of Representatives depicted in most textbooks as a place of reasoned debate, predictable processes, and restrained partisanship had simply disappeared. This came as no surprise to me. I had witnessed the coarsening of politics firsthand as chief of staff to Republican leader Bob Michel. His battles not only with Democrats but also with hard-edged Republicans led by Newt Gingrich warned of the decline in civility and comity that became evident to all in the 104th Congress.

Just a few examples. On the floor of the House, Bob Dornan (R-CA) charged President Clinton with "giving aid and comfort to the enemy" during the Vietnam War—Dornan was formally sanctioned. John Mica

(R-FL) violated House decorum when he called the president "the little bugger." Wes Cooley (R-OR) offered to punch a pregnant member of the press in the nose. Jim Moran (D-VA) shoved Duke Cunningham (R-CA) after a testy debate on Bosnia, promoting a general melee and an urgent summons to the Capitol police.[2] Democrat Maxine Waters ordered New York Republican Peter King to "shut up" during a Banking Committee hearing.

The lack of respect extended to the very highest levels of leadership in the House. The charges and countercharges swirling around Newt Gingrich's behavior had a predictable impact on the relationship between the Speaker and minority leader Dick Gephardt. The two of them went 18 months without a single private conversation. By contrast, Minority Leader Michel had met at least once a week with Democratic leaders.[3] The relationship between the leaders in the 104th Congress was a far cry from the days when Tip O'Neill and Michel famously played golf together.[4]

What occurred in Congress, of course, mirrored changes in American society at large. A survey conducted in 1996 for *U.S. News and World Report* found that 89 percent of Americans thought incivility to be a serious problem; 78 percent of those surveyed believed the problem had become worse in the last decade.[5] Examples of what one scholar called "differences of opinion taken to absurd lengths" included abortion-clinic doctors murdered by abortion opponents, the Oklahoma City bombing, and a culture of "unrestrained rage, sadism and insult on the Internet."[6] Organizations such as the National Commission on Civic Renewal, headed by retiring senator Sam Nunn (D-GA) and conservative writer William Bennett, and the Institute for a Civil Society's New Century/ New Solutions led by Patricia Schroeder, a former House member, sought remedies within broader society. Even Miss Manners weighed in—"What's changed is the society," she wrote. "The House of Representatives is in danger of sinking to the level of its constituency. It's the same problem affecting everyday life."[7]

Scholars and pundits confirmed what those of us in Congress felt simply by being there. *Congressional Quarterly* analyzed congressional votes since 1954 to find that partisanship had reached its peak in 1995, when 73 percent of all roll-call votes in the House and 69 percent in the Senate broke down roughly along party lines. The partisanship index dropped some in 1996 to 56 percent in the House and 62 percent in the Senate, but in the previous 40 years even those levels had been surpassed only three times in the Senate and seven times in the House.[8]

All of us in the House, Democrats and Republicans, understood that we had been elected to debate hotly contested issues and then to vote. We expected, even welcomed, the competition among ideas. We had legitimate policy differences. To conduct ourselves without restraint and mutual respect, however, was a recipe for disaster. Harvard professor Michael Sandel put it well:

> The incivility now rampant in American life will not be cured by exhortation or by a muting of political differences. It is a symptom of a problem with our public life more fundamental than can be solved by a softening of partisan voices. Americans' worries about incivility express a deeper fear that the moral fabric of community is unraveling around us. From families and neighborhoods to cities and towns to schools, congregations and trade unions, the institutions that traditionally provide people with moral anchors and a sense of belonging are under siege.[9]

Proposing the First Civility Retreat

But what could I, a freshman congressman, do about it? The answer came soon enough. David Skaggs, a Democrat from Colorado, approached me in June 1996 about co-organizing what he called a "civility retreat" for House members. So began an assignment that I took on for the next eight years—leading efforts to change the culture of the House. By the end of my career there, I was more closely identified with the civility initiative than with any piece of legislation or formal committee assignment.

The evolution of these efforts from 1996 until 2005 demonstrated why reform was so difficult to accomplish in the House. Despite repeated efforts by scores of members to instill in the House mutual respect in personal dealings and in formal debate, we succeeded only marginally. After four civility retreats, we called it quits in 2004.

But back to the beginning. Congressman Skaggs and I were contemporaries, both in our mid-50s in 1996. The two of us had served on congressional staffs—David for his predecessor, Tim Wirth, and I for Tom Railsback and Bob Michel. Both of us had served in state legislatures, too —David for three terms in Colorado, I for a single term in Illinois. David had won the first of his six terms in the House in 1986, so he preceded me by eight years. The House lost a first-rate member when he retired in 1998 to direct the work of the Center for Democracy and Citizenship at the Council for Excellence in Government.

David came up with the idea of a civility retreat following a string of embarrassing incidents. The straw that broke the camel's back for Skaggs occurred when Sam Gibbons (FL), ranking Democrat on the Ways and Means Committee, threw down a pile of papers in front of Republican chair Bill Archer of Texas, called the Republicans a "bunch of fascists" and "dictators," stalked out of the committee room, and yanked on the necktie of California Republican Bill Thomas—all over issues related to Medicare. The press dubbed the incident "the brawl in the hall."[10] As Skaggs recalled, "In the back of everybody's mind, I think, is the realization that we're better than this. We're all serious-minded people. We ought to be able to figure this thing out a little better."[11] David had sounded out a couple other members before he approached me. He and I were not close friends, so I was surprised when he asked me to co-sponsor the retreat initiative. I suspect that my reputation as a fair-minded presiding officer and as Bob Michel's chief of staff had something to do with his invitation. Whatever his reasons, I jumped at the idea. I, too, was weary of the constant bickering and bothered that people back in my district bad-mouthed Congress as a result of hearing about such incivility.

In hindsight, it may seem remarkable that a casual encounter on the House floor with a colleague from the other side of the aisle, someone I did not know well, led to one of the most important assignments I took on in my career. Much of the important business of the House took place in this manner, however. We got a lot of work done by informal conversation. It didn't always take formal hearings or office appointments.

David and I knew that support from Speaker Gingrich and Minority Leader Gephardt would be crucial to the success of our proposal. The two of them epitomized the problem. The ill will between Gingrich and Gephardt was legendary and palpable. But Skaggs agreed to draft letters to them hoping to appeal to their better natures and explaining what we intended to accomplish. He would vet the letter with Democrats; I agreed to do the same with Republicans. What follows is the letter we began to circulate to colleagues in late June.

> Dear Mr. Speaker:
>
> The ability of the House of Representatives to deal successfully with the challenges facing the nation depends on the level of trust and the working relationships that exist among members. We believe there is a real need for a considered and concerted effort to improve the House in this respect.
>
> Without belaboring the experience of the last several years, we all seek a greater degree of civility, mutual respect and—when possible—bipartisanship. We believe this can be accomplished without having to compromise vigorous debate or legitimate disagreement. But it will take work and a certain commitment.
>
> We are writing you and the Minority Leader to suggest that you agree to set aside a long weekend early in 1997 for the entire membership to meet together informally at an appropriate site near Washington.

It would be premature now to try to lay out any very detailed agenda. The main purpose would be to permit members to get to know each other before the difficult work of the 105th Congress begins in earnest and to establish a more constructive spirit and ethic for member-to-member relations.

We hope you agree that such a session would help create a more congenial and productive work environment, regardless of who may have the majority after the election. We recommend that you appoint a planning committee drawn equally from each party to develop a specific proposal that could be approved by the joint leadership before *sine die* adjournment of the 104th Congress.

Thank you very much for your consideration.[12]

On July 16, Skaggs's office issued a press release announcing that the member-initiated effort had received support from 21 Democrats and 10 Republicans. David Broder broke the story of our work five days later. The *Washington Post* columnist called it "a simple, almost simple-minded idea. But it signals a change in the atmosphere on Capitol Hill, and it could have important consequences."[13] He quoted Zoe Lofgren, a freshman Democrat from California, who said, "The only time we saw the freshman Republicans during the orientation period [prior to the opening of the Congress in 1995] was when we stood on the Capitol steps to have our pictures taken. That is not healthy."[14]

Partly because of Broder's favorable column, we enlisted additional signers. On July 25, Skaggs and I, joined by Amo Houghton (R-NY) and Tom Sawyer (D-OH), personally delivered the letters to Gingrich and Gephardt. Forty-four Republicans and 42 Democrats co-signed. "My colleagues' reaction to this idea has been very positive," Skaggs said in a press release the next day. "They know we've got to improve the working environment in the House, especially after this rancorous year. Our ability to do the nation's business depends on having a basic level of mutual trust and respect, and that depends on our getting to know and understand each other a little better."[15] Skaggs said the response to our idea had been "uniformly positive," adding that when he showed people the draft of the letter to the leadership, "it was like bringing a canteen to a thirsty traveler."[16] We were further heartened by a survey of 50 members indicating that between 60 and 70 percent either were "very likely" to or would "probably" attend a retreat.

The entreaty to the leaders worked. Gingrich and Gephardt approved our proposal and appointed a formal planning committee. Skaggs and I were joined by Republicans Houghton, David Dreier (CA), Tillie Fowler (FL), and Jo Ann Emerson (MO). Democrats who served were Sawyer, Charlie Stenholm (TX), Eva Clayton (NC), and Ruben Hinojosa (TX). Debbie Dingell, wife of John Dingell (D-MI), represented the congressional spouses.[17] These members spanned differences in ideology, geography, ethnicity, gender, and seniority. Skaggs and I had looked at several lists of potential members—these folks had demonstrated by their actions a willingness to set partisan differences aside.

Staff from the Aspen Institute, the Congressional Institute, and the Campaign for Common Ground provided able and skillful assistance. In addition, we solicited advice from several sources, among them the Pew Charitable Trusts, the Congressional Research Service, the Congressional Management Foundation, the Brookings Institution, and the Faith and Politics Institute. In July, the House Democratic Caucus had taken testimony before its Committee on Organization, Study, and Review Regarding Bipartisan Cooperation in Congress, which also proved useful.[18]

At our first full-fledged planning committee meeting on September 11, David Dreier proposed that Skaggs and I serve as co-chairs, and we subsequently alternated in leading the meetings. We worked out issues by consensus, not by vote. Since not all members could attend all meetings, some issues surfaced repeatedly, even when we had thought them resolved. One staff member dubbed the process a "rolling consensus." Admittedly, this was a time-consuming way to conduct business, but it worked. Skaggs said it was clear to everyone that "we needed to demonstrate in the way we planned the retreat that its underlying premise was, in fact, valid—that it was possible for representatives of the two parties, motivated by good will toward themselves and each other and the institution, to get something done together."[19]

In late September and early October, the committee heard proposals from several nonprofit organizations based in Washington that had experience designing, organizing, and running conferences. We eventually tapped Mark Gerzon, co-director of the Campaign for Common Ground, a nonpartisan initiative to raise the level of political discourse among adversaries, to provide staff leadership. Gerzon had co-founded and directed The Common Enterprise, a network of programs to rebuild common ground in American communities administered by the Rockefeller Foundation.

Gerzon expressed initial skepticism about the proposed retreat when he met with us, but he soon warmed to the task. He spoke of the House as a community and of the need to build a sense of community among its members. Toward this end, Gerzon proposed that our retreat focus on getting the members talking and working in small groups rather than listening to outside speakers. He also urged us to plan the conference sessions ourselves rather than turning the task over to outsiders.[20]

GUIDING PRINCIPLES

Even at this early stage, I had decided to argue for a few basic principles in our planning. First and most important: improving member-to-member *relationships* was the key to restoring civility in the House. I believe that all members of Congress arrive in Washington with the same motivation— to act on behalf of our constituents to solve problems. Naturally, there are differences between (even within) the two parties about how to solve problems, but if members could carry out debate and dialogue in a civil way, it would lend a lot more credibility to the institution. As I told one reporter, "I don't think we're going to pass any more bills. I don't think we're going to lessen some of the controversy that swirls around some of these issues. But if people know one another, there will be a better understanding and a more civil tone to the debate."[21]

It may seem silly to talk about something as fuzzy as relationships. After all, no politician can succeed without developing, nurturing, and cultivating personal associations—that's how we get elected in the first place. But electoral politics gives them an unfortunate twist. We spend our whole careers in a political party where we build relationships among us or *against* them. How do you go into a colleague's district, campaign against them, then find out that they've won and you have to work with them in Congress? You treat them as enemies one minute and as colleagues the next—it's a tough trick to pull off.

I remember a story Bob Michel would tell about how he and Dan Rostenkowski (D-IL) spent time on the road together driving back and forth from Washington to Illinois in the 1950s. "In those days," Michel would say, "we were only reimbursed for one trip a year back to our districts.... Those of us who were raising families saved money by piling in the dog-gone station wagon."[22] Their routine formed the basis for a lasting friendship across the aisle as Michel became the Republican leader and Democrat Rostenkowski rose to chair the Ways and Means Committee.

What a contrast to today's routine. Members flee the Capitol every Thursday afternoon, jump on an airplane, and head home to campaign. We may be more familiar to our constituents as a result, but we are obviously less in touch with our colleagues. Our spouses don't know each other; our kids don't attend the same schools; we don't socialize across party lines.[23] Relationships suffer.

Even in our more official roles, the opportunities to establish friendships have declined. Through most of the 1970s and 1980s, after each election the freshmen of both parties went off for a week to Harvard's Kennedy School of Government for discussions with faculty about some of the issues new members were likely to face. "It helped cleanse some of the contentiousness of a just-completed campaign," recalled Tom Sawyer, who went through the process in 1986, "and it was a wonderful bonding experience. It let people get to know each other on a personal level and to recognize the genuinely complex mosaic of opinion that Congress is."[24] But when we Republicans won control of the House in 1994, one of our very first acts was to throw out that tradition. Instead of attending the bipartisan orientation session at Harvard, our party sent the freshmen to the Heritage Foundation, a conservative think tank in Washington, for policy briefings.[25] At Gingrich's direction, then, we eliminated the first opportunity for new members to get to know one another in a bipartisan setting.

Norman J. Ornstein, writing in the Capitol Hill newspaper *Roll Call*, prefaced his analysis of our retreat proposal by noting, "the institution has to find rules and norms that allow the conflicts to be vented without seeing them turn violent, and without having them reach a corrosive enough level that the outcome, and ultimately the institution, lose their legitimacy." Ornstein likened the tone on the floor to a Hatfield/McCoy feud, "with people on each side vowing to get revenge for current and past transgressions, and no end to the escalation in sight." Ornstein worried that a civility retreat would not be enough:

> But I also know that many, many Members on both sides have become radicalized by the past few Congresses. They have no interest in fraternizing with the enemy, and are looking for more opportunities to exact revenge for previous or current slights or outrages. A simple pledge to make nice will not do it. It will take more than that.[26]

How true, certainly for the emboldened conservative Republicans recruited by the Speaker.

I acted based on a couple of other principles, too, in addition to the importance of cultivating relationships. Any retreat should take place outside Washington, I believed. The program should avoid a public policy emphasis, especially if it risked raising issues on which members had already staked out partisan positions. The experience had to include families and offer opportunities for socializing. Finally, the retreat had to be funded privately. As I explained to a reporter from the *New York Times*, "All we've tentatively decided is what we *won't* be doing. We won't be holding a bunch of seminars on the three most important issues facing the country. The objective, I think, is to build better relationships among members of the House of Representatives."[27]

When Skaggs testified before the Subcommittee on Rules and Organization of the House in September, he hit the nail on the head: "It seems to me that what we are really talking about here is changing a culture and creating a different sense within the membership of the House of Representatives as to what norms are here and what is appropriate and what isn't."[28] Porter Goss (R-FL), a member of the subcommittee, quipped that "if we get that [culture change], the Nobel Prize should be liberally dispersed" among members. I recalled for the panel that Bob Michel's tenure was marked by "partisanship when it was needed on issues [and] bipartisanship when it was needed to get things done."[29]

We knew we faced an uphill climb even after the Speaker and minority leader announced their support. When informed of our plans, Sam Gibbons, whose behavior had prompted Skaggs to approach me in the first place, told a reporter,

> Good luck! Most of the time these sorts of ideas are put forth by do-gooders who want to protect themselves from scrutiny. I just don't believe you can reform this place into a nice-boys' club. The way Newt has run this place, the House membership has almost become superfluous. Newt and his staff set the agenda. He's the one who's done more than anyone else to discredit the Congress. He's been quoted numerous times as saying that in order to rebuild this country, you have to first tear it down.[30]

Regrettably, Gibbons was not alone in his pessimism. Charlie Rangel (D-NY) recalled a recent conversation with a longtime Republican colleague who had pleaded, "We've been friends for 20 years. Can't we go back to being friends?" Rangel's reply: "Being friendly with you is the same thing as being friendly with Gingrich. We'll go back to being friendly when the Democrats are back in the majority."[31] Too many members shared the opinions voiced by Gibbons and Rangel. "There's real anger on the Democratic side, a visceral anger at Republicans, and a sense of egregious injustice," a Congressional Research Service report on decorum in House debate put it. "It's hard for them to treat their former minority adversaries with respect. The 104th Congress has been terrible because of the psychological maladjustment."[32]

Setting Goals, Planning the Program

Our planning committee meetings dealt with a range of issues. Naturally, the logistics of organizing a retreat away from the nation's capital posed real challenges; our staffs worked with consultants to manage these important details. More significantly, we wrestled with how to create an environment in which participants could be candid without fear that what they said would be used against them. We discussed how to engage members and get them to commit to attending, how to fund the enterprise, the need for guidance under House ethics regulations, and what sort of follow-up would be required, among other topics. At the broadest level, we posed this question: Could we effect meaningful change by addressing the *behavior* of members, or should we address the *root causes*, those societal issues outside the congressional arena, of member behavior? I'm not sure we ever came down emphatically on one side or the other, but for this first retreat we focused on member behavior.

We struggled to some degree about the specific purposes and goals of the retreat. Some people thought it should do more than provide an opportunity for members to get to know each other and to establish personal relationships. They thought it should also educate members about the cultural, social, and economic transformations that create conflict in society. Others thought the program should explain mediation techniques and teach members to use them. We went round and round to balance the need for content with a desire not to bring in lots of outside speakers. Eventually, we were able to work through these issues successfully.[33]

In early fall, the committee began to recruit members to attend the retreat. We did not have a handle on the program at that point, but we knew members needed to put the event on their schedules. Skaggs and I wrote in a Dear Colleague letter in mid-September that "the goal of the retreat is to improve bipartisan collegiality, civility, and, so, the working environment in the House."[34] We followed up the next week with a second Dear Colleague signed by the entire planning committee membership and enclosed a survey to determine members' likelihood of attending and to ask for agenda ideas.[35] A week after that, on September 26, Sawyer, Clayton, and Houghton briefed members under a Special Order on plans for the first retreat. "I believe that there is an enormous appetite for this kind of effort," Sawyer said. "People across not only this Chamber, but throughout the country, have commented on the wide variation in the level of discourse that we have encountered in recent years, and many of us believe that some of that can be overcome, not solved, but overcome, by simply getting to know one another." In Clayton's words, "Our goal is a simple one: to fan the flames of cordiality and congeniality, with the hope of producing harmony."[36] I wasn't so sure about fanning the flames of anything, but Clayton got the main point right.

Meanwhile, planning continued in the background. Skaggs prepared the first formal retreat proposal draft for the planning committee's review on October 21. His purpose statement captured my sense of the task perfectly:

> Many House Members have become increasingly concerned about the tone of debate and quality of the work environment in Congress. Incidents in which Members treat each other inappropriately are more frequent, and are broadcast over C-SPAN and highlighted in the general media. There are regular disputes

in committee and subcommittee meetings that violate basic standards of civil behavior. While vigorous debate is to be expected in our two-party political system, personal animosity between Members and disrespect for House Rules get in the way of the work of the House and set a bad example for political discussion in the country generally.

We believe that a major cause of incivility in the proceedings on [sic] the House is the absence of good personal relationships between Members across the aisle. A number of factors have led to a House in which many [M]embers know each other only as political adversaries. One of those factors is simply a lack of opportunity for Members to get to know Members from the other party and their families outside the political arena.

The purpose of the bipartisan retreat is to provide that opportunity—to give Members of the House a moderately structured occasion to get to know each other and their families in a setting that is free of the pressures of political competition. We feel strongly that the retreat can greatly improve the chances of developing productive, trusting relationships between Members of different parties, regions, and backgrounds. Those relationships, in turn, can help establish an environment in which vigorous debates and mutual respect can co-exist.[37]

Throughout the fall, the planning committee met frequently to discuss logistics, format, and purpose. On November 14, Gingrich, Majority Leader Armey, and Gephardt signed a Dear Colleague letter urging members and their families to keep March 7–9, 1997, open: "This unique retreat is intended simply to improve the working environment in the House. By enabling Members to spend quality time with each other, along with their families, we are hopeful we can establish a more collegial atmosphere, and, thereby, better working relationships."[38]

David Broder revisited the civility initiative in a column on November 28 in which he applauded our efforts. I explained to Broder that the event would "focus on how we do our work, not on what we're working on."

Skaggs added: "It's not about eliminating disagreements; it's about how to handle disagreements."[39]

December brought welcome news. The Pew Charitable Trusts had awarded the project a $700,000 grant to be administered through the Aspen Institute, which we had selected to coordinate the retreat. We had approached Pew in early August after obtaining clearance from the Committee on Standards of Official Conduct, the body with jurisdiction to issue advisory opinions on ethics regulations.[40] From the beginning, the trusts had three concerns: the retreat should be attended by at least one-third, but preferably half, of the members of the House; participation should be truly bipartisan, with virtually equal representation from the two parties; and the members should undertake "substantive" work— that is, the retreat should not be primarily social, recreational, or even educational. The substantive work, Pew stipulated, should address issues of relationships, not policy, with a goal of developing "social trust" among the members. These three objectives were formally written into the eventual grant award as "special conditions."[41]

MAKING THE CASE

Despite having sent a series of Dear Colleague letters, though, we failed to generate much enthusiasm for the retreat. I told the press that we hoped to attract 300 members and their families, split evenly between Republicans and Democrats. We were running short of that, however; numbers were more in the 240 range. The planning committee authorized Mark Gerzon to find reasons for the shortfall by interviewing members. He reported his results in January. "You guys haven't made your case yet," he quoted a Democrat. A Republican added, "What will I get out of it?"[42] Gerzon's findings forced the committee to be more specific about why members ought to attend. We decided to appeal blatantly to members' self-interest and came up with nine enticements, which Gerzon phrased as the following:

Curiosity. Who are those people on the "other side"? What are they like? If you spend time with them, will they become friends? Or are they in fact another breed altogether?

Humility. As one leading Republican put it: "We don't have all the answers. Neither do the Democrats." The retreat is a chance to be honest about that, to stop posturing, and to see where humble dialog leads.

Partisanship. As any good partisan knows, gathering information about the other side makes good strategic sense. The more you know your opponent, the better you can advance your own causes. One reason to attend is to make sure your side learns as much as possible about the other.

Bipartisanship. Some policy issues require collaboration. What are they? How can the two sides work together? The retreat is a chance informally to begin to find out.

Image. To counteract public perceptions of House members squabbling like kids on the playground, each trying to bully the other and gain an advantage, coming to the retreat makes good sense. It conveys a public image of trying to find common ground.

Ambition. Some of the best legislation is co-sponsored by members of both parties working as partners. You can demonstrate leadership, and advance your career, by having a bipartisan strategy as well as a partisan one.

Enjoyment. The retreat could be a lot of fun.

Family. Much of the time is free for informal socializing. Your family can get to know the families of others and support each other in dealing with the lifestyle challenges that face any national leader's family life.

Community. If Congress is a community, then it must assemble as a community. Partisan retreats are simply not sufficient for genuine community-building.[43]

One of the constant complaints we heard throughout the process was that we were trying to stifle debate. I addressed this privately with every member who brought it up, and we went public, too. Skaggs told the press on one occasion, "We're not talking about getting rid of disagreement. We're not pretending that in a country as big and diverse as ours, there aren't going to be huge differences of opinion on huge issues." The point, he said, was for politicians to have their arguments while maintaining at least "some minimum regard for each other and some minimum respect of each other's motives." I readily conceded that some saw the civility campaign as "dumb" and "silly," but I argued that disrespect of politicians for one another and for one another's arguments lay at the root of many *substantive* shortcomings in Congress.[44]

We also composed a set of talking points for the committee to use in responding to the charge:

> The idea behind the retreat is a simple one—members of Congress and their families will spend the weekend together so they can get to know each other better, examine the current working environment in the House, and figure out what can be done to improve it. We're hopeful that this weekend will help build trust among members of Congress and diffuse the partisan rancor.

> We are not trying to create the "mushy middle"—to eliminate disagreements over policy matters, or discourage healthy debate about the issues facing the nation. These are facts of life in a functioning democracy with a range of views held by a diverse citizenry. We are, however, trying to honor our democracy with debates that are more civil, more respectful, and ultimately more productive.[45]

Avoiding the mushy middle was the least of our problems. The atmosphere in the House deteriorated in early 1997. On January 21, Newt Gingrich became the first sitting Speaker to be reprimanded by his colleagues for violations of House ethics rules. He had acknowledged in December that he had failed to properly manage the financing of his political activities through charitable foundations. It was a sign of hubris that he also admitted giving the House Committee on Standards of Official Conduct misleading statements in the course of its investigation—this after spending two years denying any wrongdoing. Related events included a televised committee hearing on January 17, accusations against a committee member that he had leaked tape recordings of conversations among Gingrich and his allies, and the levying of a $300,000 fine against the Speaker. This unfortunate juxtaposition of debilitating events in the House with our efforts to gin up enthusiasm for the retreats repeated itself in the next three retreats.

In response, the planning committee authorized the communications director at the Aspen Institute to develop and carry out a media plan to encourage members to attend the retreat and to give the public accurate information about it. The plan called for Skaggs and me to send a letter to newspaper editors suggesting that they write an editorial about the purpose and outline of the retreat. This produced a number of editorials, by and large supportive of the idea and cautiously optimistic that it might make a difference in the level of civility in the House. On February 5— a month before the retreat—all 10 members of the planning committee met with 24 representatives of the press for a one-hour press roundtable. A week later, we held a similar event with the regional press.[46]

Against what can be described truthfully as an inhospitable backdrop, the retreat, set for March 7–9, was fast approaching. We had selected the Hershey Lodge and Convention Center, one of the few facilities willing to accept the event on short notice and to close its doors to other guests, a condition we set. Hershey, Pennsylvania, known as the "sweetest place on earth" and located about 120 miles from Washington, just happened to be Speaker Gingrich's old stomping grounds. His mother still lived in nearby Middle Paxton Township. As a young boy, he used to ride the train to Hershey to go swimming. Truthfully, we were not so clever as to have selected Hershey because of this coincidence—it was a matter of logistical convenience.

NOTES

1. RL, "Civility and Congress," *Dirksen Congressional Center Report*, Spring 1998, RLP-Peoria-TBS, f. Civility (1).
2. Lloyd Grove, "Politics of Politeness," *Washington Post*, ca. August 1996, RLP-DC-S, f. Civility Retreats. 1997. Press (1).
3. Norman J. Ornstein, "Can This Congress Be Saved?" *Roll Call*, January 27, 1997, RLP-DC-S, f. Civility Retreats. 1997. Press (2).
4. David Broder, "The Atmosphere on Capitol Hill," *Washington Post*, July 21, 1996, RLP-DC-S, f. Civility Retreats. 1997. Press (1).
5. Brett Lieberman, "Outcry Rises for a More Civil Society," *Patriot-News*, Harrisburg, PA, March 9, 1997, RLP-DC-S, f. Civility Retreats. 1997. Press (2).
6. Jill Lawrence, "Wanted: Good Citizens, Close Communities," *USA Today*, December 16, 1996, RLP-DC-S, f. Civility Retreats. 1997. Press (1). Judith Rodin, president of the University of Pennsylvania, opened the first meeting of the Penn National Commission on Society, Culture, and Community with these remarks.
7. Lieberman, "Outcry Rises."
8. Janet Hook, "Lawmakers Plan Retreat from Rancor of Congress," *Los Angeles Times*, March 7, 1997, RLP-DC-S, f. Civility Retreats. 1997. Press (2).
9. Michael Sandel, "Making Nice Is Not the Same as Doing Good," *NYT*, December 29, 1996, RLP-DC-S, f. Civility Retreats. 1997. Press (1).
10. Frank Ahrens, "Putting 'Polite' into Politics," *Washington Post*, March 6, 1997, RLP-Peoria-TBS, f. Civility (2).
11. Grove, "Politics of Politeness."
12. Dear Colleague, June 28, 1996, RLP-DC-S, f. Civility Retreats. 1997. Correspondence.
13. Broder, "Atmosphere on Capitol Hill."
14. Ibid.
15. News release, July 26, 1996, Office of Congressman David Skaggs, RLP-DC-S, f. Civility Retreats. 1997. Press (1).
16. Broder, "Atmosphere on Capitol Hill."
17. Only Houghton and Stenholm joined me in organizing all four retreats.
18. Ralph Neas to RL, 4 October 4, 1996, RLP-DC-S, f. Civility Retreats, 1997, Correspondence.

19. Donita M. Moorhus, "The Bipartisan Retreat at Hershey: A Turning Point?" n.d., RLP-DC-S, f. Civility Retreats. 1999. Correspondence. 1996–1998.

20. Moorhus, "Bipartisan Retreat."

21. Bureau of National Affairs, Inc., newsletter, December 13, 1996, RLP-DC-S, f. Civility Retreats. 1997. Press (1).

22. Timothy J. Burger and Jim O'Connell, "Michel Quits after 38-Year Career Filled with Bipartisanship, Congress Boosting, and Song," *Roll Call*, October 3, 1993, RHMIF, f. Biographical.

23. Lawrence, "Wanted: Good Citizens."

24. Broder, "Atmosphere on Capitol Hill."

25. Ibid.

26. Norman J. Ornstein, "Road to Bipartisanship in the Next Congress Must Be Paved Now," *Roll Call*, July 29, 1996, RLP-DC-S, f. Civility Retreats. 1997. Press (1).

27. Grove, "Politics of Politeness."

28. Quoted in testimony by Don Wolfensberger before the Subcommittee on Rules and Organization of the House, April 17, 1997, RLP-Peoria-TBS, f. Civility (1).

29. Jennifer Bradley, "Date, Site Picked for Bipartisan Retreat," n.d., Bipartisan Congressional Retreat Packet, RLP-Peoria-TBS, f. Civility (2).

30. Grove, "Politics of Politeness."

31. Grove, "Politics of Politeness."

32. Grove, "Politics of Politeness."

33. Moorhus, "Bipartisan Retreat."

34. Dear Colleague, September 13, 1996, RLP-DC-S, f. Civility Retreats. 1997. Correspondence.

35. Dear Colleague, September 20, 1996, RLP-DC-S, f. Civility Retreats. 1997. Correspondence.

36. *Congressional Record*, September 26, 1996, H11362.

37. "Draft Bipartisan Retreat Proposal," October 21, 1996, attached to RL and Skaggs memo to committee, November 18, 1996, RLP, DC, Subject, f. Civility Retreats. 1997. Bipartisan Congressional Retreat Planning Committee. Also attached to Charles to Diane, October 21, 1996, "Draft Bipartisan Retreat Proposal," RLP-DC-S, f. Civility Retreats. 1997. Proposals.

38. Dear Colleague, November 14, 1996, RLP-DC-S, f. Civility Retreats. 1997. Correspondence.

39. David Broder, "Restoring Civility," *Peoria Journal Star*, November 28, 1996, RLP-DC-S, f. Civility Retreats. 1997. Press (1).

40. Various to Rimel, August 2, 1996, RLP-DC-S, f. Civility Retreats. 1997. Correspondence.
41. Moorhus, "Bipartisan Retreat."
42. Gerzon to RL and Skaggs, January 21, 1997, RLP-DC-S, f. Civility Retreats. 1997. Correspondence.
43. Gerzon to RL and Skaggs, January 21, 1997.
44. E. J. Dionne Jr., "Anything but Being 'Nice'," n.d., RLP-DC-S, f. Civility Retreats. 1997. Press (2).
45. "The Bipartisan Congressional Retreat," n.d., RLP-DC-S, f. Civility Retreats. 1997. Talking Points.
46. Moorhus, "Bipartisan Retreat."

CHAPTER 5

THE FIRST BIPARTISAN
CIVILITY RETREAT

By early March 1997, we had commitments from enough members to proceed with the first civility retreat. Although press accounts would peg the final tally at 200 members, the actual attendance amounted to 197 House members, 165 spouses, and 100 of their children. The bipartisan leadership was well represented: the Speaker, majority whip, minority leader, and minority whip attended. In addition, 45 of the 74 freshmen elected in November 1996 took part. I was a little disappointed, however, that so many senior members skipped the event. Senior Democrats, for example, so disliked the Republican leadership that they opted out, as did many older members whose children were grown.

THE LAUNCH: MARCH 7, 1997

The bipartisan congressional retreat began early Friday morning, March 7, 1997, when staff gathered in the Rayburn House Office Building courtyard—an area known as the Horseshoe—to welcome members and their families. At 9:00 a.m., the group climbed into chartered buses for the 10-minute ride from Capitol Hill to Union Station, where everyone boarded a chartered Amtrak train for the three-and-a-half-hour ride to Harrisburg, Pennsylvania, a short distance from Hershey. We departed at 11:00 a.m.

As the House chaplain, Dr. James Ford, noted, "Hershey began as soon as we got to the railroad station." The train provided a unique, casual means of transporting several hundred people together in security and comfort; there were no planned activities and no assigned seats. Members walked up and down the aisles introducing themselves to each other. The kids and families made the trip informal and welcoming. Members played cards, bragged about their kids, talked about how they got to Congress, and discussed problems in their districts. Gingrich and his wife joined us on the train. Gephardt and his wife came later in the day by car.[1]

Four working sessions for members and spouses formed the core of the retreat. The formal program began at 4:00 Friday afternoon following welcoming remarks by the leadership team. Gingrich admitted to the group that "we weren't very good at being in the majority, and Democrats weren't very good at being in the minority." He blamed the nature of the issues confronting the House, such as welfare reform, which he called big, polarizing issues.[2] "I'm interested in doing two things," he promised:

> Finding as many opportunities for bipartisan activities where Democrats and Republicans are jointly trying to solve problems. If we're both in the ditch trying to get the wagon back on the road, you just build a kind of team attitude which is different. The other thing is finding opportunities for our families to get together. Having these children here is invaluable.... If we bicker like children, how can we turn to these kids and tell them we need to behave like adults? ... We've got to learn to explain and defend legitimate social gatherings and this is one of them.[3]

To put the breakdown of relations in the House in perspective, the planning committee had commissioned a 12-minute video presentation, heavy with images of the Capitol and featuring the voices of ordinary people expressing their views on Congress. The video reviewed the history of the institution with emphasis on the values of a new nation. It depicted the diversity of our country expressed through the Constitution. The production company had brought in actors to repeat lines penned by Benjamin Franklin, Alexander Hamilton, and others. To move the focus to the contemporary Congress, the presentation recorded observations from librarian of Congress Daniel Boorstin, former Republican leader Bob Michel, and former Speaker Tom Foley. We had taped four experts who offered their opinions on the need for change in congressional behavior: Kathleen Hall Jamieson, professor and dean of the Annenberg School for Communication of the University of Pennsylvania; Thomas Mann, Brookings Institution congressional scholar; Norman J. Ornstein, congressional expert with the American Enterprise Institute; and *Washington Post* columnist William Raspberry.[4]

After the video, Amo Houghton introduced our only outside speaker, historian and Pulitzer Prize–winning author David McCullough, for an inspirational 30-minute speech. Using marvelous examples from John Adams and the Constitutional Convention, he implored lawmakers to put aside their differences and provide leadership for the country. He pleaded the lessons of history: "History is an aid to navigation in troubled times; history is an antidote to self-pity and to self-importance. And history teaches that when we unite in grand purpose there is almost nothing we cannot do." Saying that our country deserved better from "all of us," McCullough quoted Adams:

> We may please ourselves with the prospect of free and popular governments. God grant us the way. *But I fear that in every assembly, members will obtain an influence by noise not sense, by meanness not greatness, by ignorance not learning, by contracted hearts not large souls* [emphasis added]. There is one thing my dear sir that must be attempted and most sacredly observed or we are all undone. There must be decency and respect and veneration introduced for persons of every rank or we are undone. In a popular government this is our only way.[5]

Adams captured the essence of our challenge in that highlighted sentence, I thought.

Following McCullough's speech, members and spouses broke up into 12 groups of about 30 people. Each group had an equal number of Republicans and Democrats. We tried to achieve geographical diversity, too, as well as a balance between new and long-term members. Every group had Republican and Democratic co-leaders. We met in separate rooms and used an outside facilitator if we came to an impasse. The first small-group session on Friday had a single purpose: each working group was divided into two smaller groups, and each participant had one minute to introduce himself or herself and briefly state reasons for attending the retreat.

Saturday began with a family breakfast. I thought that we should emphasize families in any retreat since they are, obviously, so important to building relationships among members. Debbie Dingell, who represented the Democratic spouses group on the planning committee, deserved the credit for making the retreat so family friendly. For example, she put together a series of events for kids. Children were divided into four age groups with names appropriate for the occasion: Hershey's Kisses for the youngest, Reese's Peanut Butter Cups and Hershey's Milk Chocolate Bars for the middle two groups, and Twizzlers for the teens. We offered day care, a visit to the zoo, story time, a puppet show, a culinary workshop, a carnival, pony rides, movies, arts and crafts, sports, video games, and dances. For the members and their spouses, we held family dinners and social events on Friday and Saturday evening. The family orientation proved key to our future retreats; when members who were not quite sure about attending heard from their spouses and kids about how enjoyable (and rare) it was to spend time together in such a setting, that often made the decision easy.

The real work for us began Saturday morning. The conference organizers had distributed a briefing book ahead of the retreat in order to jump-start these small-group conversations.[6] We asked the participants to read five selections. An executive summary titled "Civility in the House of Representatives," by Kathleen Hall Jamieson, addressed two questions: Had the level of civility in the House changed? If so, how, why, and what could be done about it?[7] Dan Yankelovich provided a draft of his work in progress, "Doing Dialogue," which stressed the importance of conversation in helping participants resolve values conflicts and tensions. Among his conclusions: "Civil society stands or falls on this foundation of feelings. As we have seen, the magic of dialogue is that it really does enhance mutual understanding, respect and acceptance of others. Without dialogue, people stereotype one another in a manner that prevents mutual understanding and acceptance. With dialogue the stereotypes melt away, often replaced by good will and mutual understanding."[8]

We also included the chapter "Toward an Integral Politics" from Steven Carter's *Integrity*. He warned of the threat "from the increasing alienation of people from their government, a trend that, if not halted, may yet spell the end of genuine democracy in America."[9] James Morris traced the coarsening of society before concluding, "What's being lost is the sense that there can be national norms for ordinary behavior. A nickel notion of democracy and difference, as if respect for every view meant that no view goes unchallenged, threatens to absolve us of the need for civility. It's leveling the nation to the mean."[10]

The final entry in the briefing book consisted of George Washington's "School Exercises: Rules of Civility and Decent Behavior in Company and Conversation," which included among Washington's 110 rules such gems as "Shew Nothing to your Friend that might affright him."[11]

In the first Saturday session, we asked members and spouses to respond to the question *How has the quality of discourse in the House of Representatives affected me personally?* This question was an invitation to unburden, and people did—generally more in sorrow than in anger. It seemed to me that the folks in my group were relieved to be able to talk about their frustrations, many of them stemming from the recent campaign. The next task for the breakout groups was to identify the obstacles to improving the quality of discourse in the House. Acting upon Gerzon's advice, we had set up a requirement that in order to "post a barrier" on the board, a person had to find someone in his or her group *from the other party* who would agree that this was a problem. Each group completed a third task, too, by deciding what could be done, individually and collectively, to overcome these obstacles.[12] In a nutshell, we expected this process to reveal what we could do to improve the operation of Congress as an institution.

I was one of the small-group co-leaders. Each of us had attended two training sessions led by Mark Gerzon. As he explained it, our job was to create the conditions for more civil and productive dialogue in our respective groups. We were to help to define the issues clearly, allow sufficient time for deliberation, and assist participants in seeing the issues from other points of view. If we were successful in creating these conditions, participants would experience some of the initial rewards of genuine, sustained civil dialogue—at least, that was our assumption.[13]

Julian Dixon (D-CA) and I co-led Group F. We set out the ground rules (i.e., allow equal time for speakers, listen with intent to under-stand, demonstrate openness to other points of view, treat sessions as confidential, avoid personal attacks, and arrive on time) and began a round-robin conversation with two to three minutes for each opening statement, followed by reflections from the group members. Group F consisted of these members and spouses (in the case of couples, the man is the representative):

> Doug and Louise Bereuter (R-NE)
> Tom and Susanne Campbell (R-CA)
> Chris and Rebecca Cox (R-CA)
> Danny and Vera Davis (D-IL)
> John and Debbie Dingell (D-MI)
> Julian Dixon (D-CA)
> Michael and Barbara Forbes (R-NY)
> Virgil and Lucy Goode (D-VA)
> Ron and Tawni Kind (D-WI)

Ray and Kathy LaHood (R-IL)
John Lewis (D-GA)
Bill and Darlene Luther (D-MN)
Juanita Millender-McDonald (D-CA)
Rob and Jane Portman (R-OH)
John and Kitty Sununu (R-NH)
Jim and DeDe Walsh (R-NY)

Over the course of three and a half hours, we identified more than a dozen obstacles to civil discourse. They ranged from the one-minute rule and party-driven agendas to family separation resulting from the legislative schedule. Among six solutions, we discussed longer congressional terms, creating a common cloakroom, and holding bipartisan orientations for new members. Other groups followed the same procedure. Some of them generated scores of ideas. Group H, for example, led by David Skaggs and Jo Ann Emerson, identified 78 obstacles to civil discourse, along with 23 "Implications/Next Steps."[14]

Taken together, the 12 groups meeting in Hershey identified 505 obstacles to achieving civility and 231 solutions. Of the 505 obstacles, 154 were attributed to external factors, 306 to internal rules and procedures, and 45 to social or cultural factors (see table 1).

In the category of personal behavior, one group offered a simple solution: "Remember your Mom is watching you."[15]

For a change of pace, we spent Saturday afternoon touring and taking part in social activities with our families. Late in the afternoon, our facilitators gathered the notes from the separate group meetings, synthesized them, and presented the compilation to the co-leaders. We compared notes, reviewed the material, and tried to formulate suggestions to present on Sunday morning. The long day concluded with a reception, dinner, and evening entertainment.

Table 1. 505 obstacles to achieving civility and 231 solutions.

Category in order of frequency	Obstacles	Solutions
Personal behavior	76	15
Media	58	11
Internal culture	53	57
Campaigns	49	4
Rules/procedures	47	35
Public attitudes	43	7
Planning/scheduling	26	19
Political parties	24	1
Ideology	23	0
Socializing	22	15
Leadership	18	18
Issues	14	5
Family	12	4
Related to the one-minute rule	11	12
Speed of change	8	0
Terms	7	2
Orientation	6	13
Staff	4	5
Cloakroom	4	3
Travel	3	5

The working session on Sunday morning—a plenary session—was, by all accounts, both the literal and emotional culmination of the weekend. We co-leaders summarized the discussions of our breakout groups on Saturday. Sawyer and Houghton presented a list of more than 60 possible action steps and then co-chaired a two-hour open-microphone opportunity. Members and spouses had the chance to give one-minute reactions to what they had experienced during the weekend and to express their ideas about next steps.[16]

Hershey I, as it came to be known, exceeded my expectations. It proved to be the largest gathering of House members outside of the Capitol in the nation's history. I was certain that we had started to build friendships and relationships that would last far beyond our careers in Congress. I believed that a greater spirit of cooperation and bipartisanship would be the immediate result. I was not alone in these beliefs. Charlie Stenholm (D-TX) told the press, "There are going to be some friendships made, and I think when you do that, you're going to have a better chance of working together."[17] According to Robert Franks (R-NJ), "This is the first time I've ever had the opportunity to get to know people as human beings rather than as political entities. People will be far more reticent to engage in verbal warfare now that we understand the human dimensions of members."[18]

The Speaker and minority leader attended all sessions during the weekend, talked to each other, and appeared open to the suggestion that the House leadership have regular joint meetings. On the floor of the House the following week, Gingrich said that the retreat had produced "measurable progress" regarding the complex challenge of how to debate and legislate with respect. Gephardt, too, spoke positively about the retreat, calling it "a historic event, the only time that I know that members from both sides of the aisle and their families have had a two-day period to understand how we could better work together to solve the problems we are all trying to solve."[19]

One of my partners on the planning committee had a more reserved reaction, however. New York Republican Amo Houghton told the press, "I have high secret hopes, but low public expectations. I think we can overpromise, we can overindulge ourselves because we've all had such a wonderful time."[20] The press also called a few members who had not attended and hit upon an attitude that would confound us as we planned future retreats. An aide to Michael Oxley (R-OH), who did not attend, put it this way: "He's not going because the people who need to go won't. The people who are already civil will show up."[21] For the time being, I chose to be optimistic—an attitude that, unfortunately, would change over the next six years.

The talking points we developed as the retreat ended still serve as a succinct summary of what we had hoped to accomplish:

> For any legislature to function, its members must have a level of trust in each other. And that trust can only develop when legislators have an opportunity to get acquainted, as people, across the aisle, outside the arena of partisan combat. When people know each other, they are less likely to question the other person's motives, or to let policy differences turn into personal hostility.

> Our mission for three days has been as confounding as it has been simple. We came together to bring greater civility to the House of Representatives. No legislative business. No political games. Just members and their families taking time together, to get to know one another better, to examine the environment in the House and figure out what can be done to make it better.

> The nation is well-served by healthy and vigorous debate. That's essential to a functioning democracy. There are real and significant differences between Republicans and Democrats, and we have no desire to blur those distinctions. Rather, the retreat has been about handling those disagreements constructively, and honoring our Republic with debates that are more civil, more respectful, and ultimately more productive.

As there is no simple cure for the incivility we see too often in American society generally, there is no simple cure for the rancor and mistrust in the House. The retreat is no panacea, but it is a start. As members of Congress, we have an enormous responsibility to the nation. With some luck and good will, what has begun this weekend will help us better meet that responsibility.[22]

Now What?

Immediately following the retreat, we began to compile the findings and to circulate drafts of action steps. One report listed 231 suggestions coming out of the small-group discussions organized under these headings: campaigns (4 suggestions), cloakroom (3), family (4), internal culture (57), issues (5), leadership (18), media (11), one-minutes (12), orientation (13), personal behavior (15), planning/scheduling (19), political parties (1), public attitudes (7), rules/procedures (35), socializing (15), staff (5), terms (2), travel issues (5).[23]

We parsed these ideas in every way imaginable. For example, one draft organized the suggestions according to the action necessary to improve civility:

> Suggestions that could be implemented by action of the Speaker, e.g., move one-minutes to the end of the day, try to make the legislative schedule family-friendly, and allow the use of signal lights for each floor manager to ask his or her counterpart to seek civility among members on that side of the aisle during debate

> Suggestions that could be implemented by joint leadership action, e.g., joint leadership meetings, joint meetings of the conference/caucus, and bipartisan social events

> Suggestions that could be implemented by changes in the House rules, e.g., admit spouses to the floor during late sessions and make the ethics process less subject to abuse

Suggestions that could be implemented by Retreat Planning Committee action, e.g., distribute the opening video to all members, obtain a Special Order to explain what happened in Hershey, and hold media, staff, and committee retreats

Suggestions that could be implemented by administrative action, e.g., commission a group photo of the entire membership and provide on-going facilitation coaching for members

Suggestions that could be implemented by ethics rulings [none listed]

Suggestions that might need funding, e.g., provide member name tags, publish a spouse directory, and sponsor a lecture series

Suggestions that might involve family participation, e.g., more use of the family room and periodic functions for families

Suggestions that could be implemented by individual member action, e.g., participate in a District of Columbia clean-up day, wear name tags, mingle, and improve the tone of campaigns.[24]

At least for the next two months, the retreat seemed to have a catalytic effect. On March 12, David Skaggs and I each attended the other's leadership meetings to discuss the retreat. The Speaker had sent a memo to Skaggs and me: "You have already done a tremendous amount of work but could you codify the best advice of the Hershey retreat in terms of action steps, experiments, ideas worth exploring? I would be delighted to meet with your steering committee in the near future," the Speaker continued, "to see what we should do next. We ought to have the first meeting before the Easter break."[25] Gingrich granted an interview to *Congress Daily* during which he listed three specific actions he would consider: moving the one-minutes to the end of the day, convening regular meetings of the two parties' leaders, and holding occasional joint sessions of the party conferences.[26] The reporter quoted Tom DeLay, his whip: "It'll be interesting to see if we actually get the two leaders to spend time in [each other's] conferences. The leaders have to set an example. Most of the civility ought to be done by example with peer pressure from the leaders."[27]

The Speaker and minority leader took the floor the next day to highlight the retreat. Gingrich noted that the retreat had addressed

> one of the most difficult and complex things people do: How to engage in passionate and difficult differences, how to bring to this room 435 people who represent the entire country, and how to do so in a way in which disagreement does not become disagreeable and in which the fact that people may have different dreams and different visions and sometimes different ideologies does not become so separating us [*sic*] so divisive that it becomes difficult or impossible for us to do the people's business.

He expressed the hope that "we begin to set this House back on a track of working together, of getting things done ... and that if we work at it, together we can do a better job for all the American people."[28]

For his part, Minority Leader Gephardt thought the retreat succeeded if only because new "human relationships," his words, were established. "From the Democratic side, I pledge our best efforts to carry the spirit of that meeting forward with tangible results in trying to work together better in a variety of ways."[29] Columnist David Broder took note of remarks by Gingrich and Gephardt in a piece about the retreat suggesting that the two "embraced the notion" of civility as much as many others who had attended did. Of the retreat, Broder concluded, "it is clear that it was a mind-changing experience."[30]

We appreciated the Speaker's and the minority leader's expressions of support, which, as we wrote them, "sent a strong message of affirmation to the Members and families who attended." Our letter applauded their recently announced decision to hold regular joint meetings and urged them to announce "an agreement in principle of this idea before the recess begins on March 20. Such an announcement would be a timely demonstration that Hershey mattered and that we can make progress.

It would provide important reinforcement to the sense of hope about positive change which people expressed as they left the Retreat."[31] Regrettably, the leaders never carried through on their promise. I suspect they were well intentioned, though I'm less convinced that was the case with Gephardt. Yet neither he nor Gingrich put civility near the top of the already crowded agendas. Perhaps more important, we could never convince their staffs to follow through.

On March 13, members of the civility task force met to discuss the retreat and to begin laying out a list of about 40 rule changes to make the House less combative.[32] Although some of the suggestions should have been easy to implement, I noted that others were a "little like walking through a minefield. You have to do it very delicately if you want to get it done."[33] We also considered a proposal from one member entitled "Hershey Accords," which listed four general rules that this member recommended his colleagues follow in the wake of the retreat:

> 1. No member shall speak ill of another Member on the House floor, in Committee proceedings, or to the media.
> 2. When rumors are heard, do not assume that another Member has disparaged you. Take the time to check it out and resolve the conflict amicably and privately.
> 3. Always make positive contributions—when you do this you bring honor to the House, your district, and your colleagues.
> 4. Keep your debate and legislative agenda issue-oriented. Constituents expect us to be above making personal attacks.[34]

Ironically, *Roll Call* reported that all four accords had been compromised within a week's time.[35] On the day we met, the House broke out in partisan warfare over funding for committee budgets and voted, after acrimonious debate, to ban the practice of partial-birth abortion. The *Peoria Journal Star*, the largest paper in my district, carried a story at the end of March that summed up in a headline our uphill battle: "Sweet Lessons of Hershey Already Forgotten."[36]

Evidence to support the story abounded, unfortunately. Congressman Lloyd Doggett (D-TX), for example, was upbraided for making disparaging remarks about Gingrich's ethics problems. Only a couple of weeks later, Tom DeLay and David Obey (D-WI) got into a shoving match on the House floor over allegations that lobbyists had written legislation in DeLay's office. In that instance, DeLay poked at a newspaper story Obey was waving at him. Then DeLay shoved Obey with both hands. DeLay could be heard shouting a vulgar expression before an aide stepped between the lawmakers to separate them.[37] In mid-April, a hearing on civility before the Subcommittee on Rules and Organization of the House[38] had to be suspended because of an outbreak of incivility on the House floor.[39] All of this served to illustrate what we were up against. As I told a reporter from the *Journal Star*, "I think our group needs to discuss ... whether you can really compel members not to say something [bad] about another member. I have a sense of hope based on the enthusiasm and energy that came from the 200 members who attended Hershey. When you have 435 people, it's difficult to keep them all in tow."[40]

In early April, I joined Skaggs, Sawyer, and Houghton on a panel at a meeting attended by 300 members of the American Society of Newspaper Editors (ASNE). We wanted two things from ASNE. First, was there a role for newspapers in maintaining a more respectful dialogue? Second, would the press work with members to "resist catchy sound bites and headlines and thus increase stability and the quality of public discourse?" I told the group,

> [We] come to Congress to try to use the institution to better the society that we live [in]. But the class that I came with, I think, was different from that. Many of us live in our districts; our families live in our districts; we come here on Tuesday; we leave here on Thursday.... There are no opportunities for members to get to know one another. Hershey is not the answer. It's not the solution, but it's the beginning, the beginning of building a friendship and relationship that I believe will last way beyond many of our congressional careers.[41]

Work continued over the next several weeks to analyze the retreat's conclusions and to decide on a course of action. Jerry Climer of the Congressional Institute prepared a statistical review of the obstacles and proposed next steps, a summary of the ideas generated by the 12 groups sorted according to common categories, and a short list of distilled action steps.[42]

We seemed to be spinning our wheels. No one, including me, took on the civility initiatives as a full-time responsibility; it was too easy for all of us, members and staff, to return to our normal routines. As a result, we lost momentum. Climer reminded us that neither Skaggs nor I, and not even the committee as a whole, had what he called "sanctioning power." We could advocate change, but we lacked the power to impose it without the approval of others. He recommended that we start with pilot projects that stood a good chance of success before moving to action items likely to encounter more resistance. He warned that simply knowing who could effect change did not mean that change would result. "In fact, just handing over ideas to those with the power to make the change without going through certain advocacy steps first is probably the surest way to fail at making change," he said. "If you seriously want to pursue some of these changes, you'll have to do more than report to the true sanctioners of change." We were bound to fail, Climer concluded, "If you simply present your colleagues with a shopping list of change ideas and transactionally include as priorities those with the most support among Co-Team Leaders."[43] The next decade would prove the wisdom of Climer's analysis. We could propose change; we could not impose change.

We did attempt to pick the low-hanging fruit. We followed through on the idea of holding a special program for members who had not attended Hershey—we showed the 12-minute video and gave them copies of McCullough's speech. Gingrich spoke about the retreat, and members who had attended were encouraged to talk about it with members who had not. Unfortunately, not many members attended this "make-up" retreat, largely owing to scheduling problems.

We also decided to expand the planning committee to include members who had served as co-leaders at Hershey. To foster the relationships that began in the working groups, the expanded planning committee proposed that groups of members and spouses meet for small, informal dinners in Washington. The scheduling obstacles were so numerous, however, that only two or three groups met. Undaunted, the committee proceeded to plan more retreat-style events in 1997 built around White House functions that would draw spouses to Washington (e.g., the May luncheon with the First Lady, the congressional picnic, and the White House Christmas party).[44] We also asked the Committee on House Oversight to authorize the sergeant at arms to produce name tags for members to wear on the floor and to produce a members and spouses directory.[45] Even this simple request went unanswered, although Amo Houghton wore his Hershey name tag on the floor a few times. Seized with the spirit of Hershey, he also hosted a series of bipartisan dinners in his home.

In early June, Skaggs, Houghton, Sawyer, and I met with the Speaker armed with a list of requests and action items growing out of Hershey and refined during planning committee discussions. In addition to proposing a bipartisan retreat for the 106th Congress, reciprocal leadership visits, a retreat for staff, and admission to the floor for spouses during late sessions, we raised the vexing issue of scheduling the one-minute speeches.

The one-minutes—time given to members for general announcements or short statements of policy and scheduled to begin at 9:00 a.m.— had turned into a free-for-all that I and many others thought created a poisonous atmosphere. In most jobs, you walk into the office, greet your staff, perhaps engage in small talk. But in the House, following the opening prayer and Pledge of Allegiance, we immediately launch into what had become personal attacks. Bill Archer (R-TX) and Tony Hall (D-OH) made a special plea to change the one-minutes because "it is counterproductive to start our legislative day with a negative tone." They noted that members debated bills with courtesy and respect for the most part. In contrast, they observed, "one-minutes have become sound-bite assaults with rhetoric normally reserved for campaign commercials."[46] We wanted to move the one-minutes to the end of the day, and we had 50 members who added their support to our recommendation. The House leaders ignored us.

We also tried to establish a home for the bipartisan civility effort by merging our planning committee with the Advisory Board of the Members and Family Room. In 1994, with the strong support of the Speaker's wife, a room had been designated as the Members and Family Room, a place for quiet retreat and a venue for bipartisan and nonpartisan activities. The spouses' organizations managed the room but lacked any staff support. The leaders did accept our proposal and appointed Skaggs and me as co-chairs of a new, official committee to oversee the room.

A Preliminary Evaluation

At least by some standards, Hershey I improved the climate in the House. Research conducted later by Kathleen Hall Jamieson looked at a variety of indicators of incivility during House floor action. Her analysis of members' calling each other names or accusing one another of lying showed improvement in the tone of debate following the retreat.[47] She also collected references to our work in the *Congressional Record*. She discovered that during contentious floor debates on the budget, health care, National Endowment for the Arts appropriations, Environmental Protection Agency policies, Social Security, and campaign finance reform, members reminded each other of their pledges in Hershey to maintain high standards for debate and personal interactions.[48] Jamieson provided three specific examples:

> Example 1
> X: "I did not go to Hershey, PA at the bipartisan retreat, but if I had and would have come on the floor for this debate this evening, I do not believe I would have used words like 'absurd,' 'mush,' things of that sort.... I do not think they help us."

Y: "If I said anything that is personal to the gentleman, I apologize. I was characterizing the ideas that are in debate."
X: "My good friend Y meant nothing personal toward me, nor did I take it as such."

Example 2
X: "The Chair would require all Members to be respectful of each other anywhere on the floor. Hershey was only 3 weeks ago."

Example 3
X: "The gentleman is doing real well for a new guy."
Y: "The gentleman is, too, and I like his hair in the spirit of Hershey and comity."
X: "I thank the gentleman."

Jamieson's conclusion: "By a number of measures the first session of the 105th sustained improvement in civility that had occurred in the last session of the 104th. In some respects, the first session of the 105th improved on its immediate predecessor."[49]

I knew from talking with my colleagues that at least on a person-to-person basis, the retreat did some good. Sawyer made the point that Hershey had provided a framework in which it was possible to measure one another's behavior against a standard that had been largely lost. Skaggs agreed with me that the relationships established there made a difference in the quality of the debate and in the level of across-the-aisle empathy. Eva Clayton (D-NC) expressed the connection between the retreat and debate on the floor in graphic terms: "It is very difficult to stand on the House floor and yell and scream obscenities at somebody if you know their 12-year-old and you've been visiting with them or been at a picnic with them recently."[50]

We may have made some progress individual to individual, but we failed to make the institutional changes we sought. One meaningful example is this: the two leaders had it within their power to move the one-minute speeches on the House floor from the beginning to the end of the day. That might seem like a small thing, but the one-minutes issue took on a symbolic importance—dozens of members on both sides supported that change but to no avail. Again, this was a case in which we could not convince the leadership staff to pursue the matter. Of course, the members who abused one-minutes opposed the change, too.

NOTES

1. Donita M. Moorhus, "The Bipartisan Retreat at Hershey: A Turning Point?" n.d., RLP-DC-S, f. Civility Retreats. 1999. Correspondence, 1996–1998.

2. Brett Lieberman, "A Memorable Homecoming," *Patriot-News*, Harrisburg, PA, March 9, 1997, RLP-DC-S, f. Civility Retreats. 1997. Press (2).

3. Lieberman, "A Memorable Homecoming"; Jim Strader, "House Members Complete Retreat Upbeat, Hopeful," *Times-Picayune*, New Orleans, March 10, 1997, RLP-DC-S, f. Civility Retreats. 1997. Press (2).

4. "Congressional Retreat Video," Tatge/Lasseur Productions, January 28, 1997, RLP-DC-S, f. Civility Retreats. 1997. Welcome/Orientation.

5. David McCullough, Plenary remarks, RLP-DC-S, f. Civility Retreats. 1997. Plenary Session. Emphasis added.

6. Aspen Institute, "Bipartisan Congressional Retreat Briefing Book," 1997, RLP-DC-S, f. Civility Retreats. 1997. Briefing Book.

7. The 10 pages in the briefing book summarized a 1997 Annenberg Public Policy Center Report consisting of 108 pages with 13 chapters on topics ranging from the social and cultural context, a historical perspective, the rules of the House, factors contributing to a perception of incivility, situations in which incivility is more likely to occur, and author's recommendations. See Aspen Institute, "Briefing Book."

8. Daniel Yankelovich, "Doing Dialogue," December 2, 1996, Aspen Institute, "Briefing Book."

9. Steven Carter, "Toward an Integral Politics," in *Integrity* (New York: HarperCollins, 1996), 206, RLP-DC-S, f. Civility Retreats. 1997. Briefing Book.

10. James Morris, "Democracy Beguiled," *Wilson Quarterly* 20, no. 4 (Autumn 1996): 32, RLP-DC-S, f. Civility Retreats. 1997. Briefing Book.

11. RLP-DC-S, f. Civility Retreats. 1997. Briefing Book.

12. Gerzon to All Participants, March 5, 1997, RLP-DC-S, f. Civility Retreats. 1997. Correspondence.

13. "Working Sessions: Co-Leaders Manual," March 5, 1997, RLP-DC-S, f. Civility Retreats. 1997. Facilitators.

14. Small Group H Report, RLP-DC-S, f. Civility Retreats. 1997. Work Group Recommendations.

15. Small Group I Report, RLP-DC-S, f. Civility Retreats. 1997. Work Group Recommendations.

16. Moorhus, "Bipartisan Retreat."

17. Mary Jacoby, "No Tie-Yanking Allowed, and Don't Shout 'Shut Up,'" *Chicago Tribune*, March 8, 1997, RLP-DC-S, f. Civility Retreats. 1997. Press (2).

18. Brett Lieberman, "Retreat Declared Success," *Patriot-News*, Harrisburg, PA, March 9, 1997, RLP-DC-S, f. Civility Retreats. 1997. Press (2).

19. Moorhus, "Bipartisan Retreat."

20. Strader, "House Members Complete Retreat."

21. Janet Hook, "Lawmakers Plan Retreat from Rancor of Congress," *Los Angeles Times*, March 7, 1997, RLP-DC-S, f. Civility Retreats. 1997. Press (2).

22. "The Bipartisan Congressional Retreat," n.d., RLP-DC-S, f. Civility Retreats. 1997. Press (2).

23. RLP-DC-S, f. Civility Retreats. 1997. Follow-Up Suggestions; Climer to RL and Skaggs, April 8, 1997, "Hershey Breakout Discussion of Next Steps," RLP-DC-S, f. Civility Retreats. 1997. Next Steps (1).

24. Ibid.

25. Newt [Gingrich] to RL and Skaggs, n.d., RLP-DC-S, f. Civility Retreats. 1997. Correspondence.

26. *Congress Daily*, March 12, 1997, RLP-DC-S, f. Civility Retreats. 1997. Press (2).

27. *Congress Daily*, March 14, 1997, RLP-DC-S, f. Civility Retreats. 1997. Press (2).

28. Cong. Rec., H951 (March 13, 1997).

29. Cong. Rec., H951–952 (March 13, 1997).

30. David Broder, "The Rediscovery of Civility," *Washington Post*, March 30, 1997, RLP, Peoria, TBS, f. Civility (2).

31. Skaggs and RL to Gephardt and Gingrich, March 14, 1997, RLP-DC-S, f. Civility Retreats. 1997. Correspondence.

32. See appendix B.

33. Ed Henry, "Partisanship Thrives," *Roll Call*, March 24, 1997, RLP-DC-S, f. Civility Retreats. 1997. Press (2).

34. "Hershey Accords," First Draft, n.d., RLP-DC-S, f. Civility Retreats. 1997. Talking Points; Henry, "Partisanship Thrives."

35. Henry, "Partisanship Thrives."

36. Dori Meinert, "Sweet Lessons of Hershey Already Forgotten," *Peoria Journal Star*, March 28, 1997, RLP-DC-S, f. Civility Retreats. 1997. Press (2).
37. "Bringing Civility to the House," *Peoria Journal Star*, April 11, 1997, RLP-DC-S, f. Civility Retreats. 1997. Press (2).
38. Subcommittee press release, "Civility in the House of Representatives," April 16, 1997, RLP, Peoria, TBS, f. Civility (2).
39. Statement by Don Wolfensberger before the Subcommittee on Rules and Organization of the House, April 29, 1999, RLP-DC-S, f. Civility Retreats. 1999. Subcommittee on Rules and Organization of the House.
40. Meinert, "Sweet Lessons."
41. Tom Blount, "Bipartisan Group Talks Lawmaker Civility," *American Editor*, June 1997, RLP-DC-S, f. Civility Retreats. 1997. Press (2). See also "Public Incivility: Does the Media Have a Role?" RLP-DC-S, f. Civility Retreats. 1997. Talking Points.
42. Climer to RL and Skaggs, April 8, 1997, RLP-DC-S, f. Civility Retreats. 1997. Correspondence.
43. Ibid.
44. Henry, "Partisanship Thrives."
45. RL and Skaggs to Thomas and Fazio, April 10, 1997, RLP-DC-S, f. Civility Retreats. 1997. Correspondence.
46. Archer and Hall to RL, January 26, 1999, RLP-DC-S, f. Civility Retreats. 1997. Correspondence.
47. Kathleen Hall Jamieson and Erika Falk, "Civility in the House of Representatives: An Update," March 1998, RLP-DC-S, f. Civility Retreats. 1999; Jamieson and Falk, "Civility in the House of Representatives: The 105th Congress," March 1999, RLP-DC-S, f. Civility Retreats. 1999.
48. "A Proposal to the Pew Charitable Trusts for a Third Bipartisan Congressional Retreat," June 23, 2000, RLP-DC-S, f. Civility Retreats. 2001.
49. Jamieson and Falk, "Civility in the House."
50. Moorhus, "Bipartisan Retreat."

CHAPTER 6

IF AT FIRST YOU DON'T SUCCEED

LOOKING FOR KISSES AT HERSHEY II AND BEYOND

Yes, we were disappointed that the first civility retreat failed to improve House decorum. But we moved ahead, buoyed by support from the members, and even more from their spouses, who had attended Hershey I.

On July 22, 1998, Gingrich and Gephardt announced their appointment of the 1999 Bipartisan Retreat Planning Committee. "We believe that it is important to build on the relationships developed as a result of the first retreat and forge new relationships among those who were not able to attend last year," the leaders said in a joint statement. "It is important for our Members to begin the difficult work of the 106th Congress in a spirit of bipartisanship with our goal being to create an effective, productive environment." The press release quoted me as saying, "Hershey has become synonymous with civility. Hershey kisses are the new congressional symbol for congeniality."[1]

Tom Sawyer, a Democrat from Ohio, joined me as co-chair, David Skaggs having announced his intention to retire from the House. The Democratic committee members were David Bonior (MI), Eva Clayton (NC), Anna Eshoo (CA), Charlie Stenholm (TX), and a freshman member to be selected after the November elections. Republicans Chris Cox (CA),

Jo Ann Emerson (MO), Tillie Fowler (FL), Amo Houghton (NY), and an incoming freshman joined them. Debbie Dingell and Sandie Knollenberg represented the Democratic and Republican spouses, respectively. Bonior was an especially noteworthy addition to the group because of his position as minority whip. He had been such a vehement critic of Gingrich that we felt adding him might persuade the most partisan Democrats of the retreat's value.

Our planning committee set the dates and location for the second retreat: March 19–21, 1999, again at the Hershey Lodge and Convention Center. We also agreed that the second retreat ought to focus on seven objectives:

> 1. Help members learn about each other and understand their partnership
> 2. Focus on the process, culture, and role of the House, both now and in the 21st century
> 3. Aim to boost House productivity
> 4. Give members permission to be friends and a safe place in which to do this
> 5. Look into alternative techniques for debating issues
> 6. Provide for team building
> 7. Talk about civility in the House[2]

As 1998 drew to a close, however, two events cast a pall over the House and threatened the civility initiative. The first was the impeachment of President Clinton and the myriad events surrounding that drawn-out affair, culminating in the impeachment debate in the House, December 17–19. Until that debate, the first session of the 105th Congress had seemed more hospitable than the first session of the 104th in terms of procedural measures (i.e., requests to take down words, words taken down, and words taken down that go to a ruling by the chair).[3] As the Clinton matter played out in the second session, however, the atmosphere deteriorated. Nonprocedural indices (i.e., name-calling, vulgarity, aspersion, pejorative speech, hyperbole, and synonyms for lying) suggested that contrary to the norm of past Congresses, civil behavior crumbled and partisanship climbed.[4] Bonior told us in early January that the Democratic leadership had discussed the retreat, "and there was a lot of feeling that it should be cancelled."[5]

The midterm elections in 1998 also proved ominous; the Republican majority was whittled down to six, and this was followed by the resignations of Speaker Gingrich and Speaker-designate Bob Livingston. Our hold on the House was tenuous, to say the least. Republicans scratched for every advantage. Democrats complained, for example, that Republican leaders treated them unfairly in determining the number of seats each party received on House committees. Democrats had a point. We were overrepresented on committees, especially the power committees, including Rules and Ways and Means.[6] We had not readjusted the lopsided Republican majorities since 1995, despite our party's losses in the subsequent two elections.

These two events—the Clinton impeachment and the 1998 election results—fostered rancor and bitterness in the House. "You would think politicians would not need lessons in listening to each other. But after a year of hectoring over President Clinton's personal conduct, they are not a bad idea," editorialized the *New York Times* on March 1 before warning that "no amount of happy talk will raise Congress's esteem."[7] We intended Hershey II to result in more than happy talk.

Roll Call, the Capitol Hill newspaper, cautioned that lingering resentments within the Democratic caucus might lead numerous Democrats to skip our retreat. "If the [Hershey] retreat creates the illusion of bipartisanship without the substance of bipartisanship, then it's not very useful," said Democratic Steering Committee vice chair Steny Hoyer (D-MD). In their first formal meeting of the new year, Democrats went so far as to instruct Gephardt to deliver a bill of particulars dealing with committee ratios, among other grievances, to Denny Hastert, who had assumed the speakership.[8]

After a drawn-out lobbying effort, the planning committee finally convinced the leadership to endorse the retreat. On January 22, Hastert,

Gephardt, Armey, and Bonior sent a Dear Colleague letter urging members to attend. "Solutions to our country's problems can only be found in an environment in which we trust one another's word," they wrote, "and recognize that each member is equally important to our overall mission of improving life for the American people. We can respect one another, even as we disagree on particular issues."[9]

Drumming up attendance proved to be a continuing headache given the ill will fostered by the impeachment proceedings. In my conversations with members, I tried to make the point that everyone who had gone to the first retreat as a Republican had come back a Republican, and vice versa. The program was designed not to eliminate partisan positions but to generate respect for each other so that differing views could be discussed in a civil manner.[10]

Talk of a Democratic boycott continued, however. On February 24, Bonior addressed his party's caucus on the upcoming civility retreat only to be greeted by hissing and booing.[11] "A lot of our people are angry," said a Democratic leadership aide. "There's no reason to think that after what we just went through, with them trying to throw out the leader of our party [President Clinton], that we're all suddenly going to be buddies. That's absurd." Some on our side of the aisle were reluctant, too. Amo Houghton told one reporter that the Republicans who refused to attend were the ones who "need it most." When asked at a press conference how many members of the House Judiciary Committee would attend, I replied quickly, "Next question!"[12]

In total, 450 persons from the congressional community took part in Hershey II, a number that included spouses and children. We lacked for members, however. Ninety-four Republicans and 92 Democrats turned out, disappointing numbers and fewer than the 197 who had attended Hershey I.[13] Many who led the impeachment fight were absent. Aside from Asa Hutchinson and James Rogan, the only other House manager present was George Gekas, a Republican who represented Hershey in Congress. Judiciary Committee chair Henry Hyde was home in Illinois.

Also absent were Bob Barr, one of the president's most vociferous critics, and Barney Frank, the committee's dogged impeachment opponent. Speaker Hastert attended, however, as did Minority Leader Gephardt.

Upon reflection, and despite our best efforts and countless hours of staff work, the second retreat simply did not achieve what we on the planning committee had hoped. In some sense, it represented a step backwards. It did not help that Dick Gephardt told one reporter, "Hersheys come and Hersheys go. But the bottom line is, do we ever have any real change?"[14] John Dingell, the most senior member of the House (who attended only because his wife, a co-organizer, made him) called the retreat "a prodigious waste of my time."[15] When asked to explain his lack of attendance, Barney Frank bragged, "I have no trouble being civil when I think civility is appropriate."[16] One press report about poor attendance concluded, "But the failure of a majority of House members to come to Hershey, the self-christened 'sweetest place on earth,' underlined a feeling among many that all they would get here were empty calories. Several of them said the event was a futile charade, more useful for public relations than political harmony."[17]

In an interview with *Roll Call* at the end of March, I gave Hershey II a positive spin. "The picture that was the most lasting for me was Mel Watt [D-NC] carrying [Charley] Canady's [R-FL] newborn baby for almost an hour, walking around the room. I think that captures the essence of Hershey," I told the reporter. "It will be pretty difficult for Mel to get in an acrimonious dispute with Charley, having had an opportunity to cuddle his baby." I conceded, however, that "some things were brought up that were uncomfortable for a lot of people. Democrats want certain things like committee ratios and funding, and Republicans want Democrats to stop misrepresenting them on certain issues." At the most fundamental level, I knew that good will was not enough to restore a tone of civility to the House. "I go back to the notion that politics is about relationships," I said. "But we also ought to be able to manage our relationships if we're going to get anything done. That's what we're trying to get people to understand. It's one thing to know each other, but we've got to pass legislation."[18]

The planning committee distilled the lessons of the second retreat into 11 action steps:

> 1. Create a bipartisan mechanism to address scheduling
> 2. Create a bipartisan mechanism to address members' financial needs
> 3. Establish a bipartisan committee on fairness and integrity in the political process and campaigning
> 4. Create a bipartisan mechanism to address floor proceedings (e.g., one minutes, open rules, minority party substitutes)
> 5. Establish a bipartisan institutional fairness committee
> 6. Increase communication/coordination between parties with regular leadership meetings; consider [a] "mini-Hershey" for chairs and ranking members
> 7. Create a bipartisan mechanism to address committee ratio and resource issues
> 8. Improve freshman orientation, establish cross-party mentorships, and have freshmen CODELs [congressional delegations]
> 9. Revisit the ethics committee process; revise rules to be clear, flexible, and supportive of families
> 10. Establish bipartisan policy forums and field hearings
> 11. Develop a program of bipartisan service activities/community projects[19]

We believed that presenting what we called "mechanisms" instead of a long list of rule changes created a better chance of success. Regrettably, nothing of substance came out of hearings held by the Subcommittee on Rules and Organization of the House, which reviewed our recommendations. Nor did my meeting with the Speaker in June produce results. But the postretreat evaluation gave reason for at least tempered optimism. Of the 52 members who returned surveys, 81 percent said they would attend another retreat in 2001—only one said no. The three most-cited reasons for showing up were "I hoped to improve bipartisan relations,"

"I wanted a chance to meet colleagues and their families," and "It was a chance to discuss what improvement can be made in the House."[20]

On the strength of members' continuing interest, albeit expressed formally by just 52 of the 186 members who attended the 1999 retreat, we proceeded to plan a third edition in 2001, this one to follow the presidential election of 2000.

ENTHUSIASM WANES

Our first challenge was to fund a third retreat in the absence of measureable progress following the first two. It took a series of negotiations with the Pew Charitable Trusts to resolve their very legitimate concerns about continuing to invest in the civility initiative. By the end of June 2000, the planning committee had developed our formal response to Pew.[21] "The environment that will greet the 107th Congress next January will be as difficult as ever, following what clearly will have been another very partisan, rancorous election season," it began. "The opening for improved conditions that will exist will be equaled by the challenges. A new Administration is a certainty, and with it comes a certain opportunity to set a fresh tone in executive-legislative relations. There may also be changes in control of Congress." We acknowledged that change was an inevitable source of anxiety and tension, all the more so with changes in political power. We realized that no matter what happened in the elections, roughly half the membership of the House would report for duty next year bitterly disappointed: that they had failed to gain or to keep control of their chamber, that their party had failed to gain or to keep control of the White House. All that, coupled with the difficulties of the recent past, promised to "aggravate the risk that political conflict and partisan rancor will stand in the way of effective governance for another two years."[22]

We were not prepared to give up, however. We asked the Pew Trusts for $800,000 and promised that Hershey III would "be significantly different" from the previous retreats. In fact, the committee had already agreed to move to the Greenbrier resort in White Sulphur Springs, West Virginia. Hershey III was about to become Retreat III. As the Pew Trusts demanded, the committee set out *measurable* objectives—in other words, our definition of success for a retreat. We established three major criteria: substantial and roughly equal attendance by members of both parties; major changes in approach from the previous retreats; and serious, substantive programming. In sum, we said the third retreat would "aim to expand the vision of members about the great opportunities and the challenges facing the country and Congress. In the process, it will seek also to help insure that, while dealing with those opportunities and challenges, political disagreements and debate are kept within the bounds of decency and respect."[23]

The proposal must have struck a responsive chord. Pew picked up the tab for Retreat III, a development we reported to Hastert and Gingrich on September 28, a year to the day after our negotiations with Pew had begun.[24] Planning proceeded along what were by now well-established lines. The committee selected March 9–11, 2001, as the retreat dates.

Events in the House during the two weeks leading up to the meeting at Greenbrier did not bode well. In late February, Gephardt signed the customary letter, along with Hastert, encouraging members to attend the retreat. He did so, however, only after Hastert had reluctantly agreed to Gephardt's demand that Democrats receive an additional seat on the Appropriations Committee. As part of this sideshow, Hastert demanded that Gephardt publicly credit him with trying to bring greater comity to the House by giving the Democrats the additional seat. The press, of course, reveled in reporting the tempest.[25]

Tensions escalated further when Hastert insisted that a proposed bipartisan election-reform panel comprise five Republicans and only four Democrats. Then, one day before the retreat, Republican leaders rushed through a vote on the GOP's $958 billion tax cut. "How can Democratic Members show up at a [bipartisan retreat] on a Friday when on Thursday we were denied a substitute on maybe the single biggest issue [facing] this Congress?" one Democratic aide asked a reporter.[26] Gephardt claimed that railroading the tax-cut bill followed the pattern of action set forth by the Republican leadership on other bills. Hastert had infuriated Democrats by gaveling the House into recess after just an hour of debate on one of their pet bills, thereby cutting off discussion a full three hours before the vote was to occur. "It killed bipartisanship," Gephardt told the press.[27]

Much as in 1999, talk spread of a Democratic boycott of the retreat. One unidentified Democrat who refused to attend explained his decision: "I need to walk the dog. That's all the excuse they deserve."[28] For his part, Gephardt complained on Thursday that the upcoming retreat would be his last. "Been there, done that, all I got was this t-shirt," he whined at a news conference in his office. "I don't want to go to West Virginia to be bipartisan. I want to be bipartisan in this building."[29]

With fewer members than we had hoped, about 125, the retreat proceeded. Another drama unfolded the very weekend of the retreat, however—one that proved a distraction and underlined once again the obstacles to comity in the House. Minority Leader Gephardt's office released a letter to Speaker Hastert on Friday that detailed the "indignities perpetrated" against the minority by the Speaker and the Republican leadership. Gephardt charged that then–presidential candidate George H. Bush and Hastert had reneged on their pledge to change the tone in Washington. "If anything," the letter read, "[you] have raised the level of partisan rancor to new heights." Moreover, Gephardt gave the letter to the press before he delivered it to Hastert only an hour before the two were to appear on C-SPAN. Publicly, Hastert said he was "disappointed" by the letter, but people close to him said he was fuming.[30]

At a news conference during the retreat, Gephardt reiterated his pledge that this would be his last retreat. He added, "Bipartisanship is over—not that it ever began."[31] Hastert called the retreat only a first step (although this was the third retreat, I could not help but think), backing away from a more ringing endorsement.[32] Tellingly, the leaders arrived together to talk to reporters, but they exchanged no words or looks, and they refused to take questions. They skipped the rest of the weekend, too. A few days later, an aide to Gephardt told a reporter, "Our view of these retreats is that they have yet to produce any results, and so there's no point in being there." He added that the drop-off in attendance "indicates that there's not any interest in this."[33] Another senior Democratic aide spoke volumes when he told a reporter, "It was never a leadership initiative. It was always a thing run by moderates on both sides."[34]

In early April, the Bipartisan Congressional Retreat Planning Committee met to review evaluations of the retreat, define lessons learned, anticipate future committee activities, and decide whether to hold Retreat IV.[35] Only 22 members who had attended the retreat returned evaluations, so we did not have much to go on. To sustain the retreat's impact, however, the committee did decide, somewhat tentatively, to arrange mini-retreats for committees, to sponsor a biotechnology seminar series, to consider inviting historian David McCullough to speak in the Capitol, and to assume that another retreat would occur in 2003. In hindsight, this seems like a modest agenda for action compared to that of Retreat I. Even so, we had to cancel the McCullough event for lack of participation, and none of the six committees we approached responded to the offer to host a mini-retreat just for its members.[36]

Admittedly, the time I had spent on the civility project had not paid great dividends as far as the institution of Congress was concerned. Nor did circumstances suggest a more promising future. But I was determined to make another attempt even in the face of waning enthusiasm.

"The House is and should be a place where we vigorously discuss and debate important issues facing the country—issues about which Members often hold very different views," the planning committee wrote in inviting members to attend Retreat IV.[37] We tried to head off complaints that these retreats were intended to quash debate. As our invitation read, the Retreat is *not* meant to assume, or to push Members into, some sort of false bipartisanship. It is not about glossing over our differences. We want to put to rest any notion that we seek some mushy middle, or that attending the Retreat implies a concession about your partisan identity or what may be bothering you.[38]

I could tell that eagerness for the retreats had faded, however. When I appealed to members to participate, they responded with "Forget it" or "There's no value in it" or "What's really the purpose?" It was like pulling teeth to get some of them even to consider the offer.

The political environment on the Hill proved to be as inhospitable as ever. Tom DeLay moved up from majority whip to majority leader at the beginning of the session. Hastert was entering his third term as Speaker, but now his top assistant was one of the most combative and ideologically conservative members of our party. The Democrats elected Nancy Pelosi to replace Gephardt, who stepped down as minority leader to run for president. Pelosi, an aggressive liberal, made no secret of her belief that Democrats had nothing to gain from cooperating with Republicans on anything. The result was no surprise. According to *Congressional Quarterly*'s (*CQ*) analysis of "party unity" votes in 2003—those that pitted a majority of one party against a majority of the other party—Congress was more polarized than it had been in the five decades that *CQ* had been tracking voting patterns.[39]

Retreat IV took place February 28 through March 2, 2003, again at the Greenbrier resort. We booked *New York Times* columnist Thomas Friedman, *Weekly Standard* editor David Brooks, and columnists Karen Armstrong and Georgie Anne Geyer as keynoters. The program also included Jessica Matthews, president of the Carnegie Endowment for International Peace, and Akbar Ahmed, chair of the Islamic studies department at American University. Retreat IV, the first to follow the terrorist attacks of September 11, 2001, dealt with broad themes. Friedman's session, for example, "American Values after 9/11," was designed to help us develop a better sense of how American society's central values or principles were seen by the rest of the world and how we might be more effective in that area.

We did not neglect more immediate concerns. Our committee organized a panel of former members and spouses called "Experiences and Perspectives on Life in the House: A Sense & Spirit of Community." This session looked at recent trends and forces affecting the House with an eye to understanding how we might develop a sense of community in the day-to-day life of the chamber.[40]

The planning committee surveyed the attendees, asking them to suggest follow-up activities. We received about a half-dozen suggestions, almost all of which dealt with organizing events such as bipartisan issue luncheons, committee retreats, committee dinners with families, district weekend exchange visits, and CODELs.[41] We saw the handwriting on the wall, however. The numbers slumped (only 83 attended), enthusiasm ebbed, even press coverage declined.

The climate in the House did not improve much, as illustrated by just one example, from a *Roll Call* story headed "Poisoned Political Water Breeds Acrimony, Contempt," authored by former Iowa congressman Jim Lightfoot:

> The air is poison. Tension grips even the most casual conversations, which have become an exercise in short, cryptic remarks, many times more grunted than spoken. Distrust is the order of the day. People keep looking over their shoulders to see if anyone has taken an unhealthy interest in them. The environment is hostile and does not lend itself to any degree of accomplishment.[42]

David Skaggs, in 2003 the head of the Center for Democracy and Citizenship and still involved with retreat planning, warned me in June 2004 that the future of the civility project was in peril. It was time to be "candid and highly pragmatic" in assessing what to do next, he wrote. Despite supporting the fourth retreat, the Annenberg Foundation, which had agreed in late summer 2001 to take the place of Pew as the primary funding source, "has been pretty clear that they are not inclined to fund another retreat." Skaggs believed, too, that the planning committee had lost enthusiasm and energy. For Retreat V to succeed, we would need another funding source and new blood on the committee.[43]

THE END AND FINAL THOUGHTS

In September 2004, we canceled the bipartisan civility retreat scheduled for January 2005. No, Congress had not miraculously become a more civil place. As a legislative body, we still seemed unable to conduct much business. In June, for example, Vice President Dick Cheney used the F-word during a testy exchange with Senator Patrick Leahy (D-VT) on the Senate floor. The same week, Congressman Patrick Kennedy (D-RI) called Duke Cunningham (R-CA) an idiot after hearing Cunningham make a remark about his father, Ted Kennedy.

Just two weeks away from the start of the new fiscal year, October 1, Congress had completed only one of 13 spending bills. The November elections loomed over us. Our leaders put dozens of issues on hold because the highly partisan atmosphere blocked efforts to resolve them. A study of congressional votes in 2003 found Congress more polarized than it had been in 50 years—the average House Republican toed the party line 91 percent of the time, and Democrats voted with their party at an 87 percent clip.[44]

The evidence continued to suggest that the need for civil, respectful debate had not diminished one bit. When we contacted members to determine their interest in a fifth retreat, however, only 120 members returned surveys despite repeated efforts to solicit responses. Of that number, 47 said they definitely would *not* attend a retreat. I could not justify the time and effort to organize an event few people would attend.[45] Naturally, I was profoundly disappointed.

I had spent almost a decade leading these formal efforts to promote civility in the House. I had begun with high hopes in 1996, or at least with what I thought were realistic hopes. With the benefit of reflection, however, I can say that I had vastly underestimated the challenge. So much of what I objected to in Congress either reflected larger issues in society or resulted from factors beyond the control of the members, never numbering more than 200, who sought change.

Members of the retreat planning committees could not do much about the new hyperactive media or the proliferation of interest groups or the hardening of partisan ideologies or the congressional redistricting that produced fewer competitive seats or a style of campaigning that emphasized opposition research and constant attack. Add to those factors the narrow partisan margins in the House, which meant that both parties believed it was critical to hold down defections on key votes by framing their positions in sharp contrast to each other in anticipation of upcoming elections. No wonder the public's trust in political institutions and lawmakers' ability to deal with national problems had declined precipitously.[46]

I am convinced, too, that three other forces conspired against our efforts, factors we could not influence. First, the change in party control of the House from Democrats to Republicans following the 1994 elections proved pivotal. Democrats struggled with their newfound minority status, and Republicans promoted an ambitious, aggressive legislative agenda to enact while dealing with a president of the opposite party. The federal government shutdowns in November and December 1995 marked the culmination of this partisan bickering. Newt Gingrich got it right when he admitted in remarks at the first retreat that Republicans did not wear their new majority status any better than Democrats wore theirs as the minority.[47]

The tension resulting from this House majority role reversal was compounded by two events. The impeachment controversy in late 1998, coupled with the contested presidential election in 2000, poisoned the well beyond reclaiming. I remember when Vice President Al Gore presided over the counting of the electoral votes that gave George Bush the presidency even though Gore had won the popular vote. Congressman Jesse Jackson Jr. objected every time a state's vote was cast, and Gore had to overrule him. Jackson's ploy, when the outcome was certain, put an exclamation point to the whole ordeal. Democrats never got over either the impeachment or the 2000 presidential election result. Only when they regained the majority following the 2006 elections was there any hope of moving forward.

I grant that debate—vigorous debate—and advocacy are essential to the work we do in Congress. But progress comes only within a framework of mutual trust and understanding. Maybe I'm naïve, but I believe that personal relationships built up over time in both work and social contexts create that essential trust. Partisanship is here to stay, of course. Republicans and Democrats have legitimate ideological and policy differences over issues large and small. We can't and shouldn't paper over these differences. There is no point or virtue in what we called the mushy middle. But disagreements between Republicans and Democrats should not be poisonous.

Some of us continued down the path of bipartisanship, comity, and civility. Amo Houghton hosted bipartisan dinners in his home. Even more recently, my successor, Aaron Schock, told me that during his orientation at the Harvard School in December 2008, Congresswoman Diana DeGette (D-CO) went on at length about my work to promote civility and the four retreats. Here was the chief deputy whip of the House, who attended the retreat in 1997, pointing out to incoming members more than 10 years after that event the importance of conducting oneself in a civil manner.

My own experience illustrates the rewards and frustrations of forging bipartisan relationships. One or two days after he was elected as a Democrat to the House in 2003, Rahm Emanuel called me to say that he wanted to work together, across the aisle, on behalf of Illinois. I knew him only slightly from his days in the Clinton White House, when I had worked for Bob Michel. But that phone call started a genuine friendship and a powerful working relationship. Rahm has a well-deserved reputation as a fiercely partisan Democrat. He chaired the House Democratic Caucus and orchestrated the Democratic victories in the 2006 congressional elections. Yet we worked closely together on children's health insurance. That, in turn, led us to host six bipartisan dinners at which we talked policy and politics with equal numbers of Democrats and Republicans, all in an effort to foster collegiality and bipartisanship. He chose the Democrats; I picked the Republicans. We split the check.

This initiative was novel enough that *Chicago Tribune* reporter Jill Zuckman wrote a lengthy feature about the dinners in January 2007.[48] The next day, Denny Hastert, who by then had lost the speakership but remained a member, called me. He was outraged that I would co-host dinners with Emanuel, whom he called "the devil incarnate." Hastert raked me over the coals for about five minutes, a startling reminder of how difficult it is to sustain comity in the House. I am proud to be a Republican, and I believe deeply in the core values represented in our platform. But my Republican roots have not kept me from working with Democrats on important issues. I am very proud of my work with Congressman Bill Delahunt, a liberal Democrat from Massachusetts, and with Senator Patrick Leahy (D-VT) on DNA testing standards for murder cases. I'm not sure that Delahunt would have picked up the phone to talk about the bill if we had not struck up a friendship during the retreats. Relationships matter. It is as simple as that.

Taken as a whole, however, our successes came only at the margins. I believe today that we could have achieved more. Progress was possible. A few institutional changes, such as moving the one-minutes or modifying committee ratios, would have mattered. But the retreats failed to change the culture of the House. At the end, we were not even trying. We did not infuse the institution with respect for honest differences of opinion. I'm not sure that we had the capacity to make those broad changes. We never hit upon a mechanism to ensure that our initiatives were carried through. There was no funding for it, no permanent staff, no leadership support. We simply could not sustain the momentum. The people who were interested in keeping things the way they were, the partisan forces, overwhelmed us. We could make progress one on one, as individuals, but not across Congress as an institution.

NOTES

1. Press release, "New Hershey Retreat Committee Appointed," July 22, 1998, RLP-DC-S, f. Civility Retreats. 1999. Press.
2. Minutes of the Bipartisan Retreat Assessment and Planning Meeting, April 30–May 1, 1998, RLP-DC-S, f. Civility Retreats. 1999. Planning Committee.
3. Kathleen Hall Jamieson and Erika Falk, "Civility in the House of Representatives: The 105th Congress," pre-release copy, March 12, 1999, RLP-DC-S, f. Civility Retreats. 1999. "Civility in the House of Representatives: The 105th Congress."
4. Jamieson and Falk, "Civility in the House." Don Wolfensberger offered a devastating critique of the Jamieson report in testimony before the Subcommittee on Rules and Organization of the House. See Statement by Don Wolfensberger before the Subcommittee on Rules and Organization of the House, April 29, 1999, RLP-DC-S, f. Civility Retreats. 1999. Subcommittee on Rules and Organization of the House.
5. Notes from the planning committee meeting, January 6, 1999, RLP-DC-S, f. Civility Retreats. 1999. Planning Committee.
6. Charlie Cook, "It's True: Democrats' Seats are Numbered," *National Journal*, March 6, 1999, 640–641, RLP-DC-S, f. Civility Retreats. 1999. Press.
7. "Getting Along in Congress," *NYT*, March 1, 1999, RLP-Memoir, f. Civility.
8. Ethan Wallison, "House Civility Melting Away Before March Hershey Retreat," *Roll Call*, January 25, 1999, RLP-DC-S, f. Civility Retreats. 1999. Press.
9. Dear Colleague, January 22, 1999, RLP-DC-S, f. Civility Retreats. 1999. Correspondence.
10. "Hershey II," January 25, 1999, RLP-DC-S, f. Civility Retreats. 1999. Talking Points.
11. Juliet Eilperin, "Frayed House Prepares for Its Civility Camp," *Washington Post*, February 25, 1999, RLP-Peoria-TBS, f. Civility (1).
12. Katharine Seelye, "House, with Help, Starts Push to Find the Road to Peace," *NYT*, February 25, 1999 RLP-DC-S, f. Civility Retreats. 1999. Press.

13. These numbers were used by the planning committee and reported in the press. A recapitulation of attendance in 2004, however, put the number of members attending in 1999 at only 103. See Climer to Liesman, June 2, 2004, RLP-DC-S, f. Civility Retreats. 2005. Correspondence.

14. Bob Hohler, "Veteran of Ulster Strife Talks of US House Rifts," *Boston Globe*, March 21, 1999, RLP-DC-S, f. Civility Retreats. 1999. Press.

15. Frank Bruni, "The Whirlwind Life of (Not Just) a Political Wife," *NYT*, March 22, 1999, RLP-DC-S, f. Civility Retreats. 1999. Press.

16. Hohler, "Veteran of Ulster."

17. Frank Bruni, "Lawmakers Get Away from Capital for Lesson in Being Nice," *NYT*, March 21, 1999, RL Memoir Reference File, f. Civility.

18. "Hugs and Kisses in Hershey," *The Hill*, March 24, 1999, RLP-DC-S, f. Civility Retreats. 1999. Press.

19. "Action Steps," n.d., RLP-DC-S, f. Civility Retreats. 1999. Next Steps.

20. Charles Clonts to David Skaggs, July 29, 1999, attached to Skaggs to Michael DelliCarpini, May 4, 2000, RLP-DC-S, f. Civility Retreats. 2001.

21. "A Proposal to the Pew Charitable Trusts for a Third Bipartisan Congressional Retreat," June 23, 2000, RLP-DC-S, f. Civility Retreats. 2001. Correspondence. 1999–2000.

22. Ibid.

23. Ibid.

24. RL and others to Hastert and Gephardt, September 28, 2000, RLP-DC-S, f. Civility Retreats. 2001. Correspondence.

25. Ethan Wallison, "Retreat Faces Boycott Threat," *Roll Call*, n.d., RLP-DC-S, f. Civility Retreats. 2001. Press.

26. Wallison, "Retreat Faces Boycott."

27. Martha Bryson Hodel, "Congress Seeks Civility in W. Va.," Associated Press, March 10, 2001, RLP-DC-S, f. Civility Retreats. 2001. Press.

28. Philip Shenon, "House Votes Haunt Retreat Meant to Spur Collegiality," *NYT*, March 11, 2001, RLP-Memoir, f. Civility.

29. Martha Bryson Hodel, "Politics: Can Congressional Civility Be Reached in Bucolic Setting?" Associated Press, RLP-DC-S, f. Civility Retreats. 2001. Press.

30. Ethan Wallison, "Civility Eludes House Leaders," *Roll Call*, n.d., RLP-DC-S, f. Civility Retreats. 2001. Press.

31. Shenon, "House Votes Haunt."

32. Hodel, "Congress Seeks Civility."

33. Wallison, "Civility Eludes Leaders."

34. Ibid.

35. Planning Committee Agenda, April 4, 2001, RLP-DC-S, f. Civility Retreats. 2001. Planning Committee.

36. Skaggs to RL, August 28, 2001, RLP-DC-S, f. Civility Retreats. 2003. Correspondence; "Notes of BCRIII Planning Committee," March 19, 2002, RLP-DC-S, f. Civility Retreats. 2003. Correspondence.

37. Three colleagues joined me to co-chair the 2003 retreat: Charlie Stenholm (D-TX), Amo Houghton (R-NY), and Lucille Roybal-Allard (D-CA).

38. Dear Colleague, October 10, 2002, RLP-DC-S, f. Civility Retreats. 2003. Correspondence.

39. CQ, *Congress and the Nation, 2001–2004*, vol. 11 (Washington DC: Congressional Quarterly Press, 2006), 19.

40. RLP-DC-S, f. Civility Retreats. 2003. LaHood Packet.

41. RLP-DC-S, f. Civility Retreats. 2003. Follow-Up; Skaggs and Climer to Planning Committee, May 13, 2003, RLP-DC-S, f. Civility Retreats. 2003. Planning Committee.

42. Excerpt in Climer to Liesman, March 17, 2004, RLP-DC-S, f. Civility Retreats. 2005. Correspondence.

43. Skaggs to RL and Stenholm, June 23, 2004, RLP-DC-S, f. Civility Retreats. 2005. Correspondence.

44. Dori Meinert, "Partisan Divisions Grow in Congress," *Springfield State Journal*, September 19, 2004, RL Memoir Reference File, f. Civility.

45. Bailey to Liesman, March 17, 2004, RLP-DC-S, f. Civility Retreats. 2005. Correspondence.

46. CQ, "Partisan Politics," *CQ Researcher*, March 19, 1999, 233–256, RLP-DC-S, f. Civility Retreats. 2001. Press.

47. Brett Lieberman, "A Memorable Homecoming," *Patriot-News*, Harrisburg, PA, March 9, 1997, RLP-DC-S, f. Civility Retreats. 1997. Press (2).

48. Jill Zuckman, "Emanuel Joins GOP for Dinner," *Chicago Tribune*, January 23, 2007, RL Memoir Reference File, f. Civility.

Chapter 7

Prelude to Impeachment

"Resolved, that William Jefferson Clinton, President of the United States, is impeached for high crimes and misdemeanors...."

—H. Res. 611[1]

Nothing about the first weekend in December 1998 suggested much out of the ordinary. I had spent the days following the Thanksgiving holiday touring my central Illinois congressional district, keeping a schedule typical of a member of Congress. On Friday, December 4, for example, I met with pork producers to discuss hog prices, introduced Illinois governor Jim Edgar at the noon meeting of Peoria's downtown Rotary, and attended two Christmas parties. I traveled to Chicago for a Bradley University basketball game on Saturday before returning for a private holiday party. Sunday I rested.

Monday, December 7, promised more of the same—back to Chicago for the Farm Bureau's annual conference, returning to Peoria for an open house at the Nature Conservancy of Illinois, then to a Christmas party hosted by a local hospital at the Country Club of Peoria.

As I was driving back to Peoria with my district chief of staff, Brad McMillan, my cell phone rang. Martha Morrison, a floor assistant for

Speaker Gingrich, posed a question that put me at the center of history: "Will you preside over the House during the impeachment debate?" So began my most important assignment as a member of the House of Representatives from Abraham Lincoln's old congressional district.

The Clinton Scandals

Like most Americans, I had followed the allegations of Bill Clinton's misconduct mostly in the press. In addition to the *Wall Street Journal* and the *Washington Post*, I read the *Congressional Quarterly*, the *National Journal*, *Congress Daily*, and the two Capitol Hill newspapers—*Roll Call* and *The Hill*. I did not know Kenneth Starr, the independent counsel investigating the charges against President and Mrs. Clinton. I had heard he was close to Tom DeLay, the House majority whip, and to other conservatives in the Republican Party. As far as I could tell, Starr's exploration of the Arkansas land deal known then as Whitewater, of the White House travel office firings in 1993, and of the Clintons' request for confidential FBI files hadn't amounted to much. It's fair to say I had followed the story but not with any unusual fervor.

Separate from the Starr investigation was another legal proceeding that took on increasing importance as time passed. In February 1994, Paula Jones brought a sexual harassment suit against Bill Clinton. During the discovery phase of the Jones case, her lawyers included the name of Monica Lewinsky on a list of other women alleged to have been harassed by Clinton. Lewinsky had told several friends of her affair with the president, which began in November 1995 when the young woman interned in the White House. The Jones case became forever linked to Lewinsky after a tape recording surfaced on which Lewinsky admitted that President Clinton had urged her to lie about their relationship. In January 1998, Starr received permission from the Justice Department to investigate the Lewinsky affair.

Others have told the story of the ensuing drama. I do not intend to rehash it. Suffice it to say that I did not believe the president when, on January 26, he told us, wagging his finger to emphasize the point, "I want to say one thing to the American people. I want you to listen to me. I'm going to say this again. I did not have sexual relations with that woman, Miss Lewinsky. I never told anyone to lie. Not a single time. Never. These allegations are false. And I need to go back to work for the American people."[2]

He did go back to work. The next night he delivered his State of the Union address. The president had big plans for the balance of his presidency. With allegations swirling around him, however, he faced an uphill climb. I had heard enough rumors about the president's philandering to suspect he had not been completely truthful about the Lewinsky matter.

I knew President Clinton only in passing. Kathy and I had attended the White House Christmas party for members of Congress, but those are perfunctory affairs. I'm reasonably sure that Bill Clinton could not have picked me out of a lineup even granting his remarkable memory for faces. My generally negative impressions of him had not resulted from personal contact.

The Starr investigation continued to dominate the news through the spring and summer. The White House, Hillary Clinton in particular, cast the whole thing as politically motivated by "right-wing opponents of my husband." Starr and the White House battled back and forth for months about who was to blame for illegal leaks and unprofessional conduct. I became convinced that Hillary had got it partly right—some of my Republican colleagues sought to oust the president from the Oval Office owing to personal dislike, a sense of moral outrage, or for political advantage. I could tell from the tone of Tom DeLay's statements that he wanted the House to move to impeach the president. It would not have surprised me to learn that he and others had leaked information favorable to their cause.

Lewinsky testified before Ken Starr's grand jury on August 6. She admitted to the affair but claimed that the president had not told her to lie about it. President Clinton followed on August 17 with five and a half hours of closed-door testimony. That evening the president told the American people this:

> Indeed, I did have a relationship with Ms. Lewinsky that was not appropriate. In fact, it was wrong. It constituted a critical lapse in judgment and a personal failure on my part for which I am solely and completely responsible.

> But I told the grand jury today and I say to you now that at no time did I ask anyone to lie, to hide or destroy evidence or to take any other unlawful action.[3]

His performance did not persuade me. He may have admitted a mistake in judgment, but the president did not apologize to the American people for having misled them for the last seven months. That rubbed me the wrong way. I could only imagine how the people close to him felt about having been deceived so deviously.

On August 20, DeLay sent me a letter that I assume reached every Republican member. He called on the president to resign. DeLay accused the president of "a pattern of conduct that is unacceptable for a President of the United States." The majority whip's letter criticized the president's remarks to the nation, cited his refusal to apologize or show remorse, and expressed outrage at Clinton's "lies, deceit, stonewalls, and attacks on his critics." Regardless of party affiliation, DeLay wrote, "A promise from this President has no meaning." He concluded that he could not foresee the outcome of the scandal, but "What I do know is that President Clinton has lost the moral authority to lead the nation. For the good of the country, the honorable thing for the President to do is to resign."[4] The letter struck me as DeLay-style politics as usual, more theater than substance. His hatred of the Clintons was obvious.

THE STARR REPORT

Events accelerated in early September when Starr delivered his report to Congress, on the ninth. He listed eleven "possible grounds for impeachment" organized into four categories: perjury, obstruction of justice, witness tampering, and abuse of constitutional authority.

Starr claimed that Clinton had lied, thereby committing perjury, both in his civil deposition in the Jones sexual harassment case and in his grand jury testimony in August about the Lewinsky affair. On the second count, Clinton had obstructed justice by concealing gifts he had given Lewinsky and by trying to find her a job in New York to keep her from testifying. The witness-tampering charge had to do with Clinton's efforts to mislead presidential staff members knowing that they would repeat those falsehoods in their own grand jury testimony. The last category, abuse of constitutional authority, cast a wide net. Starr alleged that Clinton's actions were inconsistent with his constitutional duty to execute the law faithfully. He cited several specifics, including Clinton's assertion of executive privilege to impede Congress's investigation into the matter.

Unfortunately, Starr neglected to alert Congress that his 445-page report was ready. It caught all of us by surprise.

In an ideal world, the Democratic and Republican leaders in Congress would have taken their time to figure out how to treat the report. That didn't happen. My party's leaders announced on September 10 that they would release the report immediately, even posting it on the Internet. The House voted overwhelmingly on the morning of September 11 to do so. I voted with all the other Republicans.[5] I didn't have a chance to read it first; to my knowledge no one else did either, including the president's attorneys. I did review the full report shortly thereafter, however.

That weekend, September 12 and 13, I made the rounds back in my district, attending a parade, a breakfast meeting, and a hog roast. A good number of my constituents, even some Democrats, wanted instant impeachment. I was surprised, though, that many others expressed doubts about what kind of punishment, if any, Congress should impose. I told a couple of reporters from the *New York Times*, "These are the people saying the guy is sick. But they are simply not sure. People are confused about whether these are impeachable offenses."[6]

Many of the folks back home expressed concern that the Starr report had been made so publicly available, particularly considering its graphic and appalling content. I, however, believed the public had a right to the information and that its release was necessary to assist all of us in understanding the issues surrounding the independent counsel's recommendations. The speed with which the report had come out, however, reinforced the view that Republicans were determined to get the president, no matter what the cost.

The White House, of course, disputed the findings and did so vigorously. They issued a point-by-point rebuttal almost as soon as the Starr report became public. The president's lawyers admitted that their client's conduct was wrong and that covering it up had been wrong. They argued, however, that Clinton's actions did not constitute "high crimes and misdemeanors," the standard required for impeachment.

I thought the president displayed the height of hypocrisy when he disparaged Starr and the investigation. As I wrote to the hundreds of constituents who had contacted me after the release of the report, "The President is the person who has dodged and weaved, ducked and evaded, while sending his lawyers to the Supreme Court in attempts to avoid testifying and delaying the investigation, costing taxpayers millions of dollars."[7] I was irritated enough by the president's actions to sponsor a House resolution requiring Clinton to reimburse the government $4.4 million—the estimated cost of the independent counsel's investigation of the Lewinsky affair.[8] Legislatively, it went nowhere.[9]

The impact of Starr's report was compounded 10 days later when the House Judiciary Committee, on a party-line vote, released videotapes of Clinton's grand jury testimony. As did millions of other Americans, I watched as the television networks replayed the tapes on September 21.

I'm not an attorney, but Clinton's answers struck me as evasive, more characteristic of a lawyer trying to parse words than of someone trying to prove his innocence. "It depends on what the meaning of the word 'is' means," Clinton infamously said in responding to a question about his previous denials of a relationship with Lewinsky. "If 'is' means 'is and never has been,' that's one thing. If it means, 'there is none,' that was a completely true statement." What a dodge, I thought to myself.

Apparently, the public did not agree with me. Although most people, including my constituents, believed that Clinton had lied under oath, polls showed the president's job approval rating going up. A *New York Times*/CBS News poll conducted in mid-September revealed that 65 percent of those surveyed did not want Congress to hold impeachment hearings. Even more thought that Starr's investigation had not been worth the trouble.[10]

My constituents weighed in, of course. A poll conducted in mid-October by Mason-Dixon Political/Media Research Inc. indicated that almost half of Illinois voters objected to Congress's removing President Clinton from office.[11] My office received 5,000 letters and messages on impeachment, with opinion split right down the middle. It was not unusual for my constituents to be of at least two minds on an issue. To this day, I don't believe that representing your constituents means holding a wetted finger in the air to see which way the wind is blowing—it does not blow it one direction; it swirls. I read these letters and considered their views. But I voted on issues based on my independent assessment. The voters respected that. I had been in office long enough to have earned their trust. They saw me presiding over the House and knew that I was engaged in the issues. My good friend Dave Leitch, who represents Peoria in the Illinois General Assembly, carries around in his wallet the famous words of Edmund Burke: "Your representative owes you, not his industry only, but his judgment; and he betrays instead of serving you if he sacrifices it to your opinion." That about sums it up.

To those who wrote about the Clinton impeachment, I responded with the following letter:

> I have received your correspondence regarding your support for Congress's impeachment inquiry of President Clinton. I apologize for the delay in responding, and I certainly understand your strongly held view about this matter. It has generated a variety of opinions throughout my district, and the country.
>
> I believe we must rise to our constitutional responsibilities to conduct a thoughtful and expeditious inquiry into the issues raised by the Independent Counsel and the Counsel for the House Judiciary Committee. The allegations are serious, and a formal impeachment inquiry is a rare and serious undertaking.
>
> This impeachment inquiry is not about sexual misconduct, just as Watergate was not about a third rate burglary. It is more about what happened after these events occurred.
>
> Telling the truth, honesty, and integrity are the lifeblood of our system of justice. We must bring this matter to an orderly conclusion by following the process outlined in the constitution [sic]. We have begun the process and are moving forward. Chairman Hyde[12] has pledged to finish the Committee's inquiry by the new year, and we are all hopeful we will have the cooperation of everyone involved to meet that deadline.
>
> For the moment, I plan to wait to hear the results of the House Judiciary Committee's deliberations regarding this matter. They have received volumes of information from the Ken Starr investigation. They have been conducting hearings in which expert witnesses have testified about this matter. And, it is my hope that we can put the entire matter behind us very soon. I am grateful for your taking time to communicate with me.
>
> Sincerely,
> [Signed][13]

By now the momentum within the House, particularly among House Republicans, to punish the president seemed unstoppable. My colleagues on both sides of the aisle began to explore impeachment, censure, and financial fines as options. Many in my party, however, thought nothing short of impeachment would fit the crime.

We Republicans brought some history to this fight. Some in our party had been frankly outsmarted by Clinton during the government shutdown in 1995—that action created a lot of animosity. Others believed the president had dealt in bad faith as our party tried to put into practice the Contract with America after we won the majority in Congress in 1994. Those with more seniority could recall the Democrats' obsession with the Iran-Contra scandal during Ronald Reagan's administration. Hillary Clinton's secretive handling of the administration's health care initiative in 1993 had stung, too.

On Thursday, October 8, I voted with the majority to direct the Judiciary Committee to open the impeachment inquiry. Nothing happened immediately, however, as the committee worked on an omnibus appropriations bill before we all went home for the November elections.

In hindsight, those elections sped up the impeachment process in the House. Our party lost ground, leaving us with only a six-seat majority in the upcoming 106th Congress and no time to conduct full-fledged hearings with scores of witnesses before year's end. In very early December, probably about the second of the month, DeLay placed a conference call to his whip organization to gauge support for continuing the impeachment effort. Most members wanted to put impeachment behind them. To delay until the following year would invite political disaster because the number of Republicans would shrink as a result of the recent election losses. The press reported that as many as 12 Republicans intended to vote against impeachment while others sat on the fence.[14]

LaHood to Preside

On December 10, the *New York Times* announced my selection to occupy the Speaker's chair during House debate on the articles of impeachment. The story noted that I had "a reputation for fairness that Republican leaders hope[d] would have a calming influence" and that "Mr. LaHood has not been associated with the rebels."[15] Neither Gingrich nor Livingston, who might have been more logical choices, wanted to take on the task.[16] According to the Associated Press, Gingrich begged off because he did not want to end his tenure running the impeachment debate (and fellow Republicans did not want him as a distraction); Livingston did not care to begin his speakership by poking the president in the eye.[17] The leaders had then asked Parliamentarian Charlie Johnson for a recommendation. As he told me later, Charlie forwarded one name—mine.

It surprised some people that I took on the assignment so readily. I was proud to have been asked, of course, and I understood perfectly the historical importance of the event. But in terms of the work involved, or the challenge, it did not seem that big a deal. I knew I would be working closely with the parliamentarian. Charlie and I had a great working relationship because I had occupied the chair on so many occasions and because I respected his scrupulous nonpartisanship. I could count on him to give it to me straight. Charlie knew me from my days working for Bob Michel. I think he appreciated that I put the institution first, before politics and personal interest. I had more than a passing knowledge of the rules, and I had earned a reputation for evenhandedness from the chair. As Charlie recounted to me as I was preparing this memoir, Speaker Gingrich's staff would call the parliamentarian's office routinely for a recommendation of someone to preside given that the Speaker rarely did himself. Charlie's office kept a list of people he felt comfortable recommending. We had tryouts, so to speak, from the day the Republicans gained the majority. I was on that roster because, as Charlie put it, the Democrats respected me. Not everyone made it. I am proud that not once during my time in the House did I refuse the Speaker's request to preside.

I have to give Newt Gingrich his due, too. I was not always a team player. I hadn't signed the Contract with America, I hadn't voted for the tax cuts (this was a great source of irritation to him), and I had criticized the Speaker on occasion. But Gingrich really did not hold that against me when it came time to select someone to preside over the impeachment debate. In the end, I don't think politics entered into my selection. I did not campaign for the job. I did not try to figure out the political angles. I did not call anyone to get their read on the politics of presiding, either. I made my decision independently.

Charlie and his staff and I went to work immediately. In order to do this the right way, the fair way, in a way that reflected well on the House, presiding had to be by the book. I've always felt that way about the responsibility, but this would end up being the most historic period during the 105th Congress, so it absolutely had to be done by the book.

Meanwhile, events continued to unfold at breakneck speed. Two days after the press reported my selection, the Judiciary Committee considered and rejected Democrats' move to censure Clinton for "making false statements." Those who favored the resolution, including some Republicans, argued that censure was a punishment more befitting the president's actions. Instead, on December 11 and 12, the committee approved four articles of impeachment.[18] The articles charged the president with obstruction of justice, abuse of power, and two counts of perjury —essentially a ratification of the Starr report. As far as I could tell, however, the committee's deliberations had produced no new evidence. It failed to call any witnesses (Lewinsky, for example) with firsthand information about the events. On December 15, Speaker Gingrich summoned the full House back into a lame-duck session scheduled to begin December 17.

Although I was never party to the insider strategizing about impeachment, I did speak privately with Judiciary Committee chair Henry Hyde, a colleague and friend of mine from Illinois, and Tom Mooney, his staff director, several times a week from mid-November through the end of the hearings. Mooney and I went back thirty years. We had both worked for Illinois congressman Tom Railsback and had remained friends. These conversations convinced me that the firebrands in the party did not control the committee—Chairman Hyde did, and he did so forthrightly and fairly, notwithstanding all of the criticism about Ken Starr's role. It did not seem to me that Gingrich had called up Hyde and said, "Look, find a way to impeach this guy. We need to find a way to get Clinton because we can't get him any other way." The process was working as it was supposed to work.

Although I did not disclose my position at the time, I had come to believe that the president had engaged in criminal activity that met the standard for impeachment. He was, after all, an attorney and a former attorney general of Arkansas. He must have known that lying to the grand jury and encouraging others to do so constituted a criminal offense.

WHY NOT CENSURE?

Democrats hoped to derail impeachment with a strategy grounded in the arcane rules of the House. Generally speaking, House rules are set up to structure debate and to ensure that unrelated issues do not bog down bills on the floor. When a bill comes to the floor, it is usually accompanied by a rule or a set of procedures for considering the bill. The rule, issued by the Rules Committee, determines the length of debate and whether amendments are permitted. I knew this procedure cold. It was the normal way of conducting business.

But an article of impeachment is considered *privileged* and follows a different process. Once the Judiciary Committee approves it, the article goes straight to the House floor. The Rules Committee does not get the chance to issue a rule. The article is not subject to amendment on the floor. Our leaders argued that because the Judiciary Committee had decided as part of its impeachment resolution to reject a censure option, that alternative could not be considered on the House floor. In parliamentary terms, it would not be considered germane.

Minority Leader Gephardt had one option, however—something called a *motion to recommit with instructions.* Such a motion, if passed, would force the House to substitute censure for impeachment. In this sense, a motion to recommit with instructions is effectively an amendment; it is an end-run around the rule prohibiting amendments to a privileged resolution.

The notion of censure as an *amendment* is the crucial issue to understanding why the debate played out in the House as it did and why the censure option did not receive a vote. The general rules of the House state that an amendment must be germane—that is, related to the subject of the underlying proposition—in order to be considered. For the Democrats' strategy to work, censure would have to be germane to the articles of impeachment. This presented a dilemma for the parliamentarian and me since no direct precedent existed. There had never been a ruling in the House involving a member who proposed impeachment and another who tried to convert impeachment to censure by amendment. As Charlie Johnson described it, he had to reason by analogy and constitutional inference to assess the germaneness of censure.

His office spent weeks looking for precedents. The Democrats did as much research as we Republicans did. We were all grasping at straws. In the end, though, the parliamentarian reached two basic conclusions. First, the Constitution did not provide for congressional censure of the president—the Constitution sanctioned only impeachment as punishment for presidential misbehavior. In a parliamentary system, by way of contrast, the prime minister can suffer a vote of no confidence, or a censure vote, because he is a member of that body. From the parliamentarian's perspective, however, the notion of a censure appeared alien to the constitutional scheme of separation of powers in the United States.

The second finding was equally compelling. Because impeachment is privileged, any member can stand up as a question of privilege to impeach a federal official. If the chair were to say that such a member could then yield to another member or that another member could offer an amendment that would convert impeachment to censure, then censure would reach the same status as impeachment. According to the parliamentarian, the rules and precedents of the House did not support such an action.

In my mind, that settled the matter of censure—it was off the table. Democrats, of course, did not feel the same way. They worked with the parliamentarian and his staff to find a path to their end. The parliamentarian did not share strategies between parties, but going into the debate, we knew what the other side intended to do. We did not expect any surprises. Henry Hyde, chair of the House Judiciary Committee, and John Conyers (D-MI), the committee's top Democrat, would lead the debate. At some point, we expected the Democrats to offer a motion to recommit with instructions to substitute censure for impeachment. After some parliamentary maneuvering, I would take Charlie Johnson's advice and rule against the motion to recommit as not germane. Democrats could appeal that ruling to the entire House, but Charlie pointed out that the chair's ruling had been reversed only four times in the last 60 years, never on a matter of national importance.[19]

Shunning the Press

In addition to taking Charlie Johnson's well-considered advice, I decided not to talk to the national press. I did so without consulting with anyone, including my press secretary, who faced the challenge of fending off scores of reporters. I had accepted the role of impartial presider. I couldn't talk about the situation because the first question would be *How are you going to vote?* I never told anyone how I intended to vote even though I had made up my mind. When asked, I simply said I was going to wait to listen to the debate. If I had answered the first question, the second would have been *How can you be fair about it?*

I recall only two exceptions. I did let CNN send a film crew to follow me as I traveled the district over the weekend of December 12 and 13. I also met with Cokie Roberts and Peter Jennings for lunch at the Capitol Hill Club in Washington on December 16. That two-hour conversation was completely off the record, however, and focused primarily on the process by which censure might be considered in the House. I consented to this lunch as a personal favor to Cokie, whom I had known for a long time and whom I respected. She was true to her word—I never read or heard a word about the meeting. So I didn't talk to the press on the record—not a popular decision, I might add. Media types from Geraldo Rivera to reporters from local papers all over the country bombarded my office with requests for interviews.

THE DAY DRAWS NEAR

I remained in central Illinois until Wednesday, December 16. My schedules for this period show the usual office appointments, social events, visits to district schools, attendance at another Bradley basketball game, a promotion for the Peoria Players Theater, and so on.

While I was there, my Washington office received a Dear Colleague letter from Henry Hyde announcing that his committee had approved the four articles of impeachment and that the House would soon convene to vote on them. "This vote will be perhaps the most important one each of us will cast as Members of Congress," he wrote. The letter transmitted David Schippers's presentation in support of the articles—Schippers was majority chief investigative counsel to the committee. Hyde also included statements in opposition from Charles F. C. Ruff, counsel to the president, and Abbe Lowell, the committee's minority chief investigative counsel. The full committee report on the articles of impeachment would be available for us to review on December 16. "It is imperative that you take the time to read the report prior to casting your vote," the chair concluded.[20] I did, of course.

My first day back in the nation's capital, the 16th, began at 9:15 a.m. with a photo op in my office. I hosted a meeting with representatives of the Environmental Protection Agency, the Renewable Fuels Association, and Pekin Energy, a district-based ethanol producer, to discuss phase two of the reformulated gasoline program. I met with Charlie Johnson about the impeachment proceedings at 10:30 a.m.

At 2:00 p.m., the Tuesday Group met in the Longworth Building. This informal group consisted of a couple dozen centrist Republicans. I'd been a member since the group formed in 1997, and we met nearly every week to discuss policy priorities, attempting to give voice to the moderate view in the Republican Party. I then returned to my office to meet with the committee that was planning, ironically enough, another bipartisan retreat. The House Republican Conference held a mandatory meeting at 5:00 p.m. I hosted an office Christmas party at Paparazzi on Wisconsin Avenue that evening.

By mid-December, the sentiment was shifting more decidedly toward impeachment. Several previously undeclared Republicans announced they would vote for one or more of the four articles. Tom DeLay worked overtime to convince the uncommitted to back impeachment, and he was now close to the 218 votes he needed. The *New York Times* reported that the mathematical possibilities of avoiding impeachment had become all but nil, "the equivalent of drawing an inside card to a royal flush." The president would need to win virtually every one of the 18 undeclared Republicans and hold almost every Democrat who was wavering in order to prevent impeachment.[21]

All sorts of compromises and options short of impeachment were bandied about between the White House and members of Congress during that period. Every one offered by moderate Republicans required a forthright admission of wrongdoing by the president. Some included a fine to help cover the cost of the investigation. Still others proposed that Clinton simply resign. I was not party to any of these initiatives, but I would not have supported any option short of impeachment, presiding officer or not.

As if the situation were not volatile enough, President Clinton decided to launch air strikes against Iraq on December 16, the night before the impeachment debate was supposed to begin. I was outraged. The president's actions struck me as a blatant political maneuver designed to distract the nation from the historic work about to be undertaken in the House. It was unconscionable. The bombing forced the House to postpone the impeachment debate for one day.

Notes

1. 144 Cong. Rec., H1174 (December 18, 1998).
2. "Clinton, 'I Did Not Have Sexual Relations with That Woman...'," January 26, 1998, YouTube, http://www.youtube.com/watch?v=KiIP_KDQmXs.
3. "Address to the Nation on Testimony before the Independent Counsel's Grand Jury," August 17, 1998, *PPP*, RLP-Memoir, f. Impeachment.
4. DeLay to RL, August 20, 1998, RLP-DC-S, f. Impeachment. Form Response.
5. The vote was 363–63 in favor of release, with all 224 Republicans and 138 of 201 Democrats supporting the measure. One Independent voted with the Republicans.
6. Lizette Alvarez and Eric Schmitt, "Gauging a Bombardment of Opinions That Could Determine Clinton's Fate," *NYT*, September 16, 1998, RLP-Memoir, f. Impeachment.
7. Sample letter, January 25, 1998, RLP-DC-S, f. Impeachment. Form Response.
8. The amount was based on a cost report prepared by the Office of Independent Counsel, September 11, 1998, and sent to David Clark in the General Accounting Office, RLP-Peoria-TBS, f. Impeachment (2).
9. Senator Frank Murkowski (R-AK) sponsored a similar resolution in the Senate. RLP-Peoria-TBS, f. Impeachment (1–2).
10. "Clinton Impeachment Polls," www.democrats.com, RLP-Memoir, f. Impeachment.
11. RLP, Springfield Office, Political Subject Files, f. Clinton Affairs.
12. Henry Hyde, Republican from Illinois and chair of the House Judiciary Committee.
13. Draft Form Letter #163, January 25, 1998, RLP-DC-S, f. Impeachment. Form Response.
14. Alison Mitchell and Lizette Alvarez, "Republicans Tell Leaders to Aim for Quick Vote on Impeachment," *NYT*, December 3, 1998, RLP-Memoir, f. Impeachment.
15. "Illinois Congressman Is Picked as Presider," *NYT*, December 10, 1998, RLP-Memoir, f. Impeachment.
16. MSNBC News, "'Classic' Choice to Run House Debate," December 10, 1998, RLP-Peoria-TBS, f. Impeachment (1).

17. Tammy Tabor, "LaHood at the Helm," *Journal-Courier*, Jacksonville, IL, December 10, 1998, RLP-Peoria-TBS, f. Impeachment (1).

18. Peter Baker, "Committee Recommends Impeachment," *Washington Post*, December 11, 1998, RLP-Peoria-TBS, f. Impeachment (2).

19. Eric Schmitt, "Democrats Plan Parliamentary Bid to Thwart Republicans," *NYT*, December 14, 1998, RLP-Memoir, f. Impeachment.

20. Hyde to Dear Colleague, December 12, 1998, RLP-DC-S, f. Impeachment. Articles Submitted by Judiciary Committee.

21. John M. Broder and Alison Mitchell, "White House Grasps at Options as Waverers Move to Impeach," *NYT*, December 16, 1998, RLP-Memoir, f. Impeachment.

CHAPTER 8

THE HOUSE DEBATES IMPEACHMENT

Nothing in my career matched the drama that unfolded during three days in mid-December 1998. I was supposed to be in the district for a round of holiday events. But there I was in Washington, about to witness the impeachment of a president.

THURSDAY, DECEMBER 17, 1998

The floor action on Thursday, December 17, began with consideration of our response to the president's precipitous decision the night before. House Resolution 612 expressed both support for the men and women in uniform engaged in the action against Iraq and commitment to remove Saddam Hussein from power. I took the chair at about 11:45 a.m. At 1:00 p.m., the House voted to pass the resolution overwhelmingly—I voted with the majority. Majority leader Dick Armey then asked for a one-hour recess to determine the schedule for the rest of the day and week.

The House returned to session at 2:57 p.m. I continued to preside. The respective party leaders proceeded to engage in a colloquy about the schedule for the impeachment debate. Armey and Speaker-designate Bob Livingston stated the case for proceeding immediately, arguing that the public wanted to end it, that members had undertaken plenty of preparation, and that President Clinton had said the debate would not compromise the military maneuvers in Iraq.

David Bonior, minority whip, stated the Democrats' position:

> It would be a grave mistake to go forward with this vote while our Nation is engaged in military action. I cannot believe that we are even having this debate.

> It was totally inappropriate, if I might say, for some in the Republican leadership, to call for the President's resignation when he was trying to bring peace just this last week in the Middle East. So it should not surprise us that this decision would flow from that.

> Our angst about moving forward rests on another pillar; and that is the inability of this side of the aisle to have the chance to offer a reasonable alternative, a censure alternative which the majority of Americans now support. It is unfair. It is wrong. There is something about this whole process that shows a lack of judgment, a lack of proportionality, a lack of common sense.

> We have time to reach some resolution on these important questions before we engage in the debate. But I think it behooves us all to take a step back, to take a deep breath. My goodness, if Bob Dole and Jerry Ford[1] could offer a way out of this mess through the censure resolution, why cannot we have that choice on the floor? Why is that fundamental choice supported by the majority of the people in this country being denied to us on the most fundamental question that we could be dealing with in this Congress?[2]

Dick Gephardt endorsed Bonior's remarks in brief comments. After three one-minute rebuttal speeches by Republicans, the House adjourned at 3:36 p.m. All this back and forth about the schedule and the appropriateness of proceeding at all came down to this: the previous agreement among the leaders of both parties to have 18 hours of debate on the articles of impeachment fell by the wayside. Instead, impeachment would be offered as a privileged resolution with just a single hour of debate.

After adjournment, I returned to my office in the Longworth Building for an interview with Peoria's NBC affiliate, WEEK-TV. I attended a Republican Conference meeting that evening in the Capitol—it was then that Bob Livingston dropped his bombshell by confessing to extramarital "indiscretions." Consider the remarkable the situation we then faced: the pending impeachment of the president, a surprise military action overseas, and the prospective leader of the House in trouble.

When asked by a reporter what to expect from tomorrow's debate, I replied that Democrats would talk about process. They would complain about the timing, about the lack of a vote on censure, about what they called a political vendetta against the president. They would not talk about the articles of impeachment themselves or about the president's conduct.

Friday, December 18, 1998

The *Washington Post* Style section on Friday carried a lengthy story by Frank Ahrens entitled "A Man to Keep the House in Order"; it was about my assignment: "LaHood's colleagues, Republican and Democrat alike, felt the 53-year-old resident of Peoria was a natural choice to lead the contentious discussion. Now, LaHood looks better with each passing day."[3]

I arrived on the floor at about 8:45 a.m. on Friday, December 18, following a meeting in Charlie Johnson's office. I wasn't the least bit anxious about wielding the gavel that historic day.[4] I had presided over several contentious House debates before, including the partial-birth abortion row. I'm not one who sits around and frets about a vote or how I'm going to vote or whether I made the right vote or how people will view my actions. I've just never become nervous about these things. I knew what I had to do as the presiding officer—conduct the impeachment proceedings fairly.

The first bit of business on the 18th involved the formality of my appointment to the chair. The process, simple as it was, took the form of a letter entered into the record from the Speaker of the House. Here is how it appeared in the *Congressional Record*:

> Designation of the Speaker
> Pro Tempore
>
> The Speaker pro tempore laid before the House the following communication from the Speaker:
>
> Washington, DC,
>
> *December 18, 1998.*
> I hereby designate the Honorable Ray LaHood to act as Speaker pro tempore on this day.
>
> Newt Gingrich,
> *Speaker of the House of Representatives.*

I gaveled the House to order at about 9:00 a.m. The Reverend James David Ford led us in prayer: "Where there is hatred, let us sow love; where there is injury, pardon; where there is discord, union; where there is doubt, faith; where there is despair, hope; where there is darkness, light; where there is sadness, joy." The prayer was followed by approval of the journal of the last day's proceedings, then the Pledge of Allegiance.

We next considered a piece of business raised the preceding day by Eleanor Holmes Norton, the delegate to the House from the District of Columbia. As a delegate, not a full-fledged member of the House, Holmes Norton joined three other delegates entitled to participate in debate, offer certain motions, and serve and vote on committees. They could not, however, vote in the full House. Given the historical importance of the upcoming actions, she naturally enough wanted to vote. Holmes Norton offered a privileged resolution aimed at securing that right with regard only to the four articles of impeachment. She argued that because the District of Columbia votes for the president, she, even as nonvoting delegate, should be allowed to vote on his removal. In my first formal ruling during the impeachment proceedings, I ruled against her. Delegate Holmes Norton could not vote in the ensuing proceedings.

Minority Whip Bonior then offered a motion to adjourn "in protest of the decision to proceed while U.S. men and women are fighting abroad." The motion failed—ayes 183, nays 225, not voting 26. Five Democrats joined 220 Republicans who voted nay. Not a single Republican voted aye.

Formal debate on the four articles of impeachment, embodied in House Resolution 611, began on the House floor at close to 9:30 a.m., when Henry Hyde, as chair of the House Judiciary Committee, called up the privileged resolution for immediate consideration. For the first time since February 24, 1868, the House contemplated the impeachment of a president. The public galleries were packed. Almost all of the House's 435 members settled into their brown leather seats (by midday, however, the press reported, the chamber itself was half-empty, and by late afternoon only 38 members remained).

Paul Hays, the House reading clerk, read the resolution: "Resolved, that William Jefferson Clinton, President of the United States, is impeached for high crimes and misdemeanors...." He read all four articles in their entirety. For each article, Hays concluded with these words: "Wherefore, William Jefferson Clinton, by such conduct, warrants impeachment and trial, and removal from office and disqualification to hold and enjoy any office of honor, trust, or profit under the United States." Following Hays's reading of H. Res. 611, I announced from the chair, "The resolution constitutes a question of the privileges of the House and may be considered at this time."

Next, I read a prepared statement to set the tone for how I intended to preside. The rules of engagement, so to speak, permitted references to personal misconduct on the part of the president but forbade personally abusive language. I also warned against "engaging in comparisons to personal conduct of sitting Members of either House of Congress." That last sentence elicited complaints from Democrats who may have been tempted to compare the president's lapses with Speaker Gingrich's. My intent, however, was simple: to keep the debate civil and respectful, a difficult chore in light of the circumstances.

At 9:45 a.m., the debate began.[5]

I heard what I expected the first day—a series of carefully prepared partisan speeches on one side and the other. Henry Hyde led off, anticipating the Democrats' objections by focusing on the perjury charge and defending the rule of law. He asserted that "no man or woman, no matter how highly placed, no matter how effective a communicator, no matter how gifted a manipulator of opinion or winner of votes, can be above the law in a democracy."[6] The chair got carried away, I thought, when he invoked the Magna Carta, Mosaic law, Roman law, Bunker Hill, Concord and Lexington, and the soldiers who fought in World War II. The Democrats must have thought so, too—they sat on their hands as the Republicans applauded.

Dick Gephardt presented the Democrats' argument. "Mr. Speaker," he said, addressing me in the chair, "this vote today is taking place on the wrong day, and we are doing it in the wrong way." By this he meant that impeachment proceedings should not take place while military action was underway. Cleverly, I thought, he then made oblique reference to Livingston's admission the previous night. As the minority leader expressed it,

> The events of the last days sadden me. We are now at the height of a cycle of the politics of negative attacks, character assassination, personal smears of good people, decent people, worthy people. It is no wonder to me and to you that the people of our country today are cynical and indifferent and apathetic about our government and our country. The politics of smear and slash and burn must end.[7]

At that point, members on both sides of the aisle rose and applauded.

As he went on, Gephardt ignored the specifics of the charges against the president. The punishment simply did not fit the crime, he argued.

And he objected to the Republican leadership's successful effort to block a vote on censure. Among his concluding words were: "All we are asking for is that we get to vote our conscience," and "In your effort to uphold the Constitution, you are trampling the Constitution." I had to rap the gavel repeatedly to restore order as the Democrats rose in unison to support their leader.

For the balance of the day, members of the House traded charges and countercharges. John Conyers (D-MI), ranking member of the Judiciary Committee, for example, called the proceedings "a Republican coup d'état," a phrase his colleagues repeated throughout the day. Others termed the proceedings "a lynching," a "Republican juggernaut, driven by the right wing," and "constitutional assassination." Bonior called impeachment "a runaway train headed for a cliff."[8] Still others brought up the impeachment of Andrew Johnson, the Watergate case, and previous Judiciary Committee decisions related to possible impeachment proceedings. The air strikes in Iraq came up frequently, too.

I just let them talk. On two or three occasions, as the debate wore on into the late afternoon and evening, I admonished those in the gallery who were disturbing the proceedings. But I was not called upon for a single extraordinary ruling.

Promptly at 10:00 p.m., the day's proceedings ended. When I returned to my office that evening, my staff told me that people were calling from all over wondering whether I had been able to take a restroom break! I had left the chair twice, but only when I was confident that the debate was well in hand.

New York Times reporter Lizette Alvarez described my role on December 18 this way:

> But today, Mr. LaHood's role was more study-hall monitor than orchestra conductor as he constantly interrupted members' speeches with a scolding gavel to admonish their colleagues who were loitering in the aisles. "I'm going to ask everyone in the chamber to take a seat," he repeatedly said. "If you want to be in

the chamber, you have to be in a seat. We have to have order. All —both sides will require order."[9]

By all accounts, the president's opponents had enough votes to impeach him and to defeat any effort to bring a censure motion forward. I thought so, too.

At the time, I believed the House had distinguished itself by the quality and tenor of the debate. I counted Hyde's and Gephardt's remarks as standouts. I was pleased with my own performance, and many Democrats and Republicans complimented me as the session ended.

But a more lasting impression has stayed with me, not a particularly positive one. After 10 hours, the members had explored every possible nuance of impeachment as a constitutional procedure, of its applicability to the Clinton case, and of the allegations against the president. Each side took a set of more or less standard talking points and wove them into individual repetitious speeches. They were calculated, orchestrated. The arguments lacked creativity. There was no true debate. The entire spectacle failed to measure up to the unique, historical importance of the situation. The back and forth had proceeded the way debate usually occurs in the House on mundane matters.

SATURDAY, DECEMBER 19, 1998

I began Saturday morning by visiting my office to pick up the local television crew that was following me those few days. We strolled across the street to the east front of the Capitol and the entrance to the House wing. Scores of demonstrators and even more media representatives were milling around on the grounds.

The House officially convened at 9:00 a.m. on the 19th for the second and last day of the impeachment debate. After a short prayer offered by Chaplain Ford, it became clear that the House lacked a quorum. The vote to approve the journal of proceedings produced the quorum, and we proceeded with the Pledge of Allegiance. Henry Hyde recognized James Rogan (R-CA), who began where we had left off the day before, with Republicans and Democrats alternating in their one-minute speeches.

At about 9:35 a.m., Chairman Hyde recognized Bob Livingston for two minutes. What followed produced the biggest surprise of the entire impeachment proceedings in the House. Livingston began:

> I very much regret the enmity and hostility that has been bred in the Halls of Congress for the last months and years. I want so very much to pacify and cool our raging tempers and return to an era when differences were confined to the debate and not of personal attack or assassination of character.
>
> The debate has done nothing to bring us together, and I greatly regret that it has become quite literally the opening gambit of the intended Livingston speakership. I most certainly would have written a different scenario, had I had the chance.
>
> We are nearing completion, and however the vote turns out, no one may say that we did not own up to our constitutional responsibility as Members of Congress in a careful, respectful and insightful debate. Much credit is due our presiding officer, the gentleman from Illinois (Mr. LaHood), who has done an outstanding job.

The chamber was uncharacteristically quiet—members who usually engaged in side conversations paid rapt attention to the Speaker-designate. Only a handful apparently knew what would come next, and I was not one of them. Livingston continued:

> Yes, our Nation is founded on law, not on the whim of man. We are not ruled by kings or emperors, and there is no divine right of Presidents. But to the President I would say:
>
> Sir, you have done great damage to this Nation over this past year, and while your defenders are contending that further impeachment proceedings would only protract and exacerbate the damage to this country, I say that you have the power to terminate that

damage and heal the wounds that you have created. You, sir, may resign your post.

He added, "And I can only challenge you in such fashion if I am willing to heed my own words."[10]

Even as he spoke this last sentence, I could hear a few Democrats shouting back. I remember in particular that Maxine Waters (D-CA) screamed, "You resign! You resign! You resign!" at Livingston. As others started to join in the taunt, John Conyers motioned them to quiet down as I called out, "The House will be in order," as firmly as I could.

Livingston ended with these words: "I was prepared to lead our narrow majority as Speaker and I believe I had it in me to do a fine job. But I cannot do that job or be the kind of leader that I would like to be under the current circumstances. So I must set the example that I hope President Clinton will follow. I will not stand for Speaker of the House on January 6th and will leave the House."

The air went out of the chamber.

I'd never seen anything like it. I certainly had no idea that Livingston intended to resign even after his disclosure to the Republican Conference the previous evening. An eerie, shocked calm replaced the boisterous atmosphere of only a few minutes earlier. People were stunned. Charlie Johnson, standing right next to me at the rostrum, called it "the most emotional moment I've ever seen."

Livingston sat down on the Republican side, lower down in the chairs to my left, so close that I could overhear Steny Hoyer (D-MD) and Vic Fazio (D-CA) trying to persuade him to change his mind. I don't know, but I suspect that the Democrats, who generally felt positive about Livingston, feared that Gingrich or DeLay or Armey would become Speaker if Livingston left. I'm sure that scared the hell out of Democrats. But Livingston soon left the chamber in the company of Dick Armey, among others. No one knew what to expect next. Two Speakers had stepped down in a matter of weeks.

The calm was replaced soon enough by chaos. Charlie Johnson remem-
bers the details better than I. A number of members came up to me and
asked, "Where are we going?" According to Charlie, I said, "We don't
know." And Fazio or Conyers said to me, "Well, why don't we recess until
your leadership tells you where we're going?" I replied, "We don't have
any leadership. We're going to go through with this." In hindsight, that
was a crucial decision. I didn't anguish over it. I knew we had to proceed
with the impeachment debate even though I did have the authority to
call a recess. In the heat of the moment, I made that decision without
consulting anyone, not even the parliamentarian. Charlie called the
decision "instinctual," and I guess it was. Mel Watt (D-NC) also lobbied
for a recess and then threw this curve: "We need a true presiding officer,"
he told me before offering to round up Democratic backing: "*We can
support you for Speaker.*" Charlie, who was still standing right next to
me, recalls the conversation as I do.

I remember my reaction to the notion that the Democratic caucus
would support me as Speaker. Aside from my surprise, of course, I
chalked Watt's comment up to the feeling that the House was pretty
much rudderless at the moment. Few people knew that DeLay had been
working behind the scenes, since learning of Livingston's intentions, to
orchestrate Denny Hastert's move into the speakership. I never thought
for a minute that I would actually become Speaker.

Order was restored after about 10 minutes. At 9:45 a.m., the normal
routine resumed with José Serrano (D-NY) speaking for one minute on
impeachment—he barely mentioned what had just happened. Marge
Roukema (R-NJ) was the first Republican to speak after Livingston. "Mr.
Speaker, I really do not know how to begin," she said, "except to say that
our prayers are with the gentleman from Louisiana. His decision must
be respected, but we are all profoundly distressed."[11]

I did have to remind speakers to observe their time limits, and I refused
Conyers's request to have a call of the House, or a quorum call. The
one-minute speeches continued until shortly after 10:15 a.m., when Tom

DeLay took the floor—DeLay, who had labored to replace Gingrich with Livingston and who now worked as hard to recruit Denny Hastert to replace Livingston.

"Mr. Speaker, I do not know if I can make this speech, but I am going to try," DeLay began. "Believe it or not, I have been very depressed about this whole proceeding. When I came to work yesterday, it really hit me what we were about to do. But after this morning, it made me realize even more what this is all about. I feel great about it, because no matter how low we think we are or depressed we are, this country shows us time and time again how great it is." The majority whip paid Livingston a compliment, saying his disgraced colleague "understood what this [impeachment] debate was all about. It was about honor and decency and integrity and the truth, everything that we honor in this country. It was also a debate about relativism versus absolute truth."[12]

For the next several minutes, a succession of Democrats spoke to Livingston's resignation before David Bonior, minority whip, offered his view:

> Mr. Speaker, this House is shocked and saddened by the Speaker-elect's announcement. The gentleman from Louisiana is a respected member of this House who has served with distinction and dedication for over 20 years. Now we find ourselves in a destructive cycle that is eating away at our democracy. The politics of personal smear is degrading the dignity of public office and we must not let it continue.
>
> We must put an end to it, and the only way we will stop this vicious cycle is if we stand up and refuse to give in to it, whether it is Bill Clinton or Bob Livingston. To the Speaker-elect I would say, "This is your decision, the decision of your family, the decision of your Conference." But for my own part I would say, "You should not allow a campaign of cynicism and smear to force you to resign from office, and you should not have called on the President to resign."

Bonior argued that the American people had sent a clear message in the November elections. "They want this President to continue to do the job they elected him to do, and yet this Congress is deliberately ignoring their will," he lectured. "Let me tell my colleagues that people are angry, and they are frustrated, and they are outraged and bewildered at what is happening here. Six days before Christmas our troops are in battle, and a lame duck Congress is rushing to overthrow the Commander in Chief." The entire predicament struck Bonior as surreal. "The scenario reads like the plot of a cheap paperback novel, not the deliberation of the [sic] history's greatest democracy." It was not too late, he concluded, to step back from the brink: "The American people desperately want us to restore some dignity and some common sense."[13]

Shortly after 11:20, I announced that time had expired, and the previous question on the resolution was ordered.

A Last Effort at Censure

As expected, the Democrats offered a motion to recommit. One of the party's at-large whips, Rick Boucher of Virginia, took the lead. His motion to recommit H. Res. 611 to the Judiciary Committee carried with it instructions to report the resolution to the House with an amendment. The amendment would strike every word after the resolving clause and insert censure language.

The censure option contained three main provisions. First, it acknowledged that Clinton had "egregiously failed" in his obligation to conduct himself "in a manner that fosters respect for the truth" as required by his oath of office, thereby dishonoring the presidency. Second, the amendment acknowledged that Clinton had made false statements concerning his "reprehensible conduct with a subordinate" and "wrongly took steps to delay discovery of the truth." As a result, the amendment stated, the president would remain subject to criminal and civil penalties. Finally, the Democrats' proposal concluded with these words: "William Jefferson

Clinton, President of the United States, by his conduct has brought upon himself, and fully deserves, the censure and condemnation of the American people and this House."[14]

After Jerry Solomon, a Republican from New York and a member of the Rules Committee, reserved a point of order against the motion to recommit, I gave each side five minutes to speak to the motion. Boucher spoke briefly in favor and then yielded the balance of his time to Gephardt, who made his first appearance on the floor since Livingston's announcement. It was shortly before 11:30 a.m. Livingston had reentered the chamber without fanfare and sat near the back, impassive.

The Democratic leader called Livingston "a worthy and good and honorable man" and termed his resignation a "terrible capitulation" to the negative forces rampant in the political system. "We need to stop destroying imperfect people at the altar of an unobtainable morality," Gephardt continued before calling for an end to the "fratricide" that "dominates our public debate ... America is held hostage with tactics of smear and fear." His remarks drew a bipartisan standing ovation.

"Our founding fathers created a system of government of men, not of angels," the House minority leader intoned. "No one standing in this House today can pass a puritanical test of purity that some are demanding that our elected leaders take. If we demand that mere mortals live up to this standard, we will see our seats of government lay empty and we will see the best, most able people unfairly cast out of public service." Although his remarks were directed at the Livingston situation, no one could mistake the larger message—that the president had been targeted unfairly. The Democratic leader then pleaded for Republicans to join in bipartisan support for censure of the president as a means to begin to heal the wounds. "We are on the brink of the abyss. The only way we stop this insanity is through the force of our own will. The only way we stop this spiral is for all of us to finally say, 'Enough.'" As Gephardt made his way up the Democratic side of the aisle, his members embraced him, shouting affirmations. The Republicans, however, remained fixed in their seats.[15]

Solomon again rose to insist on his point of order against the motion to recommit. He argued that the motion violated the long-standing germaneness rule. As the congressman explained, in order to be held germane, an amendment must share a fundamental purpose with the text it attempts to amend. Given that impeachment is the sole prescribed mechanism to address misconduct by the president, any other procedure had no foundation in the Constitution and was not contemplated by the separation of powers. Parliamentarian Charlie Johnson had reached the same conclusion. In other words, Boucher's motion to recommit did not conform to the fundamental purpose of the impeachment resolution. "It proposes a different end, a different result and a different method of achieving that end," Solomon observed before concluding, "Mr. Speaker, I urge you to continue your reputation of fairness and sustain this point of order."[16]

Debate continued for a time on the point of order, with Democrats such as Joe Moakley (D-MA) arguing that the motion for censure was, in fact, germane. At 12:15 p.m., Solomon tried to bring the debate to an end, calling the discussion "repetitive." I disagreed, ruling that as long as members spoke to the point of order, I was prepared to let the discussion continue. I thought it important not to cut off debate on the point of order prematurely. I could have ruled immediately, but the arguments created a permanent record on the germaneness issue. After about 45 minutes, I recognized Boucher as the last speaker on the point of order, as was my prerogative as presiding officer. But then I learned that Moakley, ranking member of the Rules Committee, wanted to make a different appeal, and I recognized him, urging him to be brief.

He pleaded with me to put the question directly to the House so that the entire membership could vote on Boucher's censure proposal. Moakley did so respectfully, expecting that I would rule against him. He had worked out the specifics of his argument with the parliamentarian, and he proceeded to offer precedents for consideration by the entire House. It should be noted that the parliamentarian acts in the manner of an attorney working for a client. True, he works with both sides, Republicans and Democrats, but he observes the privileged nature of his advice—I did not know how Moakley would present his case.

After hearing his presentation, I made my ruling at about 12:30 p.m. It took the form of the 1,300-word statement Charlie Johnson and I had painstakingly crafted over days and days of consultation. The full text of my ruling is located in appendix C. In a nutshell, I ruled that Boucher's motion to recommit was not germane to the impeachment resolution. I immediately recognized the minority leader, Dick Gephardt, who appealed my ruling. After some further parliamentary maneuvering, the House sustained my ruling, 230 to 204, with one not voting.

THE VOTE TO IMPEACH

At 1:05 p.m., the articles of impeachment themselves came to a vote. To this day, I do not believe that anyone was confident of the outcome. No one could have predicted the results with any certainty.

As the call for the vote on Article 1 of the impeachment came, the Democrats responded with a prearranged walkout. We knew about the protest in advance because the Democrats wanted to make sure they had enough time to leave and return for the vote. They gathered on the Capitol steps for a photo, and then came back into the chamber within the 15 minutes allotted to vote on Article 1. Otherwise, the vote proceeded normally. I did not detect any special atmosphere on the floor—the usual side conversations were evident, for example.

The vote results came in at about 1:23 p.m., and I announced the result: "The article of impeachment is adopted."[17] The House had approved the first article, which accused Clinton of having committed perjury in his August 17 grand jury testimony. The vote was 228–206 (R 223–5; D 5–200; I 0–1). The five Republicans who crossed party lines were Peter King and Amo Houghton of New York, Chris Shays of Connecticut, Mark Souder of Indiana, and Connie Morella of Maryland. Five Democrats sided with the Republicans: Paul McHale of Pennsylvania (who was retiring), Charlie Stenholm and Ralph Hall of Texas, Gene Taylor of Missouri, and Virgil Goode of Virginia. The outcome came as no surprise—experts had thought Article 1 was the most likely of the four to succeed.

We moved immediately to vote on Article 2, which charged the president with committing perjury in his deposition in the Paula Jones sexual harassment civil suit. By a vote of 205–229, the House rejected the second article. There was an interesting inconsistency here. It seemed to many that the factual evidence against Clinton was much more compelling in his civil testimony than in his grand jury testimony, which was the subject of Article 1. Yet more Republicans voted against Article 2 even though it had stronger factual support. On this article, 28 Republicans and five Democrats broke party ranks.

The House then took up the third article, which charged the president with obstruction of justice for his efforts to find Lewinsky a job, possibly in return for her silence, and his alleged witness tampering involving his personal secretary, Betty Currie. The vote was 221 to 212—five Democrats voted for this article, 12 Republicans against.

At 2:13 p.m., the House made it two for four by rejecting the last article, 148–285, which accused the president of abuse of power. This catch-all article charged Clinton with "a pattern of deceit and obstruction" in providing misleading statements in answer to questions posed by the Judiciary Committee. Only one Democrat voted for this article, while 81 Republicans, a third of the conference, voted against it.

The two articles that won support in the House deserved to pass. The two that failed may have had less legal standing, but in my opinion, they met the impeachment standard. I voted to impeach on all four articles.

My job was almost done. Following this series of votes, the House authorized the appointment of 13 Republican members of the Judiciary Committee to prosecute the case in the Senate. The vote total to authorize was announced at 2:34 p.m.: yeas 228, nays 190, not voting 17. The

Democrats refused to serve, intending to reinforce the impression that the whole impeachment proceeding was simply a matter of partisanship. The "managers," as they were called, then walked across the Capitol to the secretary of the Senate, to whom Henry Hyde presented a leather-bound book containing the two approved articles of impeachment.

I declared the second session of the 105th Congress adjourned sine die at 2:36 p.m., Saturday, December 19, 1998.

THE AFTERMATH

House Democrats, about 80 of them, then did what I still think was a distasteful thing. They marched up to the White House and appeared with Vice President Al Gore, Hillary Clinton, and the president for a press conference. Dick Gephardt went before the cameras on the South Lawn to urge the president to defy those who counseled resignation rather than face trial in the Senate. "You cannot, you must not, you cannot, you must not, you cannot, you must not resign," Gephardt pleaded. "We will stay with you and fight with you until this madness is over."[18]

The president stepped to the microphones at 4:15 p.m. He claimed he had sought to work toward a more appropriate punishment but that we Republicans had rejected the alternative. He listed issues to which he was dedicated and which would require bipartisan support. He stressed his commitment to work for the American people. He obviously wanted to put the whole thing behind him:

> We are a good and decent country. But we have significant challenges we have to face. In order to do it right, we have to have some atmosphere of decency and civility, some presumption of good faith, some sense of proportionality and balance in bringing judgment against those who are in different parties.[19]

And he pointedly said he would not resign.

After it was all over, that night, the Republicans met in conference. We went down to HC-5, a room in the basement of the Capitol. Gingrich presided. He said to my colleagues, "Look, Ray LaHood has done about as great a job as we could ever have." And there was a standing ovation by all the members. He then commanded us to get behind Hastert as the next Speaker, which sealed the deal. One other nice gesture by Gingrich: the Speaker had a tradition of presenting a gavel to members who had presided, and he presented me with the gavel I had used those last three days. Gingrich signed it, and I asked Charlie Johnson to sign it, too— we could never have got through the ordeal without the good advice of the parliamentarians.

Later that evening, I flew back to Chicago, then went on to Peoria by car. My press secretary later reminded me that he and I listened to Christmas music on that two-and-a-half-hour trip home—without a single mention of what I had just experienced.

The reception in Peoria surprised me. I attended a 5:30 p.m. Catholic mass in late December at Holy Family Church, right across the street from my home. The woman sitting behind me was the cook at the school where I had taught junior high in the 1960s. During the time in the mass when we were supposed to give the sign of peace, I turned around to wish her a merry Christmas. When the mass concluded, I turned around to shake her hand. But she, in a very bitter way, said, "You Republicans are jealous of Clinton and I don't like what you are doing to him." She had voted for me in every election. I lost her on impeachment.

I ran into several constituents over the holidays who echoed the woman's sentiment. People who had seen me presiding said I'd done a nice job, but when it came to my votes on the four impeachment articles, that was a different matter entirely. My wife and I attended a ceremony put on each year by the Salvation Army's Tree of Lights campaign. To cap it off, we would light a huge tree at our local mall to honor the community's support. When I got there, a person with an "IMPEACH LAHOOD" sign emerged from the crowd.[20] All through December, my mail had divided evenly between supporters and opponents of impeachment. Opinion turned markedly against it in my district as the year closed.

Here is what I wrote in reply to the thousands of people who contacted me:

> Thank you for contacting me regarding your thoughts on the impeachment proceedings. I apologize for this response being in the nature of a form letter but felt this was the only way I could communicate my position in a timely manner. I received approximately 5,000 letters and phone calls on this issue alone in December.
>
> As you may know, I voted in favor of four Articles of Impeachment. I reached this decision after weeks of attentive review, study, and analysis of the facts presented in the Independent Counsel's referral to the House of Representatives and the findings of the Judiciary Committee. In addition, I closely watched the debate in the Judiciary Committee and on the House floor. Finally, I carefully considered the views offered to me by my constituency.
>
> Ultimately, I concluded that there was sufficient evidence to warrant impeaching President Clinton, thus sending the matter to the Senate for trial and additional review and consideration. The evidence indicates that the President knowingly provided false statements under oath in both a civil deposition and a federal grand jury proceeding. The President also used friends and employees to cover up his misdeed, thereby obstructing justice and abusing the power of his office. These offenses are very serious matters. They go to the very heart of our justice system—the rule of law. I believe very strongly in the rule of law in our country. I believe that no person is, or should be, above the law. This is the very basis upon which our country was founded over 200 years ago.
>
> While no one wants to see a President impeached, I believe the facts of this case unfortunately warrant such action. Again, I appreciate the benefit of your views.[21]

The rest of the story is common knowledge. When the Senate convened in January 1999 for the first session of the 106th Congress, it dealt with the two remaining articles of impeachment. The saga ended on February 12, 1999, when the Senate voted not to convict on either count.

Upon Reflection

As I think back on it, the impeachment debate in the House had three significant parts. First, taking censure off the table proved crucial. Public opinion polls at the time suggested that most Americans favored censure over impeachment. Democrats in the House and more than a few Republicans preferred it, too. But House rules and precedents precluded censure. The Office of the Parliamentarian evaluated the option exhaustively and, I continue to believe, fairly and accurately.

Second, we literally could have stopped the proceedings after Bob Livingston's stunning announcement on December 19. Who would have objected? Democrats had hoped to delay the proceedings as long as possible to let public sentiment in favor of the president build. As for Republicans, we had no leaders; we could have used the time to put our house in order. No one really knew how the vote on the articles of impeachment would turn out at that moment—how many, if any, would pass. But I remain convinced that moving ahead was the correct decision for the House, the president, and the nation. That decision was mine and mine alone.

Third, those three days, December 17–19, produced the most unorthodox selection of a Speaker in history. That two Speakers were forced from office in a matter of weeks was novel enough. But Denny Hastert filled the vacuum almost without any personal effort. He never campaigned for the job. He didn't visit members' districts. He didn't reach out. He didn't make calls. He didn't count votes. DeLay did it all, and he did it twice, for Livingston and for Hastert. I don't think that Hastert's selection was a bad way to go, necessarily. I'm not sure we could have afforded a long, drawn-out campaign with all the weeks or months of uncertainty. But to say that Hastert ascended to the speakership in an unconventional fashion—that's a monumental understatement.

NOTES

1. Both former president Gerald R. Ford and former senator Robert Dole had written opinion pieces calling for censure rather than impeachment.
2. 144 Cong. Rec., H11751 (December 17, 1998).
3. Frank Ahrens, "A Man to Keep the House in Order," *Washington Post*, December 8, 1998, RLP-Memoir, f. Impeachment.
4. In the nation's history, the House of Representatives had impeached 15 federal officers, including a president, a Cabinet member, a senator, a Supreme Court justice, and 11 federal judges. See "The House Republican Conference Floor Prep," December 18, 1998, RLP-Peoria-TBS, f. Impeachment (2).
5. 144 Cong. Rec., H11771-H11775 (December 18, 1998).
6. News release, U.S. House of Representatives Committee on the Judiciary, December 18, 1998, RLP-Peoria-TBS, f. Impeachment (1).
7. 144 Cong. Rec., H11777 (December 18, 1998).
8. R. W. Apple Jr., "With Partisan Rancor, A Bitter House Debates the President's Impeachment," *NYT*, December 19, 1998, RLP-Memoir, f. Impeachment.
9. Lizette Alvarez, "Taking a Job That Others Would Not," *NYT*, 19 December 1998, RLP-Memoir, f. Impeachment.
10. 144 Cong. Rec., H11969–H11970 (December 19, 1998).
11. 144 Cong. Rec., H11971 (December 19, 1998).
12. 144 Cong. Rec., H11974–H11975 (December 19, 1998).
13. 144 Cong. Rec., H11979–H11980 (December 19, 1998).
14. 144 Cong. Rec., H12031 (December 19, 1998).
15. Alison Mitchell, "Clinton Impeached," *NYT*, December 20, 1998, RLP-Memoir, f. Impeachment.
16. 144 Cong. Rec., H12032 (December 19, 1998).
17. 144 Cong. Rec., H12039 (December 19, 1998).
18. Peter Baker, *Breach: Inside the Impeachment and Trial of William Jefferson Clinton* (New York: Scribner, 2000), Kindle edition, locations 6192–6198.
19. William J. Clinton, "Remarks Following the House of Representatives Vote on Impeachment," December 19, 1998, *PPP*, RLP-Memoir, f. Impeachment.

20. James Warren, "Some Voters Want to Take a Favorite Son to the Whipping Post," *Chicago Tribune*, January 3, 1999, RLP-Peoria-TBS, f. Impeachment (1).
21. Draft Form Letter #549, January 25, 200[9], RLP-DC-S, f. Impeachment. Form Response.

CHAPTER 9

SEPTEMBER 11 AND THE WAR ON TERROR

Only one event surpassed the Clinton impeachment proceedings in historic importance during my service in the House—the terrorist attacks of 9/11. By virtue of my committee assignments, I had a bird's-eye view of the legislative action following those horrific events.

THE HOUSE PERMANENT SELECT COMMITTEE ON INTELLIGENCE

On December 4, 1998, amidst the Clinton impeachment controversy and upheaval in the House Republican leadership, I was appointed to the House Permanent Select Committee on Intelligence (HPSCI). I had sought the assignment for a couple of reasons. During periodic sessions with members of the *Peoria Journal Star*'s editorial board, they would point out my apparent lack of engagement in foreign affairs, suggesting that a better-rounded portfolio would impress them and voters back home. My committee assignments to agriculture and transportation rarely involved foreign policy issues. I thought a post on the HPSCI was the best way to broaden my understanding of international matters. Before his untimely departure from the House, I had told Bob Livingston of my interest in the assignment, and he pledged to make the appointment. Fortunately for me, Speaker Hastert honored the commitment, although he did not have to.

The HPSCI assumed heightened importance after 9/11, of course. When I joined, however, it was considered a "mid-major" committee. Porter Goss chaired the committee; Nancy Pelosi (D-CA) was the ranking member. The committee saw its role as both oversight and advocacy, a unique dual role. We were responsible for knowing, in some detail, what was going on within the intelligence community—to ensure that the laws were followed and that money was spent properly. The committee also identified current problems and future challenges facing the intelligence community, justified funding requests to the other members of the House and to the nation, and provided guidance and direction to the intelligence community.

The first 33 months of my service on the committee focused mostly on routine items—budgets, classified reports, and the like. In the 106th Congress, for example, the committee held seven open hearings on such subjects as biological warfare threats, encryption legislation, space launch failures, and the 1999 U.S. bombing of the Chinese embassy in Yugoslavia. The committee held 32 hearings and 29 briefings closed to the public on issues involving sensitive information, intelligence sources and methods, and national security. As we warned at the time: "The committee is concerned that our intelligence capabilities have become increasingly fragile since the breakup of the Soviet Union, and we have failed to invest in new capabilities that are now critical. American interests have expanded, new threats have evolved, and the priority placed on intelligence and the role of the intelligence community has grown significantly."[1] Words that would haunt.

In January 2001, at the start of the 107th Congress, the Speaker— with great foresight, as it turned out—established within the HPSCI, a bipartisan working group that later became the Subcommittee on

Terrorism and Homeland Security. Our initial mandate was to examine the terrorist threat to the United States, the counterterrorism capabilities of America's intelligence and law enforcement agencies, and the viability of our homeland security architecture. We held dozens of classified hearings and briefings and traveled abroad to consult with some of our key allies in the war on terror to get a firsthand look at our capabilities in action. We came away generally impressed by the commitment and hard work of the men and women fighting the war on the front lines. However, we also began to identify serious and systemic management and communications shortcomings, especially at the senior levels of the CIA, the National Security Agency (NSA), and the FBI. In fact, the full committee had pointed to such deficiencies time and time again over the years, but the leaders of those key agencies had failed to respond.[2]

SEPTEMBER 11, 2001

At 8:46 a.m., hijacked American Airlines Flight 11, having originated from Boston's Logan International Airport and carrying 76 passengers and five hijackers, two pilots, and nine flight attendants, slammed into the North Tower of the World Trade Center in New York City. Seventeen minutes later, United Flight 175, also hijacked after a Boston takeoff, crashed into the South Tower of the World Trade Center. Fifty-one passengers and five hijackers, two pilots, and seven flight attendants were aboard. At 9:45 a.m., American Flight 77, hijacked from Washington's Dulles International Airport, crashed into the Pentagon, killing 53 passengers and five hijackers, two pilots, and four flight attendants. Shortly after 10:00, the South Tower of the World Trade Center collapsed. Almost 30 minutes later, the North Tower fell. In the meantime, United Flight 93, hijacked after takeoff from Newark, New Jersey, and aimed at the U.S. Capitol, crashed in rural Pennsylvania after passengers overwhelmed the hijackers. Thirty-seven passengers (including four hijackers), two pilots, and five flight attendants were aboard.[3]

Nearly 3,000 people died in the attacks.

What I remember about that day in Washington begins with the sky —absolutely clear, a brilliant blue. I arrived at the office early to read the paper and catch up with the mail. A staff member told me that a plane had crashed into a building in New York. We watched the replay on a television in my office, and I thought it was a tragic accident, a plane off course slamming into a skyscraper.

That day, I was assigned to open the House and chair the proceedings, so I left the office and crossed the street on my way to the Capitol. Shortly before arriving, I saw a plane flying very near to the Capitol, too near. I walked into the building, and within two minutes of my entering a corridor, the Capitol Hill police were shouting in their loudest voices, "Get out of the Capitol; get out of the Capitol. We think a plane is going to hit the Capitol." We all left the building and wound up on the East Lawn. All of our cell phones went dead. We had no idea what was happening. The police blocked all the roads around the building and told us to remain on the lawn. About 30 minutes later, we all heard the thundering sonic boom of another plane followed by a billowing plume of smoke made all the more dramatic with the sky as backdrop. We all knew another building had been hit, although we did not know it was the Pentagon. Eventually, we heard bits and pieces of information about the second plane in New York from the officer milling around with us.

The most striking memory I have of the next two hours, standing there on the lawn, was the lack of communication to Congress members and staff about unfolding developments. Why would they have us standing on the lawn if a plane were headed toward the Capitol? I've never understood the logic, if there was one, except to state the obvious—we were surrounded by chaos. At long last, I returned to the office and called my wife. She, a few of her co-workers, and our son Sam were safe at our apartment.

The following day, we received word that any members of Congress still in Washington were to gather with the leadership on the Senate side of the Capitol. I joined my colleagues on the Senate steps on the east side and sang "God Bless America." The leadership told us to reenter the Capitol and to proceed with legislative business. The government would not shut down. It was a powerful symbol of our resilience.

On September 14, the House and Senate passed a joint resolution, known as the Authorization for Use of Military Force, in response to the attacks. Public Law 107-40 empowered the president "to use all necessary and appropriate force against those nations, organizations, or persons he determines planned, authorized, committed, or aided the terrorist attacks" that occurred on September 11.[4] Congress also passed a $40 billion emergency appropriations bill to fund recovery efforts and to launch a war against terrorists.

In the Wake: Congress Investigates

The U.S. intelligence community failed us. Calls for investigations came immediately. On October 2, the HPSCI recommended that a "fresh look" be taken at restructuring the CIA and the rest of the U.S. intelligence community. We wrote, "It is time for the administration to be bold, innovative, and to think 'out of the box.'" Our recommendations ran the gamut from adding a clandestine service devoted to human intelligence to hiring case officers with appropriate language skills.[5]

We faced a choice in Congress between creating an independent commission to look into the attacks or using some variation of existing congressional procedures. President Bush and leaders from both parties in Congress favored the second approach, believing the first would lead to the blame game. It took some months, however, to iron out the details.

On February 14, 2002, the leader of the Senate Select Committee on Intelligence, Bob Graham (D-FL), and the head of the HPSCI, Porter Goss, announced an agreement to conduct a joint inquiry into the activities of the intelligence community. Congress had opted for the second approach. The effort had a cumbersome name, the Joint Inquiry into Intelligence Community Activities Before and After the Terrorist Attacks of September

11, 2001. For the first time in congressional history, two permanent committees would combine to conduct a single unified inquiry. It had been a decade since the two panels had held even a joint hearing. I served on the joint inquiry panel, along with nine other Republicans; eight Democrats joined us. We had three principal goals:

> 1. Conduct a factual review of what the intelligence community knew or should have known prior to 9/11 about the international terrorist threat to the United States.
>
> 2. Identify and examine any systemic problems that may have impeded the intelligence community in learning of, or preventing, these attacks.
>
> 3. Make recommendations to improve the intelligence community's ability to identify and prevent future international terrorist attacks.[6]

The culture of the committee made it an ideal body to carry out the inquiry. We all wanted to know what had happened and how to prevent future tragedies. We conducted our hearings without the press. Questioning of witnesses never took on a partisan tone. Graham and Goss ran the committee, however, and dominated the proceedings. I attended every session but, like other committee members, was lucky to get five minutes to pose my own questions. In contrast to the private meetings, I thought that the public sessions were more like media shows than working sessions.

Nonetheless, over the course of its investigation, the panel held nine public hearings and 13 closed hearings in which we reviewed classified information. In addition, the staff analyzed almost 500,000 pages of relevant documents from intelligence agencies and other sources, conducted about 300 interviews, and participated in panels and briefings involving more than 600 people from a variety of government agencies, private sector entities, and foreign governments.

As the joint inquiry proceeded, my Subcommittee on Terrorism and Homeland Security completed its work and delivered a classified report to the Speaker in July 2002. In many respects, this report anticipated the judgments reached by the joint inquiry five months later.

Not surprisingly, we concluded that the 9/11 attacks had caught the intelligence and law enforcement communities flat-footed. There was no way around the fact that this represented a massive intelligence failure. Three years before 9/11, the subcommittee had warned, and I quote, "Failure to improve operations management, resource allocation, and other key issues ... including making substantial and sweeping changes in the way the nation collects, analyzes, and produces intelligence, will likely result in a catastrophic systemic intelligence failure."[7]

The CIA's counterterrorism capabilities had eroded significantly over the course of nearly a decade, we concluded, so that by 9/11 the agency had failed to penetrate the al Qaeda network sufficiently to get at its plans and intentions. Three explanations for the failure emerged: lack of money, inadequate morale and political support from agency leaders, and the natural trend of any federal agency to become more bureaucratic over time.

Bureaucratic ineptitude proved most devastating. The number of CIA lawyers, for example, had increased exponentially over the years. Unfortunately, lawyers and spies don't mix very well. The lawyers spent much of their time finding reasons why CIA operations officers should not conduct certain operations rather than finding ways for them to do so. The most glaring example we uncovered of so-called risk aversion—and the catalyst for many of the shortcomings in the counterterrorism mission—comprised the internal human rights guidelines promulgated in 1995 by then CIA director John Deutch.

The Deutch Guidelines, as they were commonly and derisively referred to by the rank and file at the CIA, stifled counterterrorism initiatives for years by creating an overly burdensome vetting process. The guidelines left operatives with the impression than only Boy Scouts could be

recruited for intelligence gathering, even though real terrorists, some
with blood on their hands, were the only ones who had the information
that could stop a terrorist attack. We had to pass a law in 2001 to get the
CIA to repeal the guidelines, but the damage had been done.

Our review of the FBI and the NSA found similarly deep-rooted
problems. For instance, the FBI's ability to share information—even
internally—was severely handicapped by outdated communications
equipment and a management system that emphasized local control of
information. Further, the FBI was first and foremost a law enforcement
agency, not tailored to collect or analyze intelligence. I should make one
thing clear: the intelligence community's problems did not cause 9/11.
The CIA and the intelligence agencies are not to blame for the attacks. But
there is no denying that intelligence failures played a role in the tragedy.[8]

On December 11, 2002, the joint Senate-House inquiry presented its
report to the public. None of the committee members except the co-
chairs were invited to the announcement, however, confirming a fact
of life in the House—chairs rule committees. Bob Graham and Porter
Goss delivered 35 findings and subfindings divided into three categories:
factual findings, systemic findings, and related findings. Finding 5, one
of the factual findings, summarized our general assessment of the 9/11
catastrophe:

> 5. Finding: Although relevant information that is significant in
> retrospect regarding the attacks was available to the Intelligence
> Community prior to September 11, 2001, the Community too often
> failed to focus on that information and consider and appreciate
> its collective significance in terms of a probable terrorist attack.
> Neither did the Intelligence Community demonstrate sufficient
> initiative in coming to grips with the new transnational threats.
> Some significant pieces of information in the vast stream of data
> being collected were overlooked, some were not recognized as
> potentially significant at the time and therefore were not dissem-
> inated, and some required additional action on the part of foreign
> governments before a direct connection to the hijackers could have

been established. For all these reasons, the Intelligence Community failed to capitalize on available, and potentially important, information.[9]

No one will ever know, our report surmised, what might have happened had more connections been drawn among the disparate pieces of information flowing into our intelligence agencies. We will never know for certain whether the intelligence community would have been able and willing to exploit all the opportunities had they emerged. The important point, which our 838-page report emphasized, was that our intelligence agencies, for a variety of reasons, did not perform well. They failed to bring together and fully appreciate the information that was available. Had they done so, we might have averted the 9/11 terrorist attacks. I had attended all the meetings, listened to all the testimony, and read all the reports. Consequently, I endorsed the report without qualification or reservations.

THE NATIONAL COMMISSION ON TERRORIST ATTACKS UPON THE UNITED STATES

By that point, Congress had completed two investigations of 9/11—one by the Subcommittee on Terrorism and Homeland Security, the other by the Joint Inquiry into Intelligence Community Activities Before and After the Terrorist Attacks of September 11, 2001—and I had served on both. As the latter investigation proceeded, however, concern mounted over whether the joint inquiry offered the best way to get to the bottom of what had happened on September 11. We were hampered because our jurisdiction was limited to intelligence gathering. We could not, for example, look into deficiencies in other government agencies, such as the Federal Aviation Administration. Further, we depended on the agencies we were investigating to produce the evidence necessary for the investigation. Frankly, we encountered difficulty convincing the CIA and other agencies to release documents and information that would shed light on the 9/11 terrorist attacks.[10] I suspected they were dragging their feet in hopes of delaying our inquiry until the scheduled end of our investigation in early 2003.

Overall, however, I thought the joint committee approach worked pretty well. We did have internal disagreements about staffing and, to some extent, our mission. I liked Porter Goss, but his name was mentioned frequently as a potential CIA director, which created the perception of a conflict of interest. Critics had some reason to complain.

The joint inquiry might have satisfied most members of Congress. But disclosures that President Bush had known of Osama Bin Laden's terrorist threats in the United States a month before the attacks and that FBI warnings had been overlooked raised the political stakes. The press reported that the confidential President's Daily Brief (PDB) for August 6, 2001, contained a two-page section entitled "Bin Ladin [*sic*] Determined to Strike in US." The PDB referred to (1) possible hijacking attempts by Bin Laden's disciples and (2) the existence of about 70 FBI investigations into alleged al Qaeda cells operating within the United States.[11]

In frustration, and because of pressure from the families of 9/11 victims, Congress decided that setting up an outside body to expand upon our committee's investigation made the most sense. In late July 2002, the House voted to create an independent commission to investigate the intelligence community. The White House opposed the measure, but 25 Republicans joined 193 Democrats and one independent in favor of the bill to establish the 10-member panel. The measure was opposed by 188 of my colleagues. After reconciling the House and Senate versions, Congress passed the legislation in mid-November 2002. The House vote was 366–3. I opposed the measure believing that the commission would raise false hopes among victims' families and would blame innocent government officials to no good end. The joint inquiry had done good, meticulous work. I doubted that an independent commission would reach different conclusions. I feared a prolonged third investigation would waste time and money. It would draw out the healing process.

Over the course of its investigation, what came to be known as the 9/11 Commission worked with a cumulative budget of $15 million and more than 80 staff members. It interviewed more than 1,200 people in 10 countries, reviewed more than 2.5 million pages of documents, and held 19 days of public hearings at which more than 160 witnesses testified.[12] On July 22, 2004, the commission issued a final report, which represented the unanimous views of its members.

Just as the other two investigations had done, the panel discovered several operational failures that prevented the United States from detecting and disrupting the plot. But the 9/11 Commission also zeroed in on Congress. In the commission's judgment, "The Congress, like the executive branch, responded slowly to the rise of transnational terrorism as a threat to national security." In other words, we in Congress had done little to restructure ourselves to address changing threats. Our attention to terrorism, in the commission's opinion, "was episodic and splintered across several committees." We did not provide sufficient guidance to agencies on terrorism, did not reform them in any significant way to meet the threat, "and did not systematically perform robust oversight to identify, address, and attempt to resolve the many problems in national security and domestic agencies that became apparent in the aftermath of 9/11." The attacks, the commission concluded, "were a shock but they should not have come as a surprise."[13]

The report challenged Congress not only to reorganize the intelligence community but also to change dramatically the way Congress dealt with national security matters. Commission co-chair Lee Hamilton said lawmakers had told him that oversight was so lax that the secret $40 billion annual intelligence budget often was approved after just 10 minutes of debate. "That is really absurd, that is genuinely nuts," he said.[14]

Mounting the War Against Terrorism: Iraq

Historians will scrutinize the origins and conduct of the war in Iraq for decades, if not generations. My purpose here is to record my impressions as a member of the Intelligence Committee, as someone who has a special interest in the Middle East because of my Lebanese heritage, and as a representative of people living in the nation's heartland.

Although the war against al Qaeda and the Taliban in Afghanistan took top priority immediately after 9/11, the administration did not wait long to press for action against Saddam Hussein in Iraq. President Bush had made no secret of his interest in neutralizing the regime from the very beginning of his presidency, but after the September attacks his policy shifted from one of containment to one focused on regime change.

The administration's case rested on several assumptions. First, Saddam had demonstrated his willingness to use whatever weapons he had, including chemical weapons, against his neighbors and his own people. Second, Iraq was pursuing a nuclear weapons program; if it succeeded, it would destabilize the entire region and force an arms race. Third, the regime thumbed its nose at the United Nations and its weapons inspectors, confirming, it seemed at the time, the notion that Iraq was speeding up its weapons-development programs. Finally, the administration argued that Saddam was a willing host to terrorist organizations, such as al Qaeda.

For its part, the House voted 392–12 on December 20, 2001, to adopt a nonbinding resolution demanding that Iraq permit United Nations inspectors to verify that Saddam was not developing weapons of mass destruction. I supported the measure. For the next eight months or so, the president and Congress jousted over the administration's approach to Saddam's Iraq.

In August 2002, I asked my staff to conduct research to answer two questions: *What has the United States done to change the regime in Iraq?* and *Does the president currently have statutory authority to use military force against Iraq?* As a member of the Intelligence Committee, I believed it was important to prepare for the inevitable questions about the president's strategy. The Congressional Research Service (CRS) authored a series of reports related to the first question. Kenneth Katzman, specialist in Middle Eastern affairs at CRS, produced a fair-minded document describing efforts since 1991 to oust Saddam Hussein. He cited experts who believed "past efforts to change the regime floundered because of limited U.S. engagement, disorganization of the Iraqi opposition, and the efficiency and ruthlessness of Iraq's several overlapping intelligence and security forces." I also consulted his reports on Iraq's record of compliance with UN sanctions.[15]

With regard to the second question, our research centered on provisions of the War Powers Resolution; Public Law 102-1, known as the Use of Force Against Iraq Act enacted on January 14, 1991; and Public Law 107-40, signed into law on September 18, 2001. My specific concern related to President Bush's authority to commit troops to Iraq in the absence of formal congressional concurrence. The purpose of the War Powers Resolution, passed during the administration of Richard Nixon, was to ensure that Congress and the president share in making decisions that may involve the United States in hostilities. Criteria for compliance with the resolution included prior consultation with Congress, fulfillment of certain reporting requirements, and congressional authorization.[16]

After gathering this information and mulling over the findings, I began to draft what would become H. Con. Res. 460. The simplest draft expressed the sense of Congress that

> 1. The President should provide a determination to Congress that the Country of Iraq was involved with the attacks on September 11, 2001, and continues to present a threat to the security of the United States;
>
> 2. The President should seek approval from Congress before engaging in military action against Iraq.[17]

I finally settled on more general language and introduced H. Con. Res. 460 on September 4, 2002. The "enacting" language appears here:

> *Resolved the House of Representative (the Senate concurring),* That it is the sense of Congress that the President may order acts of war against a foreign or other entity only in the following circumstances: in compliance with a treaty obligation or to repel a military attack against United States territory, possessions, or Armed Forces engaged in peaceful maneuvers; to participate in humanitarian rescue operations; or in response to a declaration or resolution of prior specific approval by a majority of the Members of each House of Congress.[18]

I wrote my colleagues in the House, asking for their support and co-sponsorship. "The President needs to make the case before Congress, the American people, and the world before our military men and women are sent into harm's way in Iraq," I reminded them. "We, as the elected representatives of the American people, must have a thorough debate on this issue before military force is used."[19] The resolution was referred to the House Committee on International Relations, without co-sponsors, where it died.

During late September and early October, I wrestled with the administration's request for congressional authorization to use force in Iraq with few restraints on the president. I was not convinced yet about the urgency of attacking the country and overthrowing the government. But in early October, CIA director George Tenet briefed me and other members on confidential data about Iraq's weapons arsenal. He reported several key findings in a 25-page report:

> 1. Baghdad hides large portions of Iraq's weapons of mass destruction efforts.
>
> 2. Since inspections ended in 1998, Iraq has maintained its chemical weapons effort, energized its missile program, and invested more heavily in biological weapons.

3. How quickly Iraq will obtain its first nuclear weapon depends on when it acquires sufficient weapons-grade fissile material. If it gets such material from abroad, it could make a nuclear weapon within a year.

4. The regime has begun renewed production of chemical warfare agents, probably including mustard, sarin, cyclosarin, and VX.

5. All key aspects—research and development, production, and weaponization—of Iraq's offensive biological weapons program are active and most elements are larger and more advanced than they were before the Gulf War.

6. Iraq maintains a small missile force and several development programs, including for an unmanned aerial vehicle that most analysts believe probably is intended to deliver biological warfare agents.[20]

Tenet's briefing convinced me that the president deserved the authority to order an attack. Tenet's most chilling finding? That Iraq was close to developing nuclear weapons.

On October 4, 2002, I spoke with reporters back in my district about the resolution authorizing the use of force against Iraq. I said that President Bush had made the case for why force was needed. "If you could see what I have seen, you would be convinced as well," I explained to a reporter from my hometown paper. "It appears that Saddam Hussein is well positioned for creating a lot of mischief in that part of the world, and we have to move quickly to stop him from building up his nuclear capability." The president scored points in my book by seeking international support and by listening to concerns expressed by members of Congress. I said that my immediate goal was to get weapons inspectors back into Iraq, but I would not rule out using force and the United States having some role in "regime building."[21] I asked a member of my staff to begin drafting a statement of my support for the president, which I intended to deliver on the House floor.

On October 7, 2002, President Bush gave a speech on Iraq in Cincinnati in which he addressed the question *Why be concerned about Iraq now?* He explained how Iraq differed from other regimes with dangerous weapons, that Saddam Hussein possessed chemical and biological weapons "capable of killing millions" along with the means to deploy them, that Iraq had provided safe haven and funding for terrorists, that Saddam was intent on developing nuclear weapons, and that 9/11 had awakened us to the threat that people like Saddam posed to Americans. "Knowing these realities, America must not ignore the threat gathering against us," the president said. "Facing clear evidence of peril, we cannot wait for the final proof, the smoking gun that could come in the form of a mushroom cloud."[22]

On October 11, 2002, Congress approved H.J. Res. 114 authorizing the president to use military force against Iraq "as he determines to be necessary and appropriate in order to (1) defend the national security of the United States against the continuing threat posed by Iraq and (2) enforce all United Nations Security Council resolutions regarding Iraq." I supported the measure. Although I did not make a practice of speaking on the House floor, I made an exception in this crucial case. My statement on the House floor, probably the most important I made during 14 years there, follows:

> I rise today in support of H.J. Res. 114, a bipartisan resolution that authorizes the use of our armed forces against Iraq. I want to take a moment to applaud the President and his team for continuing to work to garner international support to bring Iraq into compliance with U.N. resolutions, for continuing to update the Congress on the situation in Iraq, and for continuing to work with Members on both sides of the aisle in formulating the resolution we are discussing today.
>
> We do not take lightly what we are voting on here today. The decision to authorize the potential use of our nation's armed forces is very difficult. However, this resolution is not a rush to war. Our immediate goal is to allow weapons inspectors complete and unrestricted access to determine Iraqi compliance with disarma-

ment requirements. This resolution explicitly expresses support for the President's ongoing efforts to work with the U.N. Security Council to quickly and decisively act to ensure Iraqi compliance with all Security Council resolutions. However, the resolution also provides the authorization for the use of military force that may be needed to protect U.S. national security and enforce Security Council resolutions if diplomatic efforts alone are no longer effective. Congress will be kept informed.

Saddam Hussein knew what was required to end the Persian Gulf War: destroy all existing weapons of mass destruction, discontinue any development of these weapons, and allow United Nations' weapons inspectors unrestricted access so compliance with these demands could be insured. Iraq has failed to comply with each and every U.N. resolution, and has continued to stockpile and develop weapons that are a threat to not only its neighbors in the Middle East, but also the entire world. Iraq's history of violations, combined with its present policy of working to acquire weapons while continuing to restrict U.N. access, lead to a future where the United States and the United Nations must be able to commit whatever resources are necessary to ensure Iraqi disarmament.

I am proud to serve on the Intelligence Committee, and have had the opportunity to carefully study the ongoing weapons development activity in Iraq. I am convinced that this resolution is needed to allow us to use every option at our disposal to deal with Iraq. We know what Iraq is capable of, and we know that Saddam Hussein is striving to expand this capability. The people of Iraq are not safe, American military personnel who serve in the Persian Gulf are not safe, and, in fact, the world is not safe if Iraq does not begin to comply with U.S. and U.N. inspection and disarmament demands.

I believe it is important for the Iraqi people to know that the United States and the United Nations will not allow the continued development and buildup of weapons stockpiles in their country. Saddam Hussein has turned these terrible weapons against his own people, who continue to suffer repression at the hands of this dictator's persistent and willful violations of his international obligations.

I am pleased that this is a bipartisan resolution. The security of the United States, and the security of the world, rises above partisan points of view. This resolution shows Iraq that we are united in our condemnation of its continued flagrant violations of all U.N. resolutions, and in our determination to achieve Iraqi disarmament.

Again, Mr. Speaker, I want to thank the President for his ongoing efforts to work with the international community and the Congress. I want to thank my colleagues for this opportunity for us to thoroughly discuss this resolution, which is one of the most significant pieces of legislation many of us will ever vote on during our time in Congress. And, most importantly, I want to thank the men and women who serve in our nation's armed forces, continually working to achieve and maintain peace, in the Persian Gulf and around the world.

I urge my colleagues to support this bipartisan resolution, and I yield back the balance of my time.[23]

The vote in the House was 296 to 133. Republicans voted 215 to 6 in favor, while Democrats voted 81 to 126 against—the lone independent voted no.[24] The president signed the resolution into law on October 16.

It was a historic action. Congress had never approved a preemptive strike against a sovereign nation. We did so without United Nations approval and without securing the support of the international community. We had no idea what a war might cost, much less how we would pay for it. We did not know how far a war might stretch our military capacity, especially considering the ongoing commitment to Afghanistan.

Not paying for the war—in hindsight, that was the most serious mistake we made. By *we*, I mean President Bush and Congress. We are living with the result today in the crushing debt we leave our children and grandchildren. It would have been reasonable and prudent for the president to come to Congress to ask for a temporary tax to pay for the war. I attended meetings at the White House at which my colleagues pleaded with the president to do so. But I think President Bush turned a deaf ear to any talk of increasing taxes. The president's position put me personally in a bind. I found it impossible to vote against the emergency supplemental appropriations required to fund the war, despite my aversion to piling on debt. I voted for every bill—to do otherwise would have undercut the men and women we put in harm's way.

NOTES

1. Frank H. Mackaman, "LaHood in a Position to Help Shape National Security," *Peoria Journal Star*, October 7, 2001, RLP-Peoria-TBS, f. Intelligence Committee.

2. RL, "America's Intelligence Community: Protecting People and Preserving Liberty" (speech, Peoria Area World Affairs Council, February 21, 2003), RLP-Peoria-TBS, f. Intelligence Committee.

3. CQ, *Congress and the Nation, 2001–2004*, vol. 11 (Washington, DC: CQ Press, 2006), 236.

4. Ibid., 967.

5. Walter Pincus, "House Panel Suggests Revamping Intelligence," *Washington Post*, October 2, 2001, RLP-Peoria-TBS, f. Intelligence Committee.

6. U.S. Senate Committee on Intelligence and U.S. House Permanent Select Committee on Intelligence, "Joint Inquiry into Intelligence Community Activities Before and After the Terrorist Attacks of September 11, 2001," H.R. Rep. No. 107–792 (December 2002), RLP-DC-S, f. Intelligence Committee. 9/11 Report.

7. RL, "America's Intelligence Community."

8. Ibid.

9. U.S. Senate and U.S. House, "Joint Inquiry."

10. CQ, *Congress and the Nation, 2001–2004*, vol. 11, 245.

11. CQ, *Congress and the Nation* [online edition], "Congressional 9/11 Probe, 2001–2002, Legislative Chronology," RLP-Memoir, f. 9/11 and Intelligence Committee.

12. CQ, *Congress and the Nation*, 278.

13. CQ, "Report of the Commission on the Sept. 11, 2001, Attacks on the United States," *Congress and the Nation, 2001–2004*, vol. 11, 977–987; Philip Shenon, "9/11 Report Calls for a Sweeping Overhaul of Intelligence," *NYT*, July 23, 2004, RLP-Memoir, f. 9/11 and Intelligence Committee.

14. Sheryl Gay Stolberg and Philip Shenon, "Congress Plans Special Hearings on 9/11 Findings," *NYT*, July 24, 2004, RLP-Memoir, f. 9/11 and Intelligence Committee.

15. Kenneth Katzman (Congressional Research Service), "Iraq: Compliance, Sanctions, and U.S. Policy," August 5, 2002, RLP-DC-S, f. Iraq. H. Con. Res. 460.

16. Richard F. Grimmett (Congressional Research Service), "War Powers Resolution: Presidential Compliance," 20 August 2002, RLP-DC-S, f. Iraq. H. Con. Res. 460.

17. Draft C in RLP-DC-S, f. Iraq. H. Con. Res. 460.

18. Expressing the sense of Congress regarding the use of force against Iraq, H. Con. Res. 460, September 4, 2002, RLP-DC-S, f. Iraq. H. Con. Res. 460.

19. Dear Colleague, September 5, 2002, RLP-DC-S, f. Iraq. H. Con. Res. 460.

20. Central Intelligence Agency, "Iraq's Weapons of Mass Destruction Programs," October 2002, RLP-DC-S, f. Iraq. H.J. Res. 114.

21. Andy Kravetz, "LaHood Backs Use of Force in Iraq," *Peoria Journal Star*, October 5, 2002, RLP-DC-S, f. Iraq. H.J. Res. 114.

22. George W. Bush, "Address to the Nation on Iraq From Cincinnati, Ohio," October 7, 2002, *PPP*, RLP-Memoir, f. 9/11 and Intelligence Committee.

23. Draft, October 9, 2002 [large-font version], RLP-DC-S, f. Iraq. H.J. Res. 114.

24. CQ, *Congress and the Nation*, vol. 11, 239.

CHAPTER 10

LEAVING CONGRESS

The four events that figured so prominently in my congressional career —the Republican Party's ascendancy in the House (although temporary), the civility initiative, President Clinton's impeachment, and 9/11—took place against a backdrop of mostly uneventful day-to-day activity typical of most House members.

Top-notch constituent service continued to be my priority. I owe a huge debt of gratitude to my staff in Washington, Peoria, Springfield, and Jacksonville. They valued public service every bit as much as I did. Never once did they ask a constituent's party affiliation. They knew, too, that anyone who wanted a personal meeting with me got one—no exceptions. We took as much pride and satisfaction in the small things —tracking down a lost Social Security check, for example—as in the big things: bringing the Abraham Lincoln Library to Springfield, redesigning Interstate 74 through Peoria, establishing the Heartland Community Health Center, and funding construction of Veterans Drive in Pekin, to name a few. I'm proud of that record.

I took my responsibility to vote seriously, too. The record I set in my first term, missing only two of 885 votes, set the pattern for my 14 years in the House. No one appointed me to office—they elected me, and I owed constituents my votes, even tough ones, including votes to impeach President Clinton and to commit troops to Iraq and Afghanistan. Truth be told, I authored little in the way of successful legislation, certainly nothing of everlasting significance on the national stage.

Although there are no laws on the books that carry my name (bills generally carry a committee chairperson's name, and I never chaired a committee), I did contribute to legislation through committee work. During my time in the House, I served on committees and subcommittees dealing primarily with agriculture, appropriations, transportation, and national security. As frustrated as I became with the lack of civility in Congress, especially on the House floor, I ended my service there impressed by the degree of collegiality and camaraderie in committees— especially in agriculture and transportation. The way these committees functioned proved to me that we could conduct business between the parties in mutually respectful ways. In those smaller groups we tended to put ideology aside, and we got to know each other in a more personal way. That agriculture and transportation are less prone to partisan divisions helped, too. I also believe that the committee chairs and ranking members set the tone—if they approached their work intending to cooperate with the other party, committee members responded in kind.

When the Democrats retook the majority following the 2006 midterm elections, I no longer enjoyed the privilege of presiding over the House chamber, and I missed it. Some of my colleagues on the other side of the aisle asked me for advice about taking the chair, and I responded with two suggestions. First, develop a style. Develop a sense that when you're up there, the members know you're going to be fair, you're going to do it by the book, you're not going to favor one side or the other. Second, listen to the parliamentarians. They are lawyers who are trained in and know the rules of the House. No member can know all the rules, precedents, and procedures. If you listen to the parliamentarians, you can almost never go wrong.

Finally, opportunities to gain more influence within the party, either through committee assignments or leadership responsibilities, continued to elude me—not for lack of trying. My last effort to crack the Republican leadership ranks typifies my increasingly exasperating attempts in the House to wield more influence. In my early terms, I could blame Newt Gingrich and his acolytes for blocking me. But Denny Hastert's speakership proved equally inhospitable. There was just one exception: I was named to the House Appropriations Committee in 2000, a post I had long sought, although it yielded only parochial benefits for my district.

BIDDING AGAIN FOR LEADERSHIP

During the spring of 2000, I decided to lay the groundwork for a new leadership bid. The only opening at the time was secretary of the Republican Conference, which did not interest me, but I thought that spending money on behalf of Republicans might help me down the road. To that end, I set up the Abraham Lincoln Leadership Political Action Committee as a means to distribute money to fellow Republicans.

My chance came in December 2001 when majority leader Dick Armey announced his retirement from the House, setting off a chain reaction. At least seven Republicans threw their hats into the ring for Armey's post, although the odds-on favorite was Tom DeLay. I set my cap for DeLay's position, the third-ranking leadership post. Whips are responsible for enforcing party discipline. They canvass party members on pending issues, give floor leaders their assessments of support or opposition, and pass political intelligence to and from the leaders. Whips are also expected to keep tabs on the whereabouts of their colleagues and make sure they are on hand to vote. Bob Michel had served as whip before becoming leader. DeLay's chief deputy, Roy Blunt (R-MO), appeared to be my stiffest competition.

On Wednesday evening, December 12, the day of Armey's announcement, I met with Speaker Hastert for 30 minutes to discuss the leadership situation. I told the Speaker, my friend for more than 20 years, that I was considering a run either for majority leader or for majority whip. He advised me to look at the whip's race. Unfortunately, as it turned out, Denny stayed out of the race and did not endorse me. In fact his spokesman, John Feehery, told a reporter shortly after my announcement, "He's [referring to the Speaker] comfortable with Roy Blunt. If Ray wants to run, he's comfortable with that."[1] A tepid recommendation at best.

The next day, I announced as a candidate for majority whip in a Dear Colleague letter. I touted my experience as a congressional staffer and seven years as a member. I pledged to support President George W. Bush, the Speaker, and the majority leader. I omitted from my announcement, however, the following paragraph from an early draft:

> As you well know, what I am not is one to do things the same way they have always been done, or to go along to get along. And that is something that one does not change. But I am hopeful these are attributes that will be conducive to innovative approaches and building new coalitions to get things done.[2]

For obvious reasons, I did not want to spotlight my independence from the party at this critical juncture.

My hometown newspaper supported my effort with an editorial that I might have written myself:

> LaHood would be a good choice for No. 3. Unlike those who see government as the enemy, he looks for ways to make it work. He lacks the hard edge that so bothers suburban soccer moms. He gives the appearance of being driven by reason, rather than ideology. He has good relationships with Democrats and, early in his congressional career, organized bipartisan retreats to promote civility.
>
> Unfortunately, these attributes may make LaHood a tough sell in a House Republican caucus that is more conservative than he is. It depends on what members want. If they want to pull the Republican Party back to its Main Street, individualistic, government off-my-

back roots, and away from the social and fiscal fringes, they'll have that chance next year.[3]

I brought some advantages to the leadership race. I was close to Speaker Hastert, of course. I had earned the respect of my colleagues on both sides of the aisle as presiding officer, which would come in handy when called upon to put together coalitions broader than my own party. The bipartisan civility retreats helped—with such a small majority, our party needed to be able to reach across the aisle. I knew how to work the process. I came from a safe district. As a moderate, I would give balance to the largely conservative leadership. I presented a fresh face, someone who could provide a kinder, gentler leadership. Tom DeLay relished being called "the Hammer." I would rather have been called "the velvet glove."[4]

I carried some baggage, too. I hailed from the same state as the Speaker, which earned me the opposition of those who sought geographical balance. Despite my indisputably conservative voting record, some of my colleagues still felt I lacked ideological purity. Admittedly, my occasional independence did not sit well with party loyalists. I had been one of seven Republican House members to vote against a $100 billion economic stimulus package approved by the House in October 2001—I thought the country had too many other pressing needs while fighting the war on terror. I was one of three Republicans to vote against the USA PATRIOT Act—it gave too much authority for wiretapping and surveillance without judicial approval and had no sunset provision.[5] To counteract the effects of these independent stances, I did not make the leadership race about issues or ideology. I made it about experience.

The final obstacle, which proved to be insurmountable, was the competition. Roy Blunt intended to move up the leadership ladder to the whip post. He had a habit of being in the right place at the right time. His first political job, at age 22, had been on John Ashcroft's congressional campaign—Ashcroft was now attorney general in President Bush's Cabinet. Blunt had emerged as one of the first members of Congress to endorse George W. Bush for president, later becoming the chief liaison between the campaign and the House Republicans. After just one term in the House, DeLay tapped him to be his top lieutenant, or chief deputy whip.

Many in my party, but particularly moderates, had two fears about elevating DeLay and adding Blunt to the leadership. First, by giving such prominence to the Hammer, we might be handing the Democrats an important weapon in what promised to be tight off-year elections in 2002. To win the whip post, I needed the votes of colleagues concerned that promoting DeLay, a tough-talking, pit-bull, abrasive conservative, might energize Democratic fundraising and put too harsh a public face on the party. As I told a local reporter, a DeLay-Blunt team "is not a good thing for the party. We need new blood, new faces, new ideas. These jobs only come around every 10 years."[6]

Our other concern was that by sheer force of personality, and with loyalists like Blunt at his side, DeLay would dominate the Republican Conference and chart the party's course without regard to more moderate voices. The dynamic boiled down to this: Should all three people at the top—the Speaker, the majority leader, and the majority whip—be products of the DeLay organization? Keep in mind that DeLay had pulled the strings to move Hastert from chief deputy whip to Speaker after the Gingrich-Livingston debacle in December 1998.

As DeLay's protégé, however, Blunt held the best cards, and I knew it. After all, he had the entire whip organization at his disposal, plus a 30-member campaign organization of his own. Moreover, he had deep ties to K Street business interests, which he courted assiduously. Although I had my supporters in the business community, too, I admit Blunt's prowess there trumped my support. *Congress Daily* quoted one business source: "Ray LaHood is a terrific guy, but with a five-seat majority, you can't afford to have a guy who is learning how to be whip. Roy [Blunt] has been sitting in that office learning how to do the job." The source also said that my "fierce independent streak" might not play well in the number three leadership slot.[7] Five days after my announcement, Blunt claimed to have 150 firm commitments.[8] He appeared to have the race wrapped up before I had left the starting gate.

With the election 11 months off, however, I kept plugging away, making calls, buttonholing. In the first two days, I called 40 to 50 lawmakers to see whether I could crack Blunt's support. I concentrated on geography, reaching out to state delegations, particularly large ones such as California, New York, Pennsylvania, Florida, and, of course, Illinois. By mid-January, I had assembled a steering committee of 25 members to help run what I expected to be a long campaign. Roy Blunt had a good head start on me, but then that's what a campaign is—a contest between competitors. Some who had committed to Blunt had done so before they learned of my interest, and I hoped to pick off a few of them. In mid-January, I asked a handful of members to call colleagues to gauge support. According to the press, Blunt now claimed over 160 "hard yeses," well above the 112 votes necessary to win in our 223-member conference.[9]

I threw in the towel a month later. After three months and a series of bad reports from my steering committee, I knew I could not win the race. I called Blunt on Tuesday, February 26, to tell him the news and to pledge my support. I was not inclined to stay in the race just to see whether the political climate would change dramatically enough to create an opening in November. Blunt had run an effective, clean campaign, and I walked away impressed by his skill and his attention to members' concerns. I did not give up my leadership aspirations at that point—I hoped there would be another opportunity. But I was left with a troubling thought: Was there a place for me in the Republican Party?

I'VE HAD ENOUGH

After seven terms in the House, I had grown increasingly frustrated. Democrats retook the majority following the 2006 midterms. In some respects, that made me a minority in the minority. As the contest for Republican whip demonstrated, our party's leadership preferred members more ideologically pure than I was for positions of influence. This despite my conservative voting record. I supported the Republican Party's position an average of almost 90 percent of the time from 2002 through 2006—a pretty strong record. Over the same period, I supported President Bush about 82 percent of the time.[10] There were more conservative members of the party, to be sure, but I did not challenge the party's orthodoxy in any fundamental way.

What could I have done differently to improve my standing in the party? I could have distanced myself from Bob Michel. Working for Bob and standing by him after he left the House meant that the true believers tarred me with the Washington-insider brush. In addition to my deep fondness for Bob and the unshakable loyalty we shared for one another, without Bob Michel I could not have won a seat in the House in the first place.

Should I have signed the Contract with America? Would that have made a difference? No and yes. Politics too often is a matter of expediency. I don't second-guess the decision—signing the contract did not make sense to me as a matter of principle or public policy. But certainly, refusing to sign closed the door to more opportunities than I ever imagined it would as I began my career.

Had I conceived of my job differently, putting less emphasis on serving my constituents and more on making my mark in Washington—would that have altered the course of my career? That's hard to say. The factors that blocked me from climbing the leadership ladder likely would have proved equally difficult to overcome in passing major legislation. Moreover, I enjoyed the work on behalf of central Illinois. We achieved more than a fair share of success. The setting back home, where we dealt with issues regardless of party or ideology, lacked the rancor of Washington, providing a welcome respite from the wrangling there.

To repeat a point I made earlier, though, I really did not anguish over lost opportunities. They do help explain, however, my restlessness as 2008 and another campaign approached. I flirted with a couple of options, including a run for governor of Illinois in 2005 and a bid for the presidency of Bradley University in 2007, but I eventually withdrew my name in both cases. In my reelection race in 2006, I had won 67 percent of the vote, suggesting that I could hold the seat as long as I wished. I was not thrilled by the prospect of running again in 2008, however.

On Thursday, July 26, 2007, while appearing on Bradley University's National Public Radio affiliate, WCBU, I announced my retirement. At 61 years of age, I found the prospect of leading an ordinary life after 30 years in politics appealing. I traveled to Springfield the next day to hold a press conference in the Press Briefing Room of the State Capitol to confirm my intentions. Recently, I discovered that Illinois Channel had filmed the 20-minute event and put it on YouTube. Even at this distance in time, I would not change a word.[11]

In prepared remarks, I made these central points: public service is a noble profession; serving in Congress is not a lifetime job, nor should it be; and the American dream is available to anyone who wants to work for it. "I feel like I'm going out at the highest point of my career," I explained. I had outlasted the hyperpartisans Gingrich, Armey, and DeLay, though I did not offer those examples at the press conference. Instead, when asked why I was retiring now, I admitted that I simply couldn't think of anything else to do. After working "1000 percent every day" for 14 years, I felt that I owed it to Kathy, our kids, and our seven grandchildren to become what I called "a normal person." When asked what my plans were, I said, "I hope the phone will ring after this announcement." I had no job lined up.

Someone in the audience asked me whether the fun had gone out of the job. "Absolutely not," I answered. "This is a great job. But it requires a lot of hard work and a lot of time." I recalled the milestones of my time in Congress—coming into the House as a member of the majority party, voting to send troops into harm's way in Iraq and Afghanistan, seeing the smoke billow up from the Pentagon on September 11, and presiding over the House during the impeachment debate. I couldn't have asked for more, I explained. "When those chapters are written about the history of America, I can say to people, 'I was there, I saw it, I saw it with my own eyes.'" I left on my own terms—I was not carried out, prosecuted out, or voted out.

David Broder paid me the compliment of writing about my retirement. "LaHood is not a familiar figure to most Americans," Broder wrote, "but he embodies the characteristics that make the House work as an institution." He noted my role in the House impeachment debate, recounted my independence from the Gingrich Republicans, and singled out my work on civility. "He takes care of his constituent duties, he carries more than his share of the legislative work and—most importantly—he cultivates the kind of personal relationships that build trust across partisan and ideological lines."[12]

When he learned of my retirement, assistant Senate majority leader Dick Durbin, the senior senator from my state and a Democrat, told one columnist, "He's one of my three best friends in the Illinois delegation. I trust Ray. I have worked closely with him. His word is always good. Ray is a real human being who always tries to find that common ground."[13]

If I had to single out one example of how civil, bipartisan relationships work in the day-to-day world of the House, I would point to my relationship with then congressman Rahm Emanuel. The day after Rahm was elected to the House in 2002, he called me and said, "Ray, I want to work with you." We both hailed from Illinois, but that's where our apparent similarity ended. Consider this: I am a Republican; he is a Democrat. I am from downstate; he is from Chicago. I am a Lebanese American; he is a Jewish American. I supported John McCain in 2008; he supported Barack Obama. But we did not let what separated us prevent us from developing a great friendship. As Rahm put it, "If we could work together, anything is possible."[14] He and I co-hosted a series of bipartisan dinners at which House members from both parties spent an evening together talking policy and politics and getting to know each other personally. We may not have solved the world's problems, but those dinners produced lasting friendships and good will.

On my last day in Congress, October 3, 2008, Rahm offered this farewell comment:

> If you look back and I think if you ask all our colleagues [whom] our framers thought of [as] a member of Congress[,] what they had in their mind's eye, that person would be Ray LaHood, whose decency, his sense of what it is that he was doing here [and] on behalf of who[m] was doing it for never changed in his 30 years. He is an individual who, while firm in his principles, was very flexible about his opinions. I say, if you spend too much time in Washington you become firm in your opinions and it is your principles you are flexible on. Ray never forgot where he was from and the people of Peoria that sent him here.

In light of what would happen in the next couple of months, I have wondered whether he had something in mind when he concluded, "I would hope that Ray could find other ways to ... contribute to his country."[15]

FOUR LESSONS OF POLITICAL LIFE

In May 2008 at Millikin University's commencement, I took the opportunity to summarize the four basic lessons that have shaped my career. The first rule is this: learn to listen. We usually think of congressmen as always talking, not listening, but Bob Michel believed that listening was the most important factor in his success. Bob knew that in politics you can't speak effectively unless you first listen carefully. It means being able to listen through the static of habit and prejudice and routine that so often prevents us from learning. When we really listen, we begin to see the question from the other person's point of view. This, in politics, is the beginning of wisdom.

The second lesson: we have to judge honestly if we are to act effectively. Judgment is a virtue that has fallen on hard times. I often hear people say, "Oh, I never want to be judgmental. Who am I to judge other people?" I will grant that there is some wisdom in that statement, but there is a difference between judging people and judging the positions they hold. In politics we are required to make judgments on what people say or do, but we can do that without passing judgment on their character or motivation—that is the rule of civility.

Choose positions prudently—my third lesson. *Prudence* entails being wise in handling practical matters by showing sound judgment and common sense. The words *wise, practical, sound,* and *commonsense* are not the kind we associate with personal charisma or thrilling oratory or swiftness in debate. Prudence involves quiet, practical virtues rather than electrifying oratory. Prudence often demands long periods of considered judgment rather than sudden bursts of flashy oratory.

The final virtue of politics, and of private life, as well, is the ability to conduct ourselves with civility, in victory or defeat. Someone once said that civility in public life is like good manners in private life: they don't solve problems, but they create an atmosphere in which problems can be solved. Looking back at my congressional career, I'm proudest of the efforts to return civility to our debates. Regrettably, that experiment largely failed. In Washington, our debates are marked all too often by the three D's: demonizing, denunciation, and disrespect. This descent into the politics of personal abuse is insidious in its effect on debate and discussion. It permeates not only government but also the media and the very nature of public debate itself.[16]

Too often political debates are still couched in the language favored by the most ideological or power hungry—the language of the battlefield. Politics, we are told, is war; those who disagree with us are the enemy; we should take no prisoners; and our disagreements are to be fought in the trenches. I take this lesson from Bob Michel, who served as a combat infantryman in World War II. He landed on Normandy beach on D-Day plus six and fought his way across France and Belgium into Germany. He was wounded by machine-gun fire and received the Purple Heart, two Bronze Stars, and four battle stars. Bob Michel knew war firsthand. But this combat veteran never referred to politics as war. He knew the difference, and he taught all who worked with him that difference. He taught us that successful public service in a democracy does not mean and cannot mean the destruction of one's enemies.[17]

I remember the words of a great Illinoisan, Abraham Lincoln, who once served my district in Congress:

> We are not enemies, but friends. We must not be enemies. Though passion may have strained, it must not break our bonds of affection. The mystic chords of memory, stretching from every battle-field and patriot grave to every living heart and hearthstone all over this broad land, will yet swell the chorus of the Union when again touched, as surely they will be, by the better angels of our nature.[18]

NOTES

1. Dennis Conrad, "Peoria Congressman Campaigns for Leadership," *Pekin Daily Times*, December 15, 2001, RLP-DC-S, f. Republican Leadership. Leadership Races, 2002.
2. Draft announcement, December 13, 2001, RLP-DC-S, f. Republican Leadership. Leadership Races, 2002.
3. "LaHood Would Put GOP on More Moderate Course," *Peoria Journal Star*, December 16, 2001, RLP-DC-S, f. Republican Leadership. Leadership Races, 2002.
4. Dori Meinert, "LaHood May Seek House Offices," *Peoria Journal Star*, December 13, 2001, RLP-Campaign, f. Whip Race.
5. I did support the bill once it was modified to include a sunset after four years.
6. Meinert, "LaHood May Seek House Offices."
7. Charlie Mitchell, "To Be Perfectly Blunt," *Congress Daily*, December 19, 2001, RLP-DC-S, f. Republican Leadership. Leadership Races, 2002.
8. "Blunt Supporters Claim Enough Votes to Win Whip's Job," *Congress Daily*, December 18, 2001, RLP-DC-S, f. Republican Leadership. Leadership Races, 2002.
9. "In House GOP Ranks, A Race Develops," *Congress Daily*, December 14, 2001, RLP-DC-S, f. Republican Leadership. Leadership Races, 2002; Kerry Kantin, "LaHood in Whip Race," *The Hill*, January 30, 2002, RLP-Campaign, f. Whip Race.
10. Jackie Koszczuk and Martha Angle, eds., *CQ's Politics in America 2008: The 100th Congress* (Washington, DC: Congressional Quarterly, 2007), 357.
11. See the YouTube feature in three parts at http://www.youtube.com/watch?v=T8sWR7EZAbk.
12. David Broder, "Departure of LaHood leaves void," *Omaha World-Herald*, August 5, 2007, the Dirksen Congressional Center, Accession 2010/9/2–1.
13. Quoted in Mark Shields, "Washington Will Miss Ray LaHood," www.creators.com, July 26, 2008, RLP-Memoir, f. Leaving Congress.
14. Shields, "Washington Will Miss Ray LaHood."
15. 154 Cong. Rec., H10812–13, (October 3, 2008), RLP, Washington Office, Personal, f. Retirement.

16. RL, "The Michel Touch," April 27, 2007, RLP-Peoria-TBS, f. LaHood Speeches.
17. Ibid.
18. RL, "The Four Basic Lessons," RLP-Peoria-TBS, f. LaHood Speeches. Lincoln's First Inaugural, March 4, 1861.

CHAPTER 11

THE OBAMA CABINET

THE PROMISE OF BIPARTISANSHIP

I served as secretary of transportation in President Barack Obama's Cabinet from January 23, 2009, when I was sworn in, to July 2, 2013, when I walked out of the Department of Transportation's (DOT) headquarters at 1200 New Jersey Avenue, SE. Those four and a half years proved pivotal in DOT's history, and I am enormously proud of the accomplishments of the 55,000 people who worked there during my service.

In a later chapter I will talk about the good work of the department, but I begin my account of serving in the president's Cabinet by considering a more general and perplexing question: Why did the promise of bipartisanship, a promise so powerfully expressed by the new president even as he campaigned, go unfulfilled? I say *perplexing* because the explanation still confounds me. The recurring partisan battles between the Democratic president and the Republican House on Obamacare, the budget, the debt ceiling, immigration, energy—you name it—testify to the pervasive ideological polarization between the two political parties. It was not supposed to be this way. Barack Obama can rightfully claim substantial, even historic, accomplishments. But the potential for more eluded him.

CONFIRMATION

In the weeks following Rahm Emanuel's call on December 17, 2008, inviting me to join the administration, I prepared for confirmation hearings before the Senate Committee on Commerce, Science, and Transportation. If the president-elect took an informal approach in selecting me as his secretary-designate, his transition team took no chances with my confirmation. The casual selection process changed abruptly on Monday, December 22, when I took part in a conference call with the transition staff, the confirmation team, and the agency review team. Yes, it took three separate teams to get Cabinet designees up to speed. Besides the deluge of forms and paperwork, we discussed communication goals and press inquiries, a schedule for courtesy calls on senators, the need to conduct a mock confirmation hearing, and DOT's role in the economic recovery plan. This first conference call identified a series of topics for issue briefings. A memo in my files listed them:

> Overall structure & functions at USDOT [U.S. Department of Transportation]
> Safety Issues
> Issues for economic recovery bill
> Constituency and member attitudes
> Aviation: Agency review, labor issues, air traffic control modernization
> Highways: Agency review, highway trust fund status
> Transit: Agency review, funding, backlog
> Rail: Agency review, implement Rail Act
> Other modes, other USDOT agencies
> Energy and environmental linkages; fuel economy standards
> Budget issues: FY09, FY10
> Agenda for first day, first week
> Changeover issues: rulemakings, personnel, Office of the Secretary organization[1]

Three days removed from the press conference announcing my selection as secretary of transportation, finally I had my first comprehensive introduction to the job ahead.

My confirmation hearing took place on Wednesday, January 21, at 2:00 p.m., before the Senate committee. John D. Rockefeller (D-WV) chaired the panel, and Kay Bailey Hutchison (R-TX) was the ranking member. Bob Michel and Dick Durbin introduced me. Durbin told his colleagues that President Obama wanted to make sure his Cabinet was bipartisan and "to show there were leading politicians who could serve in his cabinet and do so effectively." "I'll be honest with you," Durbin explained. "I went to him and said, 'I think Ray LaHood is that person.'"[2]

In my opening statement, I emphasized two principles: openness and fairness. I pledged to solicit advice from all who cared about our transportation system, to keep an open door. I suggested that being a Republican in a Democratic administration gave me a real appreciation of the value of listening to all sides. "I hope you take my selection as a signal of the President's commitment to focus his energies on policy rather than partisanship," I said.[3]

For the next two hours, I answered questions on topics ranging from modernizing the air traffic control system to the role of transportation spending in reviving the economy. I felt comfortable in the role—there were no surprises. Rockefeller cut the session off shortly after 4:00 p.m. because the Senate was preparing to confirm Hillary Clinton as secretary of state. Consequently, the committee did not vote formally on my confirmation, but Rockefeller and Hutchison conveyed to their respective leaders that I was good to go.

The full Senate confirmed me as the 16th secretary of transportation by voice vote on January 22, 2009, only two days after President Obama's inauguration. Just before 1:00 p.m. the next day, Friday, I was joined for the official swearing-in ceremony at the department by Kathy, our son Sam, and fellow Illinoisan and assistant Senate majority leader Dick Durbin. The oath of office was administered by Linda Washington, assistant secretary for administration, and took place before my new staff and members of the Department of Transportation transition team. The next Tuesday, Vice President Biden led a ceremonial swearing-in ceremony in the Old Executive Office Building for the most recently confirmed Cabinet appointees and their families.

My charge from the president was simple: "If there's a problem, I'll let you know," he said. "If you don't hear from me, you must be doing something right." As head of a department with more than 55,000 employees and a $70 billion budget, I viewed the job more broadly: help to create a bipartisan approach to governing, implement the president's plans for transportation policy, protect the president from unhappy surprises, and manage the department.

One week later, on Friday, January 30, I held my first press conference. Most of the exchange with reporters concerned the economic stimulus. "My job is more than Peoria now," I said. "I work for the Obama administration. I'm part of a team. My job is to carry out the president's agenda and to work with the states to see that the money gets out so people can go to work." I sounded the bipartisan theme, too. "The election is over. There's [sic] no labels. Everyone has one goal," I explained. "Let's get the country moving forward, let's get the economy moving forward, let's get people back to work. It has nothing to do with party labels."[4]

THE PROMISE OF BIPARTISANSHIP

I had spent a career cultivating a civil, bipartisan approach to politics and problem solving. Now I had the chance to practice that approach from an executive rather than a legislative position. Of all the Cabinet departments, DOT suited me the best. Transportation is bipartisan. When I was on the House Transportation Committee, we passed two transportation bills; both attracted more than 380 votes in the House and 80 votes in the Senate. As I have often said, "There are no Republican or Democratic bridges. There are no Democratic or Republican roads. There just aren't."

I was equally convinced that President Obama shared my optimism about the promise of bipartisanship. He had impressed me from the beginning. Dick Durbin told me eight months before the 2004 elections for the second Senate seat from Illinois to keep my eye on Chicago's Barack Obama.

Illinois had an open seat that year following the retirement of incumbent Republican senator Peter Fitzgerald after one term. Durbin believed Obama, then a state senator, would win the Democratic primary in a crowded field of nine candidates, one of whom would eventually spend $30 million in his unsuccessful effort to win the race. I had never heard of Obama—his name meant nothing to me. But Dick knew what he was talking about. Obama set up a campaign committee 21 months before the primary, lined up endorsements from key unions in the state, and secured the endorsement of four U.S. House members and the late senator Paul Simon's daughter. The hard work paid off with an unexpectedly large winning margin—almost 30 percent ahead of his nearest rival.

The state Republican Party handed Obama a gift in the general election. When its primary winner left the race for personal reasons, the party selected the inept Alan Keyes, who did not even live in Illinois, as its standard-bearer. Game over. Obama won the election with 70 percent of the vote. In a bit of historical coincidence, Senator-elect Obama would take the seat once held by Everett McKinley Dirksen (R-IL), perhaps the key senator to the passage of the Civil Rights Act of 1964.

As candidate Obama crisscrossed downstate in 2008, we did not meet. He probably didn't know me from Adam's house cat. But only two days after Obama won that Senate race, my cell phone rang. "Ray, this is Barack Obama. I'm coming to Peoria," he said. "I'd like to sit down with you and talk about how we can work together."

A week later he showed up in Peoria, and we met in my district office for 90 minutes. We talked briefly about his campaign and how he had won—his winning margin was the largest in Illinois's history for a Senate race. More importantly, he said he wanted to represent all of Illinois and was looking for people to help him. I suspect that someone, perhaps Rahm Emanuel or Dick Durbin, had put a bug in his ear that if he wanted to reach out to Republicans, I was the best guy to contact.

During his term in the U.S. Senate, Obama proved very helpful in funding projects in my district. For example, the city fathers in Pekin, a community of 32,000 just across the river from Peoria, sought funds to build a highway on the east side of town to improve access to an interstate highway. The total cost for the project amounted to $6 million. To complete an early phase, however, they approached me, their congressman, about securing $4.8 million in federal funds. I handled the matter on the House side. Obama took up the project on the Senate side. After his staff and mine had worked out the details, he and I consulted on the best way to proceed. Eventually, we appropriated the entire $4.8 million for the initial phase of Pekin's Veterans Drive. It did not matter to either of us that he was a Democrat and I was a Republican.

Our relationship went beyond a shared interest in state projects. When he opened a downstate office in Springfield, where I also had a district office, he invited me to the opening. I accepted and said a few words— believe me, it's unusual for a Republican House member to appear at a public event showcasing a Democratic senator. On projects large and small, we established a bipartisan friendship.

Obama had a gift for the personal touch, too. In his race against Hillary Clinton during the Democratic presidential primary in 2008, Obama was advised to visit several Democratic House members to get their endorsements as at-large delegates to the Democratic Convention. He did so by coming on the House floor during a vote, and I went down to talk to him. He gave me a handshake and a hug, which is his custom, and then asked, "What are you going to do after you retire?" I said I had no firm plans. He replied, "If this thing works out [i.e., winning the presidential election], I'm going to be looking for some Republicans, and I'd like to talk to you."

My point is this: here is a guy who is running for president, trying to get at-large delegates to support him, working the Democratic side of the House floor, and he thinks to ask me that question and offers me the prospect of a job. Not every politician has that gift.

My interactions with Barack Obama over four years convinced me that he appreciated the value of personal relationships, of mutual respect, of understanding based on a willingness to listen to one another, and, ultimately, of compromise. These traits are essential to working across the political aisle. Moreover, he practiced the art of building these relationships skillfully, intuitively, seemingly without effort. I assumed these qualities would stand him in good stead with Congress as he moved forward with his agenda should he win the presidency. Current wisdom may characterize the president as aloof and either unable or unwilling to practice personal politics. My experience contradicted that image.

I believe to this day that bipartisanship is built into Barack Obama's DNA. He campaigned, and campaigned emphatically, on the promise of governing in a different way. One has only to read his remarks in Springfield when he announced his candidacy for president. After describing the challenges facing the nation as the campaign began, and the inability to overcome them, candidate Obama said,

> What's stopped us is the failure of leadership, the smallness of our politics—the ease with which we're distracted by the petty and the trivial, our chronic avoidance of tough decisions, our preference for scoring cheap political points instead of rolling up our sleeves and building a working consensus to tackle big problems.[5]

He sounded this theme through innumerable campaign appearances for the next 22 months, culminating in his election-night victory speech on November 4, 2008. "In this country, we rise or fall as one nation, as one people," he declared. "Let's resist the temptation to fall back on the same partisanship and pettiness and immaturity that has poisoned our politics for so long."[6]

People elected Barack Obama at least partly out of a desire to see Washington function in a more civil, respectful, bipartisan way. A CBS News/*New York Times* poll at the end of October 2008 indicated that 70 percent of respondents answered "Will be" to the following question: "If Barack Obama is elected president, do you think he will be able to work with members of both parties in order to get things done, or will he not be able to?" In the same poll, respondents answered "Would" to this question: "If he were elected president, do you think Barack Obama would bring about real change in the way things are done in Washington, or wouldn't he do that?"[7] Americans hoped for and expected a departure from the partisan stridency that had plagued Washington.

Among the many articles forecasting the tenor of the new adminis- tration following the election, the *Tampa Bay Times* described the test ahead simply in this headline: "Can Obama Keep Promise of Bipartisan- ship?" "The tone that he sets beginning now in the transition is hugely important," said Lee Hamilton, a former Democratic Congress member from Indiana. "He really has an extraordinary opportunity. I think he has to show respect for all the parties, I think he must not claim a sweeping mandate, I think he needs to build trust," Hamilton concluded.[8]

Obama and his team seemed up to the challenge. During the transition between the election and the inauguration, the president-elect took several concrete steps toward bipartisanship. The *New York Times* reported, for example, that Obama "is working to build a cordial relationship with Republicans by seeking guidance on policy proposals, asking for advice on appointments and hoping to avoid perceptions of political arrogance given the wide margins of his victory." Obama called Republican leaders on the Hill, sent Rahm Emanuel to their meetings, and urged my House colleagues to support his economic recovery plan. "I'd say, so far so good," the *Times* quoted senator Lamar Alexander (R-TN) as saying. "If he follows through on that, he'll find plenty of Republicans willing to help him." The transition team caught flak from liberal Democrats for these overtures to the party they had just defeated so overwhelmingly. Chief of Staff Emanuel reminded them, however, "Even though the majorities [of Democrats in Congress] are big, the challenges are of such a magnitude that we're all inheriting, it's going to require bipartisanship to solve. We're not lip-synching bipartisanship here."[9]

It may seem hard to grasp in today's political climate, but even so partisan a partisan as Senate Republican leader Mitch McConnell (KY) said the administration "is off to a good start" in December 2008. "This is an opportunity to tackle big issues and to do them in the middle," he suggested, before adding that it would not be a good idea "to go down a laundry list of left-wing proposals and try to jam them through Congress." McConnell told the *Times* that if Obama nominated more than "a token Republican" to his Cabinet, it would signal the Democratic president's commitment to bipartisanship.[10] The country agreed in large measure. Nearly six in 10 surveyed in a *Los Angeles Times* poll in mid-December said Obama's Cabinet selections were consistent with his promise to promote renewed bipartisanship.[11]

Appointing me was a calculated move by the new president to soothe partisan tensions, and I wanted to support him. I was the only bona fide Republican to serve in his Cabinet. By that I mean I was the only person who had run for office as a Republican, who had won elective office as a Republican, and who was proud to be called a Republican. I had campaigned hard for Obama's opponent in 2008, serving as a delegate for John McCain at the Republican National Convention. I imagine every other Cabinet appointee either campaigned or voted for Barack Obama. McConnell may have considered mine just "a token Republican" selection, but it did not feel that way to me. Nor to the president. As he put it during his appearance at a Caterpillar plant in East Peoria (my former congressional district) a few weeks into his first term: "Ray comes from a long line of Republicans I love, starting with Bob Michel. I think there's a common-sense, Midwestern, can-do, bipartisan attitude that Ray represents, and I am so pleased that he's in my Cabinet."[12]

I had spent my congressional career battling against closed-mindedness, ideological fixation, and politics as usual. Putting that reputation to work on behalf of someone I thought could be a transformational president— what an exciting prospect. I wanted to be one voice in a rising choir that said *enough*. Enough of politics as a zero-sum game in which nobody can find room to compromise. Enough of disagreement breeding distrust rather than dialogue. Enough of all the hooting and hollering that drowns out what's really important: serving the people who sent us to Washington in the first place.[13] In accepting his invitation to serve, I had high hopes that this president would tackle and solve the daunting challenges facing the country in bipartisan fashion. By the summer of 2013, however, I had learned that hoping was not enough.

The Inner Circle

I held four expectations as I began my tenure at DOT. First, that President Obama would use my experience and network of relationships to build Republican support, chiefly in the House, for his major policy initiatives. Second, that the White House staff, if not the president himself, would consult me on the strategy for obtaining such support before taking legislation to the Hill. Third, that because I was a member of his Cabinet, my views on the substance of transportation policy would carry weight. Finally, that because of DOT's $77 billion budget and its capacity to help stoke the economic recovery, I would weigh in on decisions even beyond the department's traditional scope. At the beginning, of course, I could not know how realistic these expectations would prove to be.

Let me be clear on this point: I was not part of the administration's inner circle. As much as the president and I shared a mutual respect, I was not his confidant. Michelle Obama, Rahm Emanuel, David Axelrod, Valerie Jarrett, Robert Gibbs, and Joe Biden—those were the folks who had the president's ear on domestic policy. As far as I know, no Cabinet secretary cracked the inner circle; certainly, I did not. I do believe, however, that my experience will shed light on at least some of the reasons why an administration initially committed to a new style of governing subsequently abandoned it.

To succeed in helping the president and the administration, I needed to understand who the players were, how they made decisions, what they wanted to accomplish, and how supportive they would be of transportation issues.

The first part of the puzzle quickly fell into place. President Obama depended almost exclusively on a handful of folks situated in the White House. He rarely sought counsel outside that group. He did not, as other presidents have done, place a high value on consulting with members of Congress—a fact that made my job as informal liaison with congressional Republicans that much harder. None of this came as a surprise, however. The informal structure at the White House resembled the Obama campaign team—small and close knit, prizing loyalty, speaking with a single voice, and keeping information and decisions close to the vest. David Plouffe, Obama's campaign manager, once explained the virtue of what was known, ironically, as the Bush model of communications discipline: "We talked a lot about the Bush model, which is that there are a few people who really know everything."[14] Their approach produced one of the most successful presidential campaigns in memory—little wonder that the practice continued in the White House. How well the approach suited the task of governing, as opposed to campaigning, remained an open question.

I would count the First Lady as the most important person in the president's inner circle for obvious reasons. I did not know Michelle and had not met her until the president's inauguration. Over the next four years, I acquired a respect for her poise, her intelligence, and her passion for the issues that concerned her. I admired her decision to make the welfare of the Obamas' daughters, Malia and Sasha, her number one priority. Far be it from me to assess the quality of her advice to the president more generally. Suffice it to say I had no doubt about her influence.

My friend Rahm Emanuel, as the president's chief of staff and consigliore, played the key staff role among the president's closest advisers. He did so by virtue of his office, of course, but there was more to it than that. Rahm and the president had overlapped in Congress and knew each other well as members of the Illinois delegation. Among all the president's advisers, Emanuel had the most experience with the House. He had won three terms there, beginning in 2002, and served in two Democratic leadership positions: chair of the Democratic Congressional Campaign Committee from 2005 to 2007, and chair of the House Democratic Caucus, 2007 to 2009.

He, along with Axelrod and Biden, brought substantial political knowledge to the new administration. Rahm had worked on Paul Simon's (D-IL) first Senate campaign in 1984—Simon defeated three-term incumbent Charles Percy in a razor-thin upset. Emanuel parlayed that success into a position as national campaign director for the Democratic Campaign Committee in 1988. True to his Chicago roots, Rahm was senior adviser and chief fundraiser in Richard M. Daley's first campaign for mayor in 1989. Incidentally, Axelrod worked on both Simon's and Daley's successful campaigns, too. Emanuel directed Bill Clinton's finance committee in 1992, joined the Clinton White House staff first as assistant to the president for public affairs and then as senior adviser to the president for policy and strategy. Rahm could be ruthless when it came to politics. The public probably associated him with the story of his sending a dead fish in a box to a pollster who was late delivering his results. Rahm acquired the nickname "Rahmbo" the hard way—he earned it.[15]

As I have explained, however, he and I formed a perfectly civil, warm relationship in the House, a relationship that carried over into the Obama White House. For the first two years, until October 2010 when he resigned to run for mayor of Chicago, Rahm was my primary conduit to the White

House. We talked regularly on the phone and continued our practice of monthly dinners.

I tried not to abuse our friendship, however, and did not lean on Rahm for help very often. But I do recall one occasion when I did so. In April or May 2009, I planned to travel to Arizona to announce a $36 million light-rail project. Some unknown staffer from the Office of Management and Budget (OMB) attempted to halt the event, saying the project might not be eligible for stimulus money. My appeal to Peter Orszag, OMB's director, went nowhere. That's when I called Rahm. He took care of it.[16]

On November 20, 2008, President-elect Obama named David Axelrod as a senior adviser to his administration charged with communicating the substance of the president's agenda. I did not know him, but few would argue with Axelrod's qualifications for the job. A political science major at the University of Chicago, he had put his academic training to practical use over more than two decades as a political consultant. Like Emanuel, Axelrod first made a name for himself in 1984 when his campaign-management team defeated Chuck Percy's bid for reelection against challenger Paul Simon. Subsequently, his consulting firm enjoyed a fair amount of success at all levels of campaigns, working primarily for Democratic candidates. He met Barack Obama in the early 1990s, when Obama was a community organizer in Chicago. The two joined forces in Obama's successful run for U.S. Senate in 2004 and again in his presidential bid in 2008—Axelrod ran the candidate's media campaign.[17]

When it came to strategizing about selling the president's program, Axelrod was the go-to guy. During the first few months of the administration, he convened "the Wednesday Night Meeting," an invitation-only, two-hour session for a handful of advisers. I did not know about these sessions until they were reported by the press. I was never included even though DOT played a major role in the economic recovery effort at that time. Historians may see this as a harbinger of a governing style based on isolation rather than inclusion. In any event, I got the impression that no one carried more influence with the president on the politics of persuasion than Axelrod did. His White House office was the closest to the Oval Office, a not-so-subtle indication of his status. He reviewed every major speech the president delivered, offered advice on every major policy position the president took, and worked with Robert Gibbs, the president's spokesman, to create the message of the day. Axelrod had never worked in government, however, and had never run for elective office. In deciding how to approach Congress, those facts handicapped him. He and I never worked together even on major transportation initiatives. Maybe our policy portfolio simply did not interest him, or perhaps Axelrod failed to see the political advantages of promoting DOT's message on such broad administration initiatives as the stimulus.

Valerie Jarrett's influence with the Obamas differed from that of the others in the inner circle. As I later learned, when Barack and Michelle were young lawyers in Chicago, Jarrett had taken them under her wing; mentored them; introduced them to her wealthy, influential friends; and opened up access to the African-American community across the country. Well-connected in Chicago, Jarrett had served as planning commissioner in Richard M. Daley's mayoral administration while running a real estate company and serving on civic boards. Like Axelrod, she lacked the experience of serving in elective office. That apparently didn't matter to the Obamas. Jarrett got in on the ground floor when Barack and Michelle evaluated his chances of beating Hillary Clinton for the Democratic presidential nomination in July 2007. According to reports, Barack personally recruited Jarrett to serve on his campaign team. A Democrat close to the president said Jarrett would be "one of the four or five people in the room with him when decisions get made." As the First Lady explained to a reporter, "She knows the buttons, the soft spots, the history, the context."[18]

Jarrett, an attorney with degrees from Stanford and the University of Michigan, co-chaired the Obama transition. In that role, she helped the president choose his Cabinet, although I never interacted with her in that capacity, undoubtedly because of my long association with Rahm.

Her title in the new administration was senior adviser and assistant to the president for intergovernmental relations and public liaison (perhaps the longest staff title in the White House). In addition to counseling the president on a wide range of issues, she served as the point person for state and local officials and supervised the Office of Public Liaison. Some people in the White House found it difficult to work with her—she's smart and tough, and I figured that she was one of those advisers the president circled back to at the end of the day. But Valerie and I developed a good relationship over time because we both knew how helpful governors and mayors could be in implementing the economic recovery program. She appreciated that I paid attention to local officials, returned their calls, spent time with them, and followed through on their requests. Not every Cabinet secretary was so attentive.

Robert Gibbs's association with the Obamas began only in 2004. After stints working on Bill Clinton's 1992 presidential run and John Kerry's bid for the White House, Gibbs hooked up with David Plouffe and Axelrod on Obama's Senate campaign, serving as communications director. If 37-year-old Gibbs, the youngest of the inner circle, lacked longevity with Barack Obama, the 2008 campaign made up for it. The constant day-to-day interaction between the candidate and Gibbs gave the future press secretary an intimate knowledge of the new president. Gibbs told the *New York Times* in December 2008 that his role would include advising the president, not simply speaking for him, and Obama praised him for knowing "what is on the minds of the American people." Gibbs, he added, will be "invaluable in any discussion we're having about policy or politics. And beyond that, I trust him completely."[19] Gibbs and I never developed a working relationship, and frankly, I did not regret that.

Vice President Joe Biden's resume and qualifications are so well known that I don't intend to review them. Although Obama knew him as a colleague in the Senate, Biden was unique in the inner circle because he lacked the intimate relationship born of political experiences that the First Lady, Axelrod, Jarrett, and Gibbs shared with the president. Over time, however, Biden joined the others as one of the president's confidants. That proved especially important to me because President Obama put the vice president in charge of transportation policy. We traveled together about once a month during the early days as we visited sites throughout the country which had received DOT stimulus funds. He knew that state and local officials could move the economic recovery along with the right kind of help from the feds. More than that, the vice president respected the institutions of government, particularly Congress. He believed in the wisdom of talking to (and listening to) Republicans. Of all the outstanding people in the Obama administration, Joe Biden was the best example of someone who, in word and deed, practiced bipartisanship.

What did these folks in the inner circle have in common? They had unlimited access to the president. They enjoyed a personal relationship with him based on trust and, for the most part, lengthy service with him. With the exception of Emanuel and Biden, they had no experience with the nuts and bolts of politics on Capitol Hill. None of them knew transportation and infrastructure. Ultimately, I had an established relationship at the outset only with the chief of staff, not with any of the others.

Every president has had an inner circle of confidants, necessarily so, and President Obama was no exception. It became a parlor game in Washington to figure out who fell into that group, first in the campaign, and after the inauguration, in the administration. In April, *U.S. News and World Report* identified more than two dozen members.[20] I counted only six for domestic policy—the closer you were to these folks, the closer you were to the president. In special cases, of course, others joined the circle. For example, Larry Summers, head of the president's National Economic Council; Peter Orszag, director of the Office of Management and Budget; and Timothy Geithner, secretary of the treasury, counseled the president on economic matters. Hillary Clinton and Robert Gates, at state and defense, respectively, were the only two Cabinet secretaries to meet frequently and regularly with the president. David Plouffe, Obama's campaign manager, no doubt spoke with the president often even though he had no official appointment. But that core group of six functioned as the most intimate advisers for the duration of their service to the president.

There is a risk in relying too heavily and too exclusively on a small group for advice and counsel. As time passed, the president seemed to me to become more isolated, more insulated from those outside the in-group, less engaged with others. This unfortunate development accentuated the gap between the president's publicly articulated vision and what happened on the ground. It is arguably one reason why commentators have accused the president of losing touch with such issues as the rollout of Obamacare midway through his second term.

The Cabinet as Advisers to the President

Access to those in the inner circle represented one way to influence policy and strategy, and my opportunities seemed, quite frankly, limited. Cabinet meetings represented a second avenue. Entering office, I had expected (perhaps naïvely) Cabinet meetings to include a relatively free give and take in discussion, the president seeking advice from his appointees and building consensus for a decision. Despite my years working for House Republican leader Bob Michel, I had never attended a meeting of the Cabinet. I looked forward to joining the best minds in the administration in an ongoing conversation about the president's goals and how to accomplish them. That's not exactly what happened.

The president did not convene his first Cabinet meeting until April 20, 2009, three months after he had taken office and two months after the passage of the stimulus bill, arguably the most important bill promoted by the administration until the health care initiative. In other words, the Cabinet, as a group, had held no discussions about the stimulus. That would prove to be the rule rather than the exception.

Among the documents preserved in my personal files is an April 18 memo directed to the president from Chris Lu, assistant to the president and Cabinet secretary, and Liz Sears Smith, his deputy. It served as the briefing for that first Cabinet meeting. I don't recall how I ended up with a copy, but it is telling evidence about the structure and purpose of the president's meetings with us.

The memo identified the people who would attend and how their seats around the table were assigned, described the role of the press, allocated speaking roles very precisely, and included what was known as a "tick-tock," a minute-by-minute script for the event. According to the agenda, the press would leave the meeting following the president's welcome, and then our deliberations would begin. Here is the guidance given to the president when it came time for Cabinet members to speak:

> **YOU** [referring to the president] call on each member of the Cabinet to report (2 minutes each) on highlights from their depart-ments. You will call on the Cabinet in the order in which their departments were created, then you will call on the Cabinet rank officials, then the National Security Advisor, with the Chief of Staff concluding.[21]

In my two minutes, I focused on department initiatives that promoted economic recovery. For example, DOT had already approved more than 2,200 transportation projects and allocated more than $7.3 billion of the $48.1 billion in funding that was provided to my department under the American Recovery and Reinvestment Act. Those projects, I reported, would generate at least 37,000 new jobs.[22] We spent over an hour listening to other Cabinet secretaries make similar reports, one right after the other. The president did not question any of us, and we did not question each other. No discussion, period.

The president met briefly with reporters following the meeting. He told them that he had delivered three messages to us. First, he was proud of the work we had done and "of the talent, the diversity, and the work ethic of this team." Second, in the president's words, "we have had to take some extraordinary steps" in order to shore up the financial system and to deal with the economic crisis. Finally, he charged us with wringing out more efficiencies in our departments in order save money and to "send a signal that we are serious about changing how government operates." He told the press that we had to identify at least $100 million in additional cuts to our administrative budgets. The president answered a single question and ended the session at 1:24 p.m.[23]

I recount this first Cabinet meeting to make these points: (1) the meetings were much more highly scripted than I had anticipated; (2) the opportunity to give candid advice to the president was, frankly, nil; (3) the meetings suggested to me how isolated the president was from those who did not fall within his inner circle; and (4) we did not have the opportunity at any point in the meeting to discuss the "extraordinary steps" we were supposed to take—we accepted the president's directive without conversation.

I don't know whether other presidents have operated in this fashion, although I have a hard time believing that Lyndon Johnson did so. During my time in the Obama administration, I never attended a Cabinet meeting during which a meaningful decision was reached about important issues. It was all for show. As far as I could tell, our discussions changed not a single mind on policy questions or on administration strategy. The meetings simply allowed the president to announce that he had consulted his Cabinet about decisions he and his advisers had already made.

The administration's lack of interest in using the Cabinet disappointed and surprised me. In sounding the need for change in Washington, candidate Obama had famously referred to Abraham Lincoln's "team of rivals," a concept made popular by historian Doris Kearns Goodwin in her book by that name about the Lincoln Cabinet, as a model for his Cabinet. He told *Time* magazine's Joe Klein that as president he would surround himself with "people who are continually pushing me out of my comfort zone." He admired Lincoln's approach: "I don't want to have people who just agree with me."[24] In another interview with Klein, Obama said

> I think that the one thing I have become pretty confident about is being able to tap into the smartest people on any subject and to

draw together a lot of contrary or contradictory perspectives. And push people's arguments against each other, ask the right questions and figure out a least a framework for solving problems.[25]

Obama's statements, in the context of changing the way Washington worked, suggested to me the promise of a better use of the Cabinet than he made during my tenure in it. What happened? Scholars and pundits have pointed to several possible explanations. They range from the idea that presidents have not used Cabinets for advice since the 1950s to the claim that personal relationships between a secretary and the president count for more than a position in the Cabinet per se. Still others make the point that government has grown so large that with 15 Cabinet posts, it's no wonder presidents rely on a smaller group of advisers. For many decisions, this line of thinking goes, the president can ill afford to consume precious time running the bureaucratic gauntlet —better to decide quickly.

These reasons may make sense, but they raise this question: What prevents a new president from using the Cabinet more effectively? Simply because past presidents have not employed the Cabinet in the ways I suggest does not mean that a president is forbidden from doing so. For a chief executive who campaigned on changing the way government functions, President Obama did not use the talent in his Cabinet to seek broader judgment about his policies and strategy. That became obvious to me during congressional consideration of the administration's economic stimulus package as the president's first term began. The same held true during later efforts to reform transportation policy.

NOTES

1. "Conference Call," December 22, 2008, RLP-DOT, f. Confirmation (1).
2. "Ray LaHood Confirmation Hearing," *W[ashington] P[ost] Politics*, January 21, 2009, RLP-Memoir, f. DOT.
3. Ibid.
4. *Peoria Journal Star*, January 3, 2009, RLP-DOT, f. Clippings.
5. Associated Press, "Illinois Sen. Barack Obama's Announcement Speech," February 10, 2007, RLP-Memoir, f. DOT.
6. "Election Night Victory Speech," Grant Park, Chicago, November 4, 2008, RLP-Memoir, f. DOT.
7. CBS News/*New York Times* Poll, October 25–29, 2008, PollingReport.com, RLP-Memoir, f. DOT.
8. Wes Allison and Bill Adair, "Can Obama Keep Promise of Bipartisanship?" *Tampa Bay Times*, November 5, 2008, RLP-Memoir, f. DOT.
9. Jeff Zeleny, "Initial Steps by Obama Suggest a Bipartisan Flair," *NYT*, November 24, 2008, RLP-Memoir, f. DOT.
10. Zeleny, "Initial Steps."
11. Mark Z. Barabak, "Obama Enjoys Strong Support," *Los Angeles Times*, December 10, 2008, RLP-Memoir, f. DOT.
12. POTUS, "Remarks at a Caterpillar Plant in East Peoria, Illinois," February 12, 2008, *PPP*, RLP-Memoir, f. DOT. Bipartisanship.
13. RL, "Address to Graduates," Loras College Commencement, May 22, 2012, RL Information File, DCC.
14. Mark Leibovich, "Between Obama and the Press," *NYT*, December 21, 2008, RLP-Memoir, f. DOT.
15. "Rahm Emanuel," *Politico*, n.d.; "Rahm Israel Emanuel," *Biography Channel* website, n.d.; and Mark Jannot, "A Rahm for the Money," *Chicago Magazine*, August 1992. All in RLP-Memoir, f. DOT. Inner Circle.
16. Leibovich, "G.O.P. Résumé, Cabinet Post, Knack for Odd Jobs," *NYT*, May 5, 2009, RLP-Memoir, f. DOT.
17. Zeleny, "President's Political Protector Is Ever Close at Hand," *NYT*, March 9, 2009, and "David Axelrod," *Biography Channel* website, n.d., RLP-Memoir, f. DOT. Inner Circle.
18. Jodi Kantor, "An Old Hometown Mentor, Still at Obama's Side," *NYT*, November 24, 2008; and Kantor, "Obama Hires Jarrett for Senior Role," *NYT*, November 14, 2008, RLP-Memoir, f. DOT. Inner Circle.

19. Leibovich, "Between Obama and the Press," *NYT*, December 21, 2008, RLP-Memoir, f. DOT.
20. *U.S. News and World Report*, "Obama's Inner Circle: What Do You Think?" April 1, 2009, http://www.usnews.com/news/obama/articles/2009/04/01 /obamas-inner-circle-what-do-you-think.
21. "Cabinet Meeting," April 18, 2009, RLP-DOT, f. Cabinet Meetings, 2009.
22. "Talking Points for Secretary LaHood," April 20, 2009, RLP-DOT, f. Cabinet Meetings, 2009.
23. White House, Office of the Press Secretary, "Remarks by the President after Meeting with the Cabinet," April 20, 2009, RLP-Memoir, f. DOT.
24. Albert R. Hunt, "Why Doesn't Obama Use His Cabinet More," Bloomberg, February 10, 2013, and Todd Purdum, "Team of Mascots," *Vanity Fair*, July 2012, RLP-Memoir, f. DOT. Inner Circle.
25. Joe Klein, "The Full Obama Interview," Time.com, October 23, 2008, RLP-Memoir, f. DOT. Inner Circle.

CHAPTER 12

THE STIMULUS PACKAGE
AND WORKING THE HILL

Democrats were flying high in January 2009. In addition to welcoming one of their own to the White House, the first in eight years and only the second since 1981, Democrats outnumbered Republicans in the Senate 57 to 41 (two independents caucused with the Democrats). They prevailed over Republicans in the House, too, 257 to 178. Democrats controlled all the levers of power in the nation's capital.

Despite the deepening economic recession, the mood of the country favored the governing party. Associated Press–GfK Roper Public Affairs & Media surveyed 1,000 adults immediately after the November election. After reminding respondents that Democrats would control the House, the Senate, and the presidency, the polling firm asked respondents whether it was "good for the country, bad for the country, or [did] not really make any difference" that one party controlled all three. Forty-two percent said it was good for the country, 34 percent said bad, and 20 percent said "no difference."[1] A CNN/Opinion Research Corporation Poll confirmed the impression. In response to the same question, 59 percent said Democratic control would be good for the country; only 38 percent replied to the contrary.[2]

Those were heady times for Democrats. And they were determined to make the most of it. Senate majority leader Harry Reid (D-NV) opened the Senate on January 6. He pointed to Barack Obama's upcoming inauguration to say that Democrats, having expanded their numbers in the Senate, were prepared to deliver "the change that our country desperately needs." Reid continued:

> We're grateful to begin anew with a far more robust Democratic majority. But both parties learned an important lesson over the past two years. When we allow ourselves to retreat into the tired, well-worn trenches of partisanship, when we fail to reach for common ground, when we're unable in the words of President-Elect Obama, "to disagree without being disagreeable," we diminish our ability to accomplish real change.[3]

Immediately following her election as Speaker of the House, Nancy Pelosi addressed the chamber in remarks she entitled "Our Nation Needs Action and We Need Action Now," a phrase she repeated four times during her comments. As Reid had in the Senate, the Speaker sounded a bipartisan note when she pledged to "look forward, not backward; we will join hands, not point fingers; we will rise to the challenge, recognizing that our love of country is stronger than any issue which may divide us." Then, fully aware of the power her party wielded, the Speaker said, "Together, with our new President, we as a Congress and as a country must fulfill the rest of America's promise. All of that promise will not be redeemed quickly or easily. But it must be pursued urgently—with spirited debate, and without partisan deadlock or delay."[4]

The two Democratic leaders in Congress said the right words when they promised both action to meet the challenges facing the nation and commitment to a bipartisan approach. My optimism was tempered only by the 14 years I had spent in the House trying to restore civility to the chamber. In the case of the Speaker, for example, I had little doubt that she would readily sacrifice bipartisanship for "action." Of course, now I was part of her team, the Democratic administration's team. Time would tell whether my role as ambassador to congressional Republicans would run afoul of the demand for action.

THE PELOSI GAMBLE

Nancy Pelosi had represented California's 12th district since her first election to the House in 1987. She hailed from one of the safest Democratic districts in the country, one that included San Francisco. Her party had held the seat since 1949, and Pelosi had never faced a serious reelection threat. In 2002, her colleagues selected Pelosi to lead the Democrats in the House as minority leader—she preferred the title "Democratic Leader." She replaced Dick Gephardt of Missouri, who relinquished the post after Democrats failed for the fourth time during his tenure to regain control of the House. As the spokesperson for the minority during Republican president George W. Bush's administration, Pelosi had proved a divisive figure. "There is no question that the Democratic Party is the party of the public interest," she said at the time. "A big difference with the Republicans is they are the party of special interests; we have to make that clear to the American people."[5]

She was elected Speaker of the House in 2007, the first woman, the first Californian, and the first Italian American to serve in that position. Incidentally, Rahm Emanuel, then the incoming chair of the House Democratic Caucus and future chief of staff to President Obama, nominated her for the post. House Democrats had grown restive after 12 years of Republican control of the body, compounded by six years with George W. Bush in the White House. Democrats wanted to replace wrong-headed, in their view, Republican policies with their own on health care, fiscal policy, the environment, gay rights, and so on. Theirs was a liberal agenda; Pelosi was unabashedly liberal. House Democrats sought a strong leader; they found one in Pelosi.

She had never been shy about her ambitions. Before the 2006 midterm elections, for example, Pelosi had announced that if she were elected Speaker, her caucus would push through a series of bills during the first 100 hours of the 110th Congress—she called the plan "Six for '06." In announcing her intentions, Pelosi said that 100 hours would be enough time to begin to "drain the swamp" after more than a decade of Republican rule.[6] Democrats swept those midterms and elected her Speaker for the 110th Congress. By January 18, 2007, only 14 days after Congress convened, the House had passed every one of Pelosi's measures as they had been submitted. The Democratic majority voted to raise the federal minimum wage, allow federal funding of embryonic stem cell research, implement 9/11 Commission recommendations, cut tax breaks for big oil companies, allow Medicare to negotiate price discounts on drugs, and cut student-loan interest rates. As I watched the Speaker work her magic, I was reminded of my first few months in Congress as Newt Gingrich had rammed through the Contract with America. Pelosi kept the 233 House Democrats, a diverse bunch, together for some very tough votes. Most of the bills, however, stalled in the Senate. Nancy Pelosi was (and is) experienced, smart, shrewd, intensely partisan, opportunistic, and ambitious.

It was clear from the outset of the Obama administration that the Speaker had big plans and wielded considerable power both by force of personality and by virtue of her office. With Democrats firmly in control of the White House, the Senate, and the House, I am sure she believed she could push through a legislative program that had been blocked by President Bush and the Senate since 2007. Once the Senate became filibuster-proof in the spring, Republicans had no capacity to thwart legislation supported by unified Hill Democrats. The Speaker was not content to march to the White House drum, either. She had called out the president on subjects ranging from the auto-industry bailout to plans to investigate the recently retired Bush administration.

I have wondered whether Pelosi's new status as only the second-most important Democrat in town had anything to do with her approach to legislating on behalf of the administration. She struck the right tone in her public remarks: "It is for me thrilling to be Speaker with a Democrat in the White House. This is what we have worked for for such a long time," she said in an interview with the *New York Times*. "I feel in a stronger position now. For me, my responsibility as Speaker is enormously enhanced by a president whose vision I respect and whose agenda I will help stamp."[7] All well and good, but in hindsight those last six words stand out. Not comfortable as second fiddle, the Speaker may have intended to function as much more than the White House's messenger—at least, that was my read.

Sometime in January, although I have no hard evidence of it, I believe Obama's inner circle signed off on the Speaker's strategy for passing legislation in the House: ignore the Republicans; don't negotiate with them; Democrats have the votes to pass bills without their help. I did not participate in whatever discussions took place, but I suspect that Rahm Emanuel, who had a very close relationship with the Speaker, endorsed this way of handling the president's legislative program. For his part, the president, new to the office and unseasoned in the job, may have ignored his natural inclination to work both sides of the aisle out of deference to Pelosi. Admittedly, I am speculating. But no other explanation so well fits the events as they unfolded over the next two years.

The White House left the stimulus bill, its first consequential legislation, to the Speaker. The president provided some general guidance, but Pelosi and her allies wrote the stimulus legislation. The administration did not draft a proposal and send it to the Hill. Instead, Pelosi combined several legislative components produced by a handful of House committees, mostly headed by her allies. That process produced a bill that departed from the president's wishes in several respects. For example, although the president had said he preferred that 40 percent of the stimulus bill comprise tax cuts, Pelosi eventually cut a deal that limited that provision to just a third.[8] If the devil is in the details, Nancy Pelosi took care of the details.

By granting control of the substance and approach to the legislation to the Speaker, the president missed a prime opportunity to transform the way government worked in Washington. Instead, conventional politics ruled.

THE STIMULUS PACKAGE

The deal with Pelosi was struck without my knowledge and without a hearing at the Cabinet, which had not even met, so I approached my first opportunity to lend a bipartisan assist to the new administration in the dark. That opportunity came on January 27, when the president visited Capitol Hill to discuss his plans for economic stimulus legislation with House Republicans. For over a year, the nation's economy had been stalled. Almost a month after the November elections, the National Bureau of Economic Research announced that the economy had entered recession nearly a year earlier, in December 2007. President George W. Bush had grappled with the enormous challenge in different ways, using both monetary and budgetary policies. He signed the Economic Stimulus Act of 2008 into law on February 13, 2008, a bill I had supported as a House member. Two hundred sixteen Democrats voted for the bill, as did 169 Republicans, a show of substantial bipartisan support.

As the economic crisis worsened, Congress enacted and President Bush signed a series of measures, including the Emergency Economic Stabilization Act. This act created the infamous Troubled Assets Relief Program (TARP), which authorized the Treasury Department to buy up to $700 billion in troubled assets from financial institutions. The bill passed the House with 221 Democratic votes and 47 Republican votes, including mine. Again, Congress had acted in bipartisan fashion.

At the beginning of the 111th Congress, President Obama and congressional leaders made action on an economic recovery bill a top priority.

The American Recovery and Reinvestment Act of 2009 (ARRA), H.R. 1, was introduced on January 26, 2009, by David Obey (D-WI), chair of the House Appropriations Committee. House and Senate action on what was known as the stimulus bill came quickly. The House began consideration of H.R. 1 on January 27 and passed the bill on January 28 in a vote of 244–188. All but 11 Democrats voted for the bill, and 177 Republicans voted against it (one Republican did not vote). Bipartisan support for legislation to buck up the economy had disappeared almost overnight.

Senate consideration of H.R. 1 occurred over eight days, beginning on February 2 and ending with Senate passage on February 10 by a vote of 61–37 (with one not voting). All the Democrats voted in favor, joined by only three Republicans. That day, the House and Senate agreed to hold a conference on the bill and appointed the conferees.

The House and Senate versions of H.R. 1 were roughly comparable in scope, but there were significant differences that had to be resolved. The House-passed version would have increased the deficit by nearly $820 billion over 10 years, according to the Congressional Budget Office. In contrast, the Senate's version would have increased the deficit by about $838 billion over the same period, a pretty small difference in the scheme of things, but a difference that had to be reconciled.

After the conferees completed their negotiations, they filed their conference report on February 12. Their compromises reduced the overall impact of the bill on the deficit to $787 billion, well below the House and Senate levels. House Democrats unveiled this final version of the stimulus bill by posting it online late Thursday night, February 12. On Friday the 13th, the House approved the $787 billion package, 246–183, without a single Republican vote. Even Joe Cao (R-LA), who had sided with Democrats on an earlier vote, joined his party. Later that day, the Senate agreed to the conference report by a vote of 60–38. Every Senate Democrat and independent voted for the bill, joined by just three Republicans. The president signed H.R. 1 into law on February 17. If it was action the administration wanted, action was what it got—an impressive performance by the Democrats, but at what political cost?

ARRA was a relatively lengthy and complex act, amounting to just over 1,400 pages. The almost $800 billion it authorized would boost the economy through extensive discretionary spending, mandatory spending, and revenue provisions. The administration estimated that the act would save or create some 3.5 million jobs. The legislation funded existing and a few new programs in the 15 Cabinet-level departments and 11 independent agencies. Some of the funds were to be distributed to states, localities, other entities, and individuals though a combination of formula and competitive grants and direct assistance. In addition to new spending and tax provisions, the bill created new policies regarding unemployment compensation, health insurance, health information technology, broadband communications, and energy, among others.[9]

Behind the rapid but formal legislative process of ARRA lies the backstory of a new administration failing to gain Republican support for landmark legislation. The White House's efforts at bipartisanship proved tepid and ineffective, the result of the Speaker's ill-advised strategy. When the president visited Capitol Hill on January 27 just as the House began debate on H.R. 1, he brought along a half-dozen people. I was one of them. We were not briefed ahead of time about what the president might say or whether we were to participate. At the time, I thought this was odd but chalked it up to the staff's inexperience and to the frenetic pace of activity at the White House. The session itself was cordial enough. We gathered in the Capitol. I recall that virtually every Republican House member attended. The meeting was closed to the press. I sat in the front row and listened as the president spoke for about 20 or 30 minutes. His main message was the urgency of the economic situation, that the American people expected and deserved action, which he described as a recovery package that put people back to work, created investments in energy independence, provided an effective health care system and an education system that worked, and rebuilt the nation's infrastructure.

Even though the administration had decided to defer to the Speaker, I believe the president genuinely hoped to hear constructive suggestions from the House Republicans, ideas he could then weave into the stimulus legislation in order to attract Republican votes. He took a few questions, but it was clear to me that the folks in the room were not in a mood to respond to his appeal. They made it clear that Democrats had shut them out, that the House was not following regular order, and that committees had not had a chance to consider the package. The president responded by asking that House Republicans keep politics to a minimum. As he told reporters after the meeting, "There are some legitimate philosophical differences with parts of my plan that Republicans have, and I respect that." "I don't expect a hundred percent agreement from my Republican colleagues," he continued, "but I do hope that we can all put politics aside and do the American people's business right now."[10] In remarks directed at the Speaker, however, Congressman Scott Garrett (R-NJ) told reporters upon leaving the meeting, "We'd encourage the House leadership to emulate the President in his outreach to our party."[11]

We did not know it at the time, but Minority Leader Boehner had met with about three-quarters of the rank-and-file Republicans earlier in the day to urge them to vote against the House version of the stimulus package when it came up the next day, no matter what the president said. One news source called Boehner's message "a harsh welcome to partisan politics for a president who is making a dramatic gesture" in coming to the Hill to meet with Republicans. A press aide to the minority leader told ABC News, "While we certainly appreciate the willingness of the President to come to Capitol Hill, the problem remains with Congressional Democrats who are moving forward with little regard toward improving the bill. Unless the Speaker agrees to make changes, then congressional Democrats should not count on our support." An ABC blog post reported a message from inside the conference meeting as the Republicans discussed how the president could win GOP House support —focus the stimulus spending on infrastructure investment and tax relief. "If Mr. Obama can't convince House Democrats to cut spending," this lawmaker said in his leak to the press, "then the President will have less credibility on fiscal responsibility in the future. If he cuts this back, he will have a huge win." The same source said there was widespread belief that Republican support for the bill had dwindled after Pelosi's appearance on *This Week with George Stephanopoulos* the preceding Sunday, when she defended some of the bill's spending measures, including hundreds of millions of dollars on contraception and on coupons to help people convert to digital television.[12]

I doubt that anyone in the White House, including the president, sought to include coupons for digital TV in the stimulus package. For some reason, however, the Speaker defended them. It was just another example of her independence from the White House, although less substantive than her deal on the tax cuts.

The White House may have been content to let the Speaker control the action in the House based on the assurance that Democrats had the votes to pass H.R. 1. That did not, however, eliminate the desirability of attracting at least some Republican support. Doing so would lend a bipartisan cast to the legislation, allow the president to fulfill his pledge to play nicely with Republicans, and keep the door open to two-party cooperation down the road. To that end, and after the president's visit to Capitol Hill, Rahm recruited me to contact between 10 and 15 of my former colleagues to gain their support for the stimulus package. He and I selected mostly moderates, Tuesday Group types, such as Peter King (NY), Charlie Dent (PA), Mark Kirk (IL), Frank LoBiondo (NJ), and Rodney Frelinghuysen (NJ).[13] I heard the same complaint through my first six or seven calls: "Democrats just shut us out of the process"; "Pelosi warned her troops to stay away from us"; "Obama promised an open, bipartisan process—this has been a joke"; "Pelosi wants to jam this down our throats"; "Why should we vote for a bill we haven't even seen?" I called Rahm and said, "This is mission impossible." I stopped making calls. I did not expect Republicans to roll over and accept the president's ambitious economic recovery agenda whole cloth. But the strength of feeling against the president had taken me aback. The bitterness on the part of House Republicans was unmistakable.

It came as no surprise to me when the House vote tally showed zero Republican support. "Obviously, I wasn't very persuasive," I said at the time, "since I wasn't able to persuade anyone to vote for it."[14] Because Pelosi had failed to live up to the president's bipartisan mantra and refused to bargain with Republicans, no one from my party was willing to support the final bill. At a press conference during House action, a reporter asked the Speaker, "Is it your fault in some ways that Barack Obama's first vote was so partisan and not bipartisan?" "I didn't come here to be partisan. I didn't come here to be bipartisan," she replied. "I came here, as did my colleagues, to be nonpartisan, to work for the American people, to do what is in their interest."[15] I guess the Speaker's definition of *nonpartisan* differed from mine.

The lesson? That neither civility nor bipartisanship would come easily as the new administration took office. House Republicans deserve a fair amount of blame for the lockstep vote on stimulus. Boehner showed little willingness to meet the president halfway, or any way. Fault lies with the administration, too. The judgment to hand over decision making and legislative strategizing to Pelosi so early in the term on so critical a bill crippled efforts at bipartisanship on major policy initiatives for the next two years. The price we paid was incalculable. Her strategy nearly killed my influence with House Republicans. Now I was part of an administration that had shut them out. Once they had been excluded from the stimulus negotiations, and later from health care, they said to hell with Obama, and my value as a Republican in a Democratic administration diminished markedly. Moreover, the White House had reached this decision without consulting me, the person they had selected to promote bipartisanship. The strategy likewise betrayed the sentiment expressed by the president when he announced my appointment (and that of others, too) to his Cabinet in December—that together we would help craft what he had termed a "21st-Century Economic Recovery Plan." No. We were pointedly excluded.

The administration could have done this all differently. Instead of deferring to the Speaker, the president could have said to his inner circle, "I'm going to pick up the phone and talk to Republicans. I am going to tell the Speaker that I don't like this strategy of closing Republicans off. That's not what I campaigned on." Given his own instincts (and common sense), he should have told Pelosi before the inauguration, "That's not how we're going to operate." That would have been my advice, had I been asked. Given the solid bipartisan votes cast on the Economic Stimulus Act of 2008 and the Emergency Economic Stabilization Act during the Bush years, I believe the possibility of bipartisan support for the Obama plan was real.

In the short term, the administration's gamble had worked. Congressional Democrats, supported by the White House, muscled through the stimulus package on the strength of Democrats' votes alone.

WORKING THE HILL PART 2

The president did achieve more success attracting Republican support for some of his priorities. But that support came in fits and starts, and I do not believe the White House ever committed fully to a genuine bipartisan approach to policy making, despite the president's words to the contrary. Nor do I believe that House Republicans would have been wildly receptive following their experience with the stimulus.

With the first economic recovery battle behind us, the administration turned its attention to health care reform. I will leave it to future historians to account for this signature accomplishment in President Obama's first term. My purpose is to suggest that because the White House game plan still centered on Speaker Pelosi's winner-take-all approach, strong bipartisan support, which was what the president said repeatedly that he wanted, was a pipe dream.

President Obama announced his intention to push for health care reform in a wide-ranging address before a joint session of Congress on February 24, 2009, just two weeks after the stimulus vote. His 6,000-word speech included fewer than 500 words devoted to health care, but they signaled the beginning of a concerted effort to remake medical care in this country. "I suffer no illusions that this will be an easy process," the president said:

> Once again, it will be hard. But I also know that nearly a century after Teddy Roosevelt first called for reform, the cost of our health care has weighed down our economy and our conscience long enough. So let there be no doubt: Health care reform cannot wait, it must not wait, and it will not wait another year.[16]

The legislative process for the Patient Protection and Affordable Care Act played out over the next 12 months, from the first White House health care summit on March 5, 2009, to the bill-signing ceremony on March 23, 2010. Debate over the particulars of reform quickly took on a partisan dimension as Republicans as a bloc opposed the individual-mandate component of the Democratic package, among many other provisions. Partisan divisiveness grew to a point I had not seen since the Clinton impeachment and the contested results of the 2000 presidential election. The acrimonious climate deteriorated throughout the process both within and outside the halls of government—the tea party movement probably found its voice as a result of the administration's health care proposal.

Buffeted by these partisan voices in both the capital and the countryside, President Obama tried to cool passions in yet another address before a joint session of Congress in September. Referring to the past several months, he said, "we've seen Washington at its best and at its worst. We've seen many in this Chamber work tirelessly for the better part of this year to offer thoughtful ideas about how to achieve reform." However, he also remarked that:

> What we've also seen in these last months is the same partisan spectacle that only hardens the disdain many Americans have

towards their own Government. Instead of honest debate, we've seen scare tactics. Some have dug into unyielding ideological camps that offer no hope of compromise. Too many have used this as an opportunity to score short-term political points, even if it robs the country of our opportunity to solve a long-term challenge. And out of this blizzard of charges and countercharges, confusion has reigned.

He acknowledged that the easy route "would be to kick the can further down the road," to defer reform one more year or one more election or one more term. "But that is not what the moment calls for.... I still believe that we can act when it's hard. I still believe we can replace acrimony with civility and gridlock with progress.... That is our calling. That is our character."[17] Ironically, it was during this address that Representative Joe Wilson, a Republican from South Carolina, famously shouted "You lie!" as the president spoke.

I approached my bipartisan bridge-building on behalf of the president's health care reform plan by relying on personal friendships established over the years. My approach was unfailingly soft-sell—my job wasn't to twist arms. Using the House gym, or Members' Wellness Center as it is formally known, was part of my strategy. I worked out on a treadmill for about an hour three times a week in SB-322 in the subbasement of the Rayburn House Office Building. I had chaired an informal committee that oversaw gym operations when I was a House member, so I knew how important it was to preserve the gym as a sanctuary—no staff, no press, nobody taking notes. The civility initiative I had led in the House singled out the gym as a place to build relationships and to get beyond partisan differences. As former members of the House, Rahm Emanuel and I enjoyed gym privileges. The informality of the place lent itself to my style of persuasion. I don't know how many times House members approached me there about transportation projects in their districts, for example. That gave me a leg up during the health care deliberations, too. When members talked with me about their road projects, I took their temperature on health care. After a year of these soundings, I had a pretty good idea about the extent of bipartisan support.

Shortly after the president's September appeal, I estimated that as many as 10 House Republicans might support final passage of the bill. That didn't sound like a lot, but it was worth the effort because it would give the president some bipartisan cover in the event that no Senate Republican could be persuaded to vote for the bill.

I was optimistic about my chances because I had pulled in eight crucial Republican votes for the president's climate-change bill earlier in the year. The main provision of the controversial American Clean Energy and Security Act (ACESA) called for a cap-and-trade system to regulate greenhouse gas emissions. We knew that vote would be close because many Democrats, especially those from areas dependent on coal for electricity or from districts with a large number of manufacturing jobs, might vote against the bill. But on June 26, 2009, ACESA passed, 219–212. Without those eight Republican votes, the bill would have failed. I don't pretend to claim all the credit, although the president called to thank me, and Rahm referred to me as "his secret weapon." I did feel a sense of accomplishment, however. As I confided to my journal, "Finally, I was able to use relationships with Republican colleagues to help pass major legislation."[18]

When push came to shove on the health care bill, I hoped to repeat the success I had enjoyed with climate-change legislation. Again, my effectiveness would depend on personal relationships. I recall one specific example involving colleagues from my home state. As the day neared for the expected final vote on the Patient Protection and Affordable Care Act in March 2010, four Illinois Democrats had refused to commit to vote for the bill: Melissa Bean, Jerry Costello, Bill Foster, and Deborah Halvorson. A fifth, Dan Lipinski, had pledged to vote no if the measure provided funding for abortions. These were members of the president's own party, and he had visited Capitol Hill personally to lobby them. Yet they refused to budge, and Rahm asked me to see what I could do with my fellow

Illinoisans. He got a kick out of my assignment and teased me publicly at an awards dinner, saying to the audience I should not stay out too late, "because he still has five calls to make."[19] And I made those calls.[20]

Bean wanted more cost-containment measures in the bill and refused to commit without reading the final version. Foster, whom I knew better, told me the same thing—he intended to study the entire 2,407-page Senate-passed bill and the 153 pages of modifications sought by the House Democrats before deciding. I did not get a pledge from him. Halvorson refused to announce her position. I visited Lipinski in his office but left unsure that he would change his mind.

Jerry Costello proved a more promising target. He was the senior Democrat in the Illinois congressional delegation, having represented a downstate district since his first election in 1988. We had served together on the House Transportation Committee. In fact, the press had identified Costello as a possible candidate for secretary of transportation late in 2008. He had served on the National Leadership Committee of then senator Obama's National Catholic Advisory Council during his 2008 election campaign, so the president knew him personally. Costello was getting a lot of heat from the Catholic churches in his district, which warned him that a yes vote would be a "bad" vote.

It made perfect sense for me to contact Jerry Costello because of our shared service, even though we were of different parties. A centrist Democrat, Costello had a strong right-to-life record, as did I. I called him two or three times on the health care reform bill to make this argument: "Look, you're the senior Democrat from the president's home state. What message does it send to other Democrats if you vote against him?" But I still had no firm commitment. I called Rahm: "I think Costello is gettable. Why don't you ask the president to invite him to the White House?" The president did invite Costello and me to the Oval Office for a final pitch—never underestimate the power of a meeting in the Oval Office. President Obama greeted us warmly when we arrived, and the three of us sat down—no staff joined us until later, when Rahm Emanuel stepped in. The president was at his best, asking Costello about his family before getting down to business. The two of them talked about the upcoming vote for about 30 minutes. I sat quietly—I don't think I said a single word after the initial pleasantries. Costello did not make a commitment during the session, but President Obama had made the best case possible.

The White House had not given up completely on Republicans, either, as the process wound down, but the Speaker was of no help. With about a month left before the final vote on the health care bill, Pelosi appeared on CNN's *State of the Union with Candy Crowley*. The show opened with a video clip of Pelosi saying, "The bill can be bipartisan, even though the votes might not be bipartisan." Crowley capsulized the prerecorded clip this way: "House Speaker Nancy Pelosi on the way forward as Democrats try to pass health care reform without Republicans."[21] I did not get the Speaker's definition of *nonpartisan* in March 2009, but I did understand her meaning of *bipartisan* now. In fact, I agreed. There were several Republican ideas in the bill, including granting Americans the ability to buy health insurance across state lines, among other provisions. But my former Republican colleagues interpreted her remarks in the most negative fashion possible, as an affront to the party.

In a last-ditch effort to parlay whatever influence I had with House Republicans into votes, I went public with an op-ed in the *Chicago Tribune* on March 14, a week before the vote. I titled the piece, perhaps optimistically, "Beyond Politics: Why Republicans Should Support Health Care Reform." I pointed out that I had been a Republican all my life, that I still considered myself a fiscal conservative and an advocate for a smart but restrained government. Most people wouldn't expect me to advocate for comprehensive health care reform, I admitted, but I believed that there was "no bigger issue to solve and no better chance to solve it than now." If I were still a member of Congress, I wrote, "I would proudly vote for the bill that President Barack Obama is championing," and I would urge my colleagues to do the same, "not because I don't believe in fiscal discipline, but because I do."

I proceeded to describe the primary features of the bill and to plead that denying people access to the best health care system in the world "is morally reprehensible." I singled out three Republican ideas that had found their way into the bill before echoing Speaker Pelosi: "While the ultimate vote on health care may not be bipartisan, the ultimate bill certainly is." I closed with these words: "During my time in Congress, I was known for reaching across the aisle. I did it not for the sake of bipartisanship alone, but in order to get important things done." And I reminded my former colleagues that they had "the opportunity to change the lives of their friends and neighbors for the better by voting for health care reform."[22]

The Patient Protection and Affordable Care Act, now also known as Obamacare, passed in the House by a vote of 219 to 212. All 219 votes were cast by Democrats—Bean, Costello, Foster, and Halvorson among them. Of the five we had sought to persuade, only Lipinski held out. Republicans, acting as a bloc, provided 178 of the votes opposed. So much for bipartisanship.

The Saturday after the vote, while I was back home in Illinois, my cell phone rang. The voice on the other end said, "Please hold for the president." The president came on the line to thank me for my efforts on the health care bill and mentioned Costello's vote specifically. Before he ended the call, he invited me to play golf later that day. Of course, he was in Washington, and I was in Peoria.

NOTES

1. AP-GfK Poll, November 6–10, 2008, PollingReport.com, RLP-Memoir, f. DOT. Obamacare.
2. CNN/Opinion Research Corporation Poll, November 6–9, 2008, PollingReport.com, RLP-Memoir, f. DOT.
3. Cong. Rec., S7 (January 6, 2009), RLP-Memoir, f. DOT.
4. Nancy Pelosi, "Our Nation Needs Action and We Need Action Now," January 6, 2009, *Democratic Leader Nancy Pelosi News Room*, RLP-Memoir, f. DOT. American Recovery and Reinvestment Act (ARRA).
5. Carl Hulse, "The 2002 Election: The Democrats: Pelosi Says She's Secured Votes to Be House Democrats' Leader," *NYT*, November 9, 2002, RLP-Memoir, f. DOT. Pelosi Gamble.
6. David Espo, "Pelosi Says She Would Drain GOP 'Swamp,'" *Washington Post*, October 6, 2006, RLP-Memoir, f. DOT. Pelosi Gamble.
7. Carl Hulse, "Speaker Makes Room for New No. 1 Democrat," *NYT*, January 5, 2009, RLP-Memoir, f. DOT. Pelosi Gamble.
8. Jay Newton-Small, "Obama vs. Pelosi: Can the President Work with the Democrats?" *Time*, February 4, 2009, RLP-Memoir, f. DOT. Pelosi Gamble.
9. Congressional Research Service, "American Recovery and Reinvestment Act of 2009 (P.L. 111-5): Summary and Legislative History," April 20, 2009, R40537, RLP-Memoir, f. DOT. ARRA.
10. POTUS, "Remarks Following a Meeting with the House Republican Conference," January 27, 2009, *PPP*, RLP-Memoir, f. DOT. ARRA.
11. Newton-Small, "Obama vs. Pelosi."
12. Caitlin Taylor, "Boehner: GOPers Should Vote No on Stimulus," ABC News *The Note*, January 27, 2009, RLP-Memoir, f. DOT. ARRA.
13. I contacted three Republican moderates in the Senate, too—Susan Collins and Olympia Snow of Maine, and Pennsylvania's Arlen Specter. They pledged to support the Senate's version of the stimulus bill.
14. Josh Kraushaar, "LaHood Pushes for GOP Support," *Politico*, February 8, 2009, RLP-Memoir, f. DOT. ARRA.
15. *PR Newswire*, "Transcript of Today's Speaker Pelosi Press Conference," January 29, 2009, RLP-Memoir, f. DOT. Pelosi Gamble.
16. POTUS, "Address before a Joint Session of Congress," February 24, 2009, *PPP*, RLP-Memoir, f. DOT. Obamacare.

17. POTUS, "Address before a Joint Session of Congress on Health Care," September 9, 2009, *PPP*, RLP-Memoir, f. DOT. Obamacare.
18. RL Journal, 12, June 26, 2009, RLP-DOT, f. Journal.
19. Katherine Skiba, "Obama Team Lobbied Illinois Democrats on Health Bill," *Chicago Tribune*, March 19, 2010, RLP-Memoir, f. DOT. Obamacare.
20. RL Journal, 25, n.d., RLP-DOT, f. Journal.
21. CNN, *State of the Union with Candy Crowley*, February 28, 2010, RLP-Memoir, f. DOT. Pelosi Gamble.
22. RL, "Beyond Politics: Why Republicans Should Support Health Care Reform," *Chicago Tribune*, March 14, 2010, RLP-Memoir, f. DOT. Obamacare.

CHAPTER 13

THE TRANSPORTATION
REAUTHORIZATION CHALLENGE

My bridge-building tasks extended beyond forging bipartisan support to advance the administration's broad legislative agenda. As secretary of the department that built real bridges, I had three primary duties: (1) promote the president's vision for transportation policy, (2) support the legislation necessary to achieve his vision, and (3) manage my department.

The first two responsibilities came together as Congress considered transportation reauthorization bills from 2009 into 2013. These bills provided the funding for the department's array of surface transportation programs. Regrettably, the administration missed a golden opportunity at the beginning to do what the president had said he wanted to do—to remake transportation policy from the ground up. This opportunity closed, however, within the first year of his administration. Subsequent routine transportation reauthorizations got caught in the gears of the legislative machinery. Following the 2010 off-year elections, Republicans regained the majority in the House and promptly threw sand into those gears as normally bipartisan transportation issues fell victim to a tug of war between the parties. In the end, ambitious transportation reform

suffered from Washington's diminished capacity to accomplish big
things. In July 2013, I left the Cabinet without having solved the central
infrastructure dilemma for the 21st century: how to pay for it.

"MAKE NO LITTLE PLANS": A VISION FOR TRANSPORTATION

Candidate Obama campaigned for a progressive, innovative, comprehensive transportation program. In a letter to Transportation for America in
October 2008, Obama responded to the organization's request to discuss
his plans to refashion policy. "You've hit on one of the central challenges
facing America now," he wrote. "Our infrastructure is crumbling and
we need to rebuild it." As part of the investment "in our future and
[to] strengthen our core infrastructure," he promised to put two million
more Americans to work "rebuilding our crumbling roads, bridges and
transit systems." He repeated his campaign pledge to create a National
Infrastructure Reinvestment Bank, funded at $60 billion over 10 years.
The letter went on to outline his plans for green technology, Amtrak
funding, high-speed rail development, urban transit systems, and incentives for transportation alternatives such as bike paths and walkways.[1]
It was obvious that Barack Obama intended to transform transportation
policy, not simply tinker with it.

In December, the Associated Press reported the president-elect as
saying, "We will create millions of jobs by making the single largest new
investment in our national infrastructure since the creation of the federal
highway systems in the 1950s." At the same time I was under consideration
for secretary of transportation, the Obama transition team was working
on what became the stimulus package. It projected "tens of billions
of dollars" for highway, mass transit, airport, and intercity passenger-
and freight-rail improvements. The president-elect saw transportation
spending as a road toward economic recovery, energy independence,
and environmental protection. As the AP story summarized, "Solve road
congestion, Obama's reasoning goes, and you put people to work. Use
less gasoline and help clean the air. Build better trains and move goods

more efficiently. Get people out of their cars and reduce greenhouse gas emissions." This expansive approach placed much greater emphasis on the federal government's direct involvement in transportation investment and policy than had President Bush's preference for leadership from the private sector.[2]

The American Recovery and Reinvestment Act allocated $48.1 billion, or 6 percent of the entire $787 billion stimulus package, to my department. President Obama visited our headquarters on March 3, 2009, to announce the first infrastructure repair project funded through our share of those funds. The Pennsylvania-based family-owned company American Infrastructure received $2.1 million to resurface Maryland State Highway 650, a road that had not been fully repaired in 17 years. The president also announced the release of $28 billion in funds "to help states create a 21st century infrastructure" as part of the "largest new investment in America's infrastructure since President Eisenhower built the Interstate Highway System." Transportation, he pledged to those gathered to hear him, was central to the nation's economic recovery. Of the 3.5 million jobs he believed would be created by 2011, "400,000 will be jobs rebuilding our crumbling roads, bridges, and schools, repairing our faulty levees and dams, connecting nearly every American to broadband, and upgrading the buses and trains that commuters take every day." As he concluded, the president said:

> Throughout our history, there have been times when a generation of Americans seized the chance to remake the face of this Nation. It's what we did in the midst of the civil war by connecting our coasts with the transcontinental railroad. It's what we did in the midst of depression by putting up a golden bridge in San Francisco, and electrifying rural America, and completing a great dam in the Southwest. It's what we're doing once more, by building a 21st century infrastructure that will make America's economy stronger and America's people safer.[3]

A week later, we approved 500 more transportation projects. Two weeks after that, we signed off on another 1,000 projects. During a second visit to the department on April 13, the president announced the 2000th venture, a project to widen an interstate and rebuild an overpass in Portage, Michigan. "We're doing what we've always done in this country," the president reminded us.

> As President Johnson said more than 40 years ago when he signed the legislation creating ... the Department of Transportation, "America's history is a history of her transportation," of railroads that pushed frontiers, and waterways and highways that opened up markets, airplanes that connected us to one another and to the world.[4]

The momentum for transportation policy transformation accelerated three days later when the president, Vice President Biden, and I met at the Eisenhower Executive Office Building to announce a historic investment in high-speed rail to the tune of $8 billion from stimulus funds. Again the president recalled our transportation history before concluding, "'Make no little plans'—that's what Daniel Burnham said in Chicago. I believe that about America: Make no little plans. So let's get to work."[5]

Here's the situation we at the Department of Transportation found ourselves in by spring 2009. The president had articulated a broad vision for transforming transportation in the United States. He had named the vice president to head up the transportation initiative from the White House. He had made a down payment on the plan by funding it from ARRA. Finally, the president had called for more—to "make no little plans." We all knew that stimulus-based spending represented a stopgap approach to transportation policy, more of an effort to jump-start the economic recovery by putting people to work quickly. The task of transforming the nation's transportation policy remained to be done. The doing had begun already in the House under the thoughtful leadership of Jim Oberstar.

I had known the 74-year-old Democratic congressman from Minnesota's 8th district for years and had served with him on the House Transportation Committee. Jim Oberstar, like me, had held a congressional staff position, rising to serve as chief of staff to his predecessor, John Blatnik. First elected in 1974, Oberstar won his seat to 17 succeeding Congresses. A widely acclaimed expert on aviation and aviation safety, he sat on the House Transportation Committee his entire career, first as the top staff member on what had been the House Public Works Committee and later as chair of the renamed committee. He co-sponsored and helped to pass the 2005 SAFETEA-LU Act (short for the cumbersome Safe, Accountable, Efficient Transportation Equity Act: A Legacy for Users), a $295 billion program that funded highways, bridges, and public transportation. By 2009, Oberstar had spent nearly 15 years as the senior Democrat on the committee, with two terms as chair. His name had been circulated by the press as a candidate for the job I then held and was mentioned again later to replace me when I left office.

Oberstar sat on the opposite side of the aisle from me and had a generally liberal voting record, in contrast to mine. That didn't matter to us. Oberstar was one of the good guys in politics, a real gentleman. He ran our committee skillfully, never afraid to exercise the prerogatives of the chair but equally willing to listen to Republicans and to account for our views. He was a transportation visionary, too, and thought in large thoughts about our country's increasingly obsolete approach to transportation policy. When asked in April 2009 what needed to happen with the national transportation system, the chair replied, "The end of the interstate era and the beginning of a new period of transit.... We need to transform the entire Department of Transportation to make it work."[6] Oberstar favored a transportation policy that deemphasized the automobile in favor of intermodalism and public transportation systems that incorporate what he called "livability" criteria. Ironically, given what would happen later, Oberstar's vision fit almost perfectly the president's vision for transportation policy.

The landmark SAFETEA-LU bill adopted in 2005 was set to expire on September 30, 2009. Oberstar had been working for months on the successor bill. He was always careful to keep the stakeholders in the loop, so I wouldn't be surprised if Oberstar had met with candidate Obama to lay out his program—I know for certain that he met with the transition team in charge of transportation. In other words, we had a pretty good idea about where Oberstar was headed.

On June 18, Jim Oberstar unveiled his proposal for a six-year, $500 billion transportation spending bill summarized in a 17-page blueprint. He and ranking member John Mica (R-FL) called for a $337 billion investment in highway construction, $100 billion for public transportation, and $50 billion for the president's vision of a nationwide high-speed rail system, with the remaining $13 billion allocated to smaller initiatives. *Make no little plans* caught the spirit of Jim's plan in a nutshell.

The bill also called for streamlining DOT, cutting more than 75 federal programs and consolidating highway funding into four core formula categories: critical asset investment, highway-safety improvement, surface transportation, and congestion mitigation and air-quality improvement. Transportation programs would all be eligible for funding from a newly created "national infrastructure bank" (essentially the proposal endorsed by candidate Obama), which would provide grants, credit assistance, secured loans and loan guarantees, standby lines of credit, and allocations of tax-exempt private activity bonding authority.[7] The bill matched Jim Oberstar's vision and the president's rhetoric.

Oberstar's plan was not the only game in town, however. The administration was crafting its own version of a transportation bill that would extend the current spending bill for 18 months. We needed that much time to figure out how to fund a more ambitious program of the kind Oberstar proposed. The Highway Trust Fund, the source of funding for DOT, would run out of money in August as revenue from the federal gasoline tax continued to decline. Constrained by the lack of resources, the White House version of how to achieve the president's vision was more modest than Oberstar's.

One day before Oberstar released his blueprint, and at Rahm Emanuel's direction, I asked the chair to postpone his announcement. As widely reported by the press, we were at loggerheads over the two competing proposals for enacting transportation policy. Oberstar said he would seek to block efforts by Congress simply to extend the authorization temporarily, as I had counseled. Instead, he wanted to force lawmakers to get down to the business of transforming, not propping up, policy. Oberstar expressed his frustration to an interviewer the next day. "The reality is that the administration does not have a program," he said. "They do not have a plan. They have not given transportation any thought. I have."[8]

Oberstar knew otherwise, of course. But he could sense the White House backing away from its previous, more ambitious position. He was right. Our plan did not match the president's public statements. It was a case of vision colliding with reality. From the administration's point of view, the country could not afford Oberstar's $500 billion price tag, which represented a 75 percent increase over the current $286 billion authorization. More ominously, the Highway Trust Fund could sustain only about $236 billion in spending. Oberstar's blueprint failed to address in any detail the means to pay for his remake of the country's transportation system.

Funding transportation programs proved to be an unresolvable dilemma during my entire tenure at DOT. Since its inception in 1956, the Highway Trust Fund had provided the vast majority of dollars for road construction and public transportation. For revenue, the fund depended on receipts from the federal gas tax. But as automobiles became more fuel efficient and drivers put fewer miles on their cars and trucks because of higher gas prices and the recession, income to the fund dropped. From 2008 to 2010, Congress was forced to authorize the transfer of $35 billion from the U.S. Treasury's general fund to cover trust fund shortfalls. We were forced to rob Peter to pay Paul.

Yet the starting point for any discussion about funding for the department's surface transportation programs, then or in the future, was the trust fund and the gas tax. Oberstar avoided recommending a gas tax increase in his blueprint. He had raised the possibility, however, in an April interview with *Blueprint America*. When asked how one might obtain public support for increased transportation spending in the midst of a recession, Oberstar recalled that in 1956 Congress had funded the interstate system with a 3 percent "user fee" on a gasoline price of 30 cents. That measure passed Congress easily, as did an addition of one cent the next year. But the tax had remained unchanged since 1993 at 18.4 cents per gallon for gasoline and 24.4 cents for diesel. In an earlier time, "there was a sense of greater vision, of a greater need in America for safety, for mobility, to move people and goods and our economy more efficiently, more effectively," Oberstar observed. "And the public understood that that penny was going for those roadway improvements." The lesson was clear to Oberstar: "We need to rekindle that same spirit and understanding in America and show that an additional user fee will make life better."[9]

I couldn't help but think, wasn't that what the president sought? Hadn't he issued a call to transform transportation on the scale Jim Oberstar proposed? The breadth of the Oberstar proposal seemed to match President Obama's eloquence about the historic opportunity to bring the nation's transportation system into the 21st century. There I was, however, pushing for a simple 18-month extension to the current authorization. By the way, this right turn away from the president's vision never received a hearing in a Cabinet meeting, and I was never called to the Oval Office to discuss it.

The White House sent me out with marching orders to short circuit the Oberstar proposal. At the time I thought that was a mistake. Oberstar's bill was a bold, good bill. I knew that he had vetted his plan with his subcommittee chairs and with Republicans—Oberstar had long experience crafting complex, bipartisan bills. He typically sat down with individuals to go through a bill chapter and verse. Consequently, I was certain that we had the votes to pass the bill with Republican backing. I said so to the administration team. Were we going to seize the opportunity to make transportation and infrastructure a priority? Would we push to pass a landmark bill? Were we prepared to implement the president's transportation vision? Would we raise the revenue to do something big?

No. Rahm Emanuel, speaking for the president, told me, "You need to go tell Oberstar we are not going to support him moving ahead with a 6-year bill." In other words, we're going to kick the can down the road.

As instructed, I met with the chair, just the two of us, on June 17 in his office next to the Transportation Committee's hearing room—it was plain disheartening. I told him that his vision was not a priority for the administration; they wouldn't support it; they wouldn't support raising revenue right now. Jim Oberstar was shocked, devastated, even hurt. But he was not one to get angry and pound the table. I'm sure he wanted to appeal to the president himself, but he did not ask me to intercede. The session was painful for me, too.[10] I had served with Jim, liked him, respected him. He had spent his whole career—three decades—waiting for this moment. Assured of the votes to pass the bill and chairing a committee in the majority party, he had put the bill together, and then he was told by the guy whom he helped get elected—a president he thought was a transportation/infrastructure guy—"We are not going to support your bill." What a shame.

I was a loyal soldier, but I felt that we could have passed the bill, and I think we could have paid for the Oberstar plan. It would have required President Obama to make an aggressive play to raise the gas tax as a first step. Next, we could have cobbled together other revenue sources. I had laid out several options in an interview with the Associated Press, including tolling, public/private partnerships, and a national infrastructure bank. As it happened, I also listed a tax based on miles driven simply as one on this list of ideas, not as a formal proposal. As sometimes happens, the reporter took that out of context and questioned Robert Gibbs, the president's spokesman, about the tax at a press conference. "Has the president weighed in on this?" the reporter asked. Gibbs replied, "I don't believe the President has. I can weigh in on it and say that it is not and will not be the policy of the Obama administration." "So was Secretary LaHood speaking out of turn here?" Gibbs: "I would direct you to Secretary LaHood on that." "Well, we actually interviewed him, so..." Gibbs: "Well, call him back."[11] That was the only time I can remember getting crosswise with the White House, and I did not appreciate the way Gibbs handled it. In any event, the options for funding a vigorous transportation policy never received a full hearing at the White House.

Early in the term, the administration had bigger fish to fry. Something had to give. To this day, however, failing to seize the opportunity to redo transportation in a large way was the biggest disappointment during my time in the administration—as big for me as for Oberstar. But part of being on the team is that once a decision is made, you have to go along.

"We're Going to Kick the Can Down the Road"

The effect of backing away from Jim Oberstar's proposal was to miss the chance to transform transportation policy for the indefinite future. In July, for example, Oberstar asked the House to approve a $3 billion infusion for the Highway Trust Fund in order to head off a projected shortfall that in mid-August would halt federal payments for highway projects. Through this move, meant only as a stopgap, Oberstar hoped to buy time to push for his six-year transportation bill before the current transportation law expired on September 30.

By now a frustrating but familiar pattern was developing between the administration and key members of Congress, in this case Oberstar. We failed to communicate, to cultivate the personal relationships so necessary to getting big things done in Washington. The Obama administration came in for frequent criticism on this score—that it did not work the Hill with enough deference, with its ears open. Some of that responsibility could have fallen to me, but the White House insisted on keeping congressional liaison on a pretty tight leash. As a result, I did not take the initiative with Oberstar following my face-to-face meeting with him in

June. Our negligence in this regard became painfully clear when Oberstar answered a question about the White House's response to his proposed $3 billion infusion to the trust fund:

> I don't know. I've called—over six months—I've called; I've left messages; I've asked for their input; I've got nothing. Until finally they said, "Oh, oh my God, we can't do anything, we've got to wait 18 months and then we'll think of some good projects."[12]

September 30, the expiration date for the 2005 transportation authorization, came and went with no long-term replacement. The administration could not stomach a fight over transportation revenues when it was occupied with health care reform and climate-change legislation. Congress authorized another limited-time extension, one in a long series that would be passed throughout the next two years.

The future did not look much brighter in 2010. The administration failed to pursue major transportation legislation that year, although the president signed into law the HIRE Act (Hiring Incentives to Restore Employment Act) on March 18. Among other provisions, that bill deposited $19.5 billion into the Highway Trust Fund to ensure the fund's solvency into 2011. It also funded the federal highway program's contract authority for the 2012 fiscal year at $42 billion, up from $30 billion, returning the program to its fiscal year 2009 level. Most importantly, HIRE extended the surface transportation authorization until the end of 2010—the authorization was set to expire on March 28. These measures had one thing in common—they were all temporary stopgaps. Kicking the can down the road. *Politico* reported in May:

> So, while the nation's infrastructure continues to age and crumble, Washington is stuck with a neutered transportation chairman, a White House distracted by more pressing issues and congressional leaders who lack the political will to raise gas taxes for a new $500 billion measure.[13]

In an election year, no one in the White House wanted to raise the billions of dollars needed to fund a transportation overhaul. By the way, Jim Oberstar lost his seat in that election to a tea party favorite by 4,407 votes.

The landscape for transportation policy changed in the 2010 election, too, as Republicans regained control of the House. The White House immediately began what one source called a "charm offensive" with the new Republican committee chairs in the House. John Mica (R-FL) replaced Oberstar as chair of the House Transportation and Infrastructure Committee. We met on December 8, the same day the House passed still another extension of the surface transportation law.

Mica was first elected to the House from central Florida's 7th district in 1992, following a successful career in business. He gained the chair of the Transportation Committee in 2006, only to lose it to Oberstar when the Democrats won back the majority.[14] As the ranking minority member during the stimulus debate in 2009, Mica made sure that transportation received a large slice of the pie. He and I overlapped on the committee, too. After our December meeting, Mica told a reporter, "I know Ray and I have a lot of confidence in dealing with him."[15] I, on the other hand, doubted that Mica would lead the committee as effectively as Oberstar had.

The charm offensive failed to produce a breakthrough. The 2005 SAFETEA-LU legislation that funded the nation's surface transportation program and which would expire at the end of September 2009 still had not been replaced. Seven times since then, we had limped along with short-term extensions—halting, temporary fixes at best. The next deadline was March 4, 2011.

2011: Reauthorization Delayed

We mounted an effort in 2011 to move a new federal surface transportation authorization bill through Congress to end the practice of stopgaps. I was optimistic and said so to a conference in Atlanta on January 18. I thought that a multiyear bill to reauthorize the department's programs could be passed and signed into law before Congress's August recess. Even though Republicans now controlled the House (many of them having pledged spending austerity), I still believed that a majority of members recognized that transportation funding was, and always had been, a bipartisan issue, that such spending created jobs and benefited the country by improving roads and bridges.

In his State of the Union remarks on January 25, 2011, the president talked about "winning the future" by rebuilding America. He used familiar language, relying on the stock examples (e.g., the transcontinental railroad and the interstate highway system) he had cited repeatedly in messages about transportation. "We have to do better," he said.[16]

The president released his fiscal year 2012 budget on February 14. In a transmittal message to Congress that called for sacrifice, that proposed a five-year freeze on all discretionary spending, that froze federal workers' salaries for two years, that reduced Defense Department funding by $78 billion over five years—even in that context, the president proposed what he called "a historic investment in repairing, rebuilding, and modernizing our transportation infrastructure."[17]

His plan would invest $556 billion over six years to modernize the country's surface transportation infrastructure, create jobs, and pave the way for long-term economic growth while recognizing the need to avoid adding to the nation's deficit. In addition to a first-year funding boost of $50 billion in 2012 to jump-start investments and job growth, the plan included $30 billion over six years to capitalize a national infrastructure bank to invest in projects of regional or national significance to the economy. In a nod to the Oberstar legacy, the budget included a livability grant program totaling $4.1 billion in the first year and $28 billion over six years, $32 billion in competitive grants to encourage states to adopt safety and livability reforms, and $119 billion for public transit over six years— about double the amount set aside for transit each year by the previous transportation bill.[18] This was the scale of investment we at DOT favored.

We were deliberately vague about the perennial issue of "pay fors"—how to pay for the additional $231 billion required over six years beyond our estimates for revenue. The president's budget did not identify where that money would come from. "These estimates are a placeholder and do not assume an increase in gas taxes or any specific proposal to offset surface transportation spending," the budget document stated. "Rather, they are intended to initiate a discussion about how the administration and Congress could work together on a bipartisan basis" to pass a surface transportation reauthorization "that is both financially sustainable and meets critical national needs."[19] The hope for bipartisanship springs eternal.

February ended in uncertainty with only a week left until federal appropriations and our authorization were set to expire. At the 11th hour, however, President Obama gave us some breathing room by signing an extension, the seventh since 2009, until September 30, the end of the federal fiscal year. Congressional support for the extension was nearly unanimous. I had told a transportation group the day before that we were still working on specific legislative language for the broad reauthorization bill. If we did not get action on it by summer, however, I feared that the 2012 election would gum up the works.[20]

The Senate Finance Committee weighed several options in May to pay for a long-term reauthorization, and that month the bipartisan leadership of the Senate Environment and Public Works Committee released Moving Ahead for Progress in the 21st Century, a plan that would reauthorize the surface transportation system for six years at $339 billion. The Republican-controlled House Transportation and Infrastructure Committee responded in July by unveiling a six-year, $230 billion reauthorization proposal. Democratic House committee leaders, joined by Senate Democrats, immediately complained that the Republican-sponsored House bill would cut highway and transit investment by a third.

The Senate committee leaders went back to the drawing board. Barbara Boxer (D-CA), one of the most liberal members of the Senate, and

Jim Inhofe (R-OK), one of the most conservative, put their ideological differences aside to produce a bill that reflected the wishes of their colleagues from both sides of the aisle, and they passed a bill out of Boxer's committee without a single dissenting vote. Their two-year, $109 billion bill (now called MAP-21) would combine nearly 200 federal transportation programs into about a dozen and give states more flexibility to define transportation priorities. It preserved intact the scope of federal highway, transit, and other surface transportation projects. MAP-21 had a short time horizon of only two years, partly because of the difficulty of projecting revenue from the Highway Trust Fund as gasoline receipts continued to decline.[21] The Senate Finance Committee still had not determined how to generate the estimated $12 billion in extra revenue needed to pay for the legislation.

"We have worked together to develop MAP-21, which is a bipartisan proposal that modernizes and reforms our current transportation systems to help create jobs, jumpstart our economy, and build the foundation for long-term prosperity," Boxer said in a statement. "This bill is an investment in America's future, because the nation's aging infrastructure has not kept up with needed improvements, and now our transportation systems are falling behind other countries. We will continue to work to move the transportation bill through the EPW Committee and the full Senate."

"This is a tremendous step forward," Inhofe said:

> Chairman Boxer has shown her willingness to work with us to produce a bill that should enjoy strong bipartisan support. Our next step is crucial: given the state of our economy, and the debate here in Congress, we must work with Chairman [Max] Baucus [D-MT] and Republicans on the Finance Committee to find a way to pay for this bill. I am confident that if we continue to work together as we have thus far, we can get the job done. Doing so is vital for jobs, the economy, and our nation's infrastructure.[22]

On August 31, President Obama took to the Rose Garden to speak about the looming October 1 reauthorization deadline. If we allowed the transportation bill to expire, he said, more than 4,000 workers would be furloughed immediately without pay. "And that's just not acceptable; that's inexcusable," he said. "It's time to stop the political gamesmanship that can actually cost us hundreds of thousands of jobs. This should not be a Democratic or Republican issue." After calling on Congress to pass a clean extension of the surface transportation bill, the president said, "That's what we're going to need to do in the short term: keep people on the job, keep vital projects moving forward, fund projects that are already underway in a smarter way." Then he continued, "Of course, if we're honest, we also know that when it comes to our Nation's infrastructure— our roads, our railways, mass transit, airports—we shouldn't just be playing patch-up or catch-up, we should be leading the world."[23]

Instead of patch-up or catch-up, we played stay-put. After its summer recess, Congress returned in September and approved a six-month surface transportation extension expiring on March 31, 2012—the eighth SAFETEA-LU extension.

President Obama returned to the bully pulpit on November 2 in remarks to construction workers gathered at the Georgetown Waterfront Park in Washington. "How do we sit back and watch China and Europe build the best bridges and high-speed railroads and gleaming new airports, and we're doing nothing," he said, "at a time when we've got more than a million unemployed construction workers who could build them right here in America right now?" He called for decisive action from Congress. He asked them to vote for the jobs bill later that week.

Then the president turned his oratorical attention to the Republicans in Congress. He said he could not imagine that Speaker Boehner would oppose a bill when he represented a state in which one of four bridges was classified as substandard. He quoted Senate Republican leader Mitch McConnell, who had told him, "Roads and bridges are not partisan in Washington." He recounted a statement from Paul Ryan (R-WI), chair of the House Budget Committee, who had recently stated, "You can't deny that infrastructure does create jobs." The president summed it up this way: "Okay, so if the Speaker of the House, the Republican leader in the Senate, and the Democrats all say that this is important to do, why aren't we doing it?"[24]

The next day, Speaker Boehner told reporters that House Republicans would introduce a multiyear surface transportation bill "in the coming weeks" and "hope[d] to move the legislation through the House before the end of the year." He said the bill would expand domestic energy production to pay for transportation infrastructure, with funding levels likely to be at or above current levels. "Everybody believes we have infrastructure deficiencies and more needs to be spent to repair, replace, and—in some cases—build new infrastructure," Boehner said. "The problem is nobody wants to pay for it."[25] By linking expansion of what he called "American-made energy production" with paying for transportation improvements, the Speaker set reauthorization on a collision course with Democrats in both the House and the Senate.

By year's end, however, neither the House nor the Senate had acted. Late in 2011, I began to think about leaving the administration following the 2012 presidential election. I made no announcement at that time, and I did not speak to the president even informally. But I was mulling over the decision. If I followed through, I assumed that I would leave without having put in place the visionary policy voiced first by candidate Obama then, in succession, by President Obama and Jim Oberstar.

2012: STALLED BY PARTISANSHIP

The legislative process continued to grind along as 2012 began. There had been eight surface transportation reauthorization extensions in the 880 days since the last long-term bill had expired. Senate and House committees had not yet marked up their respective bills, much less moved them to the floor for a vote. The latest extension was set to lapse on March 31.

At long last, the Senate passed S. 1813, the Moving Ahead for Progress in the 21st Century Act (the Boxer-Inhofe version) two weeks before the March deadline and did so on a bipartisan vote of 74 to 22. This action put pressure on the House to consider the Senate bill rather than holding out for its own. "I hope the House will take this up and not listen to this shrill voice that makes up so much of the Republican caucus in the House," Senator Harry Reid, the majority leader, said.[26] "This is really a hallelujah day," I said. "Passing a bipartisan bill reflects the very best values of the Senate. Transportation has always been bipartisan and you proved that with the passage of your bill."[27] The White House issued a press release praising the Senate for bipartisan action and expressing the hope "that the House will move swiftly and in similarly bipartisan fashion to do the same."[28]

The House Republicans had produced their latest version of a transportation bill in late January: H.R. 7, the American Energy and Infrastructure Jobs Act of 2012. They labeled it a jobs bill, but its focus was on spending for surface transportation. The effort got off to a shaky start. As the New York Times reported, Chairman Mica introduced H.R. 7 to the public at a press conference accompanied only by Republicans.[29] The House Republicans didn't get it—the only way to achieve big things is to listen to the other side and compromise. House Republicans seemed intent on passing their transportation bill without Democratic support. "I believe we have the votes to pass it. If no Democrats decide that we should pass the jobs bill, the Republicans will," said one committee Republican.[30] In other words, they would do to Democrats what Pelosi had done to them. Boehner had the votes to pass the bipartisan Senate bill out of the House. Enough Republicans were prepared to join Democrats to win passage. But in a presidential election year, the Speaker was not about to hand the president a victory on any major piece of legislation, much less one that could have resulted in better employment numbers.

My reaction was blunt. The GOP spending plan was the worst transportation bill—and the most partisan—that I had seen in my 35 years of public service. It was "the most anti-safety bill I have ever seen," I told *Politico*. "It hollows out our No. 1 priority, which is safety, and frankly, it hollows out the guts of transportation efforts that we've been about for the last three years."[31] During my 14 years in the House, including six on the Transportation and Infrastructure Committee, we had all come together to support legislation reported by our committee. The chairs with whom I served never would have held a press conference with only their partisans. "The House has a lousy bill," I told reporters. "It takes us back to the dark ages. It doesn't reflect the transportation values of the country."[32]

We objected because the bill eliminated funding for several discretionary grant programs, missing an opportunity to promote competition and innovation. We objected to Boehner's attempt to link increased energy production with infrastructure investment; a trio of bills in the House sought to use expanded drilling and oil shale production to generate about $4.3 billion over 10 years for the House bill, which the White House denounced as "pay-fors that open up pristine natural habitats not suitable for resource extraction." The Speaker also said he would attach the Keystone XL pipeline to the transportation bill—the administration had rejected Republican attempts early in 2012 to fast-track the project.[33]

The bill was so bad that President Obama threatened to veto it. The press office issued a formal statement of administration policy on February 14, expressing "serious concerns" about provisions in the bill that would make the nation's roads, rails, and transit systems less safe, reduce the transportation options available to the traveling public, short-circuit local decision making, and turn back the clock on environmental and labor protections. The statement set forth a number of objections to H.R. 7, chief among them the elimination of a 30-year legacy of dedicated transit funding from the Highway Trust Fund. "Because this bill jeopardizes safety, weakens environmental and labor protections, and fails to make the investments needed to strengthen the nation's roads, bridges, rail, and transit systems," the White House statement read, "the president's senior advisers would recommend that he veto this legislation."[34]

The veto threat came just five days after the president had offered support for the Senate's MAP-21 and one day after the White House had presented its six-year $476 billion surface transportation plan in the president's budget proposal.[35] The threat must have had at least some impact. A week later, House and Senate leaders were reworking their bills to secure additional support.

The mess surrounding H.R. 7 simply showed how difficult it was to pass legislation in a partisan Congress, with control of the two chambers in different hands, with three separate proposals jockeying for support, all in an election year with a president running for a second term. Cleavages existed everywhere. Severing the link between the gas tax and federal transit funding pitted urban members of both parties against rural members. Democrats and Republicans split over any number of issues, ranging from labor provisions to environmental concerns. Very conservative Republicans opposed some of the targeted grants programs, splitting that party in the House. Others thought that $260 billion was too much to spend, let alone our budget proposal to spend $476 billion, and that transportation should no longer be a federal priority—leave it to the states, they said. Liberals opposed adding oil-drilling projects and opening the Arctic National Wildlife Refuge. Members from what would have been the Oberstar camp objected to a provision that eliminated Safe Routes to School, a program that encouraged biking and walking as opposed to driving. Members of both parties in both chambers introduced amendments on completely unrelated items—such non-germane measures are commonly known as "Christmas tree ornaments." Republicans in the Senate, for example, pitched amendments to cut aid to Egypt and to reverse the administration's policy on contraception and faith-based institutions. These Christmas tree ornaments had nothing to do with transportation, of course, but that's the way of Washington. Speaker

Boehner gave up and did not bring the bill up for consideration in mid-February as he had intended.[36]

I addressed about 200 state transportation officials and industry leaders the first week in March and pledged the administration's support of MAP-21, the Senate version of the surface transportation reauthorization, even as I highlighted the president's fiscal year 2013 budget as the best long-term solution for the nation's transportation needs. "It's a good, good budget. It's a good framework. It's a good way for Congress to go—they should take the president's blueprint and pass it," I told the group. I said the administration would oppose H.R. 7, the House bill, as too one-sided, too unbalanced. "There are no Republican or Democratic roads and there are no Republican or Democratic bridges," I said. "There are American roads built by American workers. And there are American bridges built by American workers. Infrastructure is built by our friends and neighbors ... not by some kind of political party."[37]

In testimony before the House Transportation, Housing and Urban Development, and Related Agencies Appropriations Subcommittee in early March, I continued to press for the administration's bill as presented in the budget. But the House Republicans pushed back. The subcommittee chair, Tom Latham (R-IA), said, "So far we aren't seeing any proposals —not in terms of length, cost, financing, or policy that will pass both the House and the Senate." Republicans opposed funding transportation investment by using money saved from fighting wars in Afghanistan and Iraq as the president had put forth. They opposed making certain transportation programs mandatory. They opposed our proposal to require that livability be used as a criterion for awarding funds to states and localities.[38]

Congress punted on March 30 and passed a clean 90-day extension through June 30, the ninth extension of SAFETEA-LU. Following additional parliamentary maneuvering, Congress began to move toward a more "permanent" solution by going to conference in early May. For the next two months, the 47 conferees from the House and Senate met to work out the differences between H.R. 4348, the 90-day extension of the current authorization, and the Senate's two-year, $109 billion reauthorization bill, MAP-21.

On June 29, again at the 11th hour, the House and Senate passed a new two-year, $105 billion transportation reauthorization bill, Moving Ahead for Progress in the 21st Century, with support from Democrats and Republicans. But it was a less robust form of bipartisanship than was customary with transportation bills. The measure passed the House 373–52; all 52 no votes came from Republicans, although 186 joined 187 Democrats in support. The Senate passed the bill 74 to 19—again, Republicans cast all the no votes. The act reauthorized the federal-aid highway, highway safety, and transit programs which had last been authorized in 2005. Although modest in scope compared to the administration's proposal, the act did include a few innovations. The law consolidated roughly 60 programs, for example, so that more resources would be available to the states directly. And for the first time ever, the law required the establishment of national goals, performance measures, and accountability in planning and funding transportation investments. These goals were centered on air quality, freight movement, safety, and state of good repair for both highways and transit. In terms of funding, the 599-page bill retained current funding levels through September 30, 2014, well beyond my tenure as secretary. The final agreement did not include provisions proposed by House Republicans to approve the Keystone XL oil pipeline or to prevent the Environmental Protection Agency from regulating coal ash.[39]

President Obama hailed the bill at the White House signing ceremony on Friday afternoon, July 6, in the East Room of the White House. "I'm appreciative of the hard work that Congress has done [on the bill]," he said. "My hope is ... that this bipartisan spirit spills over into the next phase."[40] As it turned out, MAP-21 was the best we could get. The administration did not go back to the well for a new transportation initiative in 2013.

An Assessment

I doubt that transportation reauthorization tops any list of most-important legislation, unless the list comes from DOT. But I have chosen to focus on it in my memoir because it illustrates so many of the general themes that have emerged in the Obama administration. The president's pledge both as a candidate and then in office to remake transportation policy seemed in line with his expansive vision and transformative aspirations in so many other fields, ranging from health care to diplomacy. Then vision collided with reality. In the case of transportation, that reality included higher priorities; decisions about when to lead and when to cede leadership to others; the unwieldy, ponderous nature of the legislative process; the impact of excessive partisanship, even on historically nonpartisan matters; and the challenge of finding the means to pay for change in trying economic times.

Let me emphasize that last point. When the new president took office, most everyone accepted the need for action on transportation. They knew where the bad roads were. They knew about bad bridges that needed to be fixed. They knew we suffered with outdated transit systems. But we could never figure out a way to pay for the fixes. The administration would not lobby for an increase in the gas tax when it had the votes. Republicans in the House would have blocked the increase once they regained control of the House. The infrastructure bank never gained traction, although it could have supplemented the Highway Trust Fund. We never figured out how to pay for a transportation bill that matched the president's rhetoric.

NOTES

1. Stephen Lee Davis, "President-Elect Obama Responds to Transportation for America," November 19, 2008, *Transportation for America Blog*, RLP-Memoir, f. DOT. Transportation Reauthorization. Although the headline refers to the "president-elect," the letter was written before the election.
2. Joan Lowy, "Obama Sees Transportation as Catalyst for Recovery," *Spokesman-Review*, December 13, 2008, RLP-Memoir, f. DOT. Transportation Reauthorization.
3. POTUS, "Remarks at the Department of Transportation," March 3, 2009, *PPP*, RLP-Memoir, f. DOT. Transportation Reauthorization; RL Journal, 4, n.d., RLP-DOT, f. Journal.
4. POTUS, "Remarks at the Department of Transportation," April 13, 2009, *PPP*, RLP-Memoir, f. DOT. Transportation Reauthorization.
5. POTUS, "Remarks on Transportation Infrastructure," April 16, 2009, *PPP*, RLP-Memoir, f. DOT. Transportation Reauthorization.
6. Tom McNamara, "Interview: Jim Oberstar on the Transportation Bill," Blueprint America, July 22, 2007, RLP-Memoir, f. DOT. Transportation Reauthorization.
7. Josh Voorhees, "Oberstar, Mica Plan $500B, 6-Year Transportation Reauthorization," *NYT*, June 18, 2009, RLP-Memoir, f. DOT. Transportation Reauthorization.
8. Madeleine Baran, "Oberstar's Transportation Bill a Direct Challenge to Administration," Minnesota Public Radio, June 19, 2009, RLP-Memoir, f. DOT. Transportation Reauthorization.
9. McNamara, "Interview: Jim Oberstar." Congress had not increased the gas tax since 1993.
10. RL Journal, 11, June 17, 2009, RLP-DOT, f. Journal.
11. Notes on a press briefing by Gibbs, February 20, 2009, RLP-Memoir, f. DOT. Transportation Reauthorization.
12. Geof Koss, "Oberstar Maps a Course for Full Highway Bill," *Roll Call*, July 27, 2009, RLP-Memoir, f. DOT. Transportation Reauthorization.
13. Elana Schor, "James Oberstar Stymied on Transit Bill," *Politico*, May 17, 2010, RLP-Memoir, f. DOT. Transportation Reauthorization.
14. U.S. Congressman John Mica website, http://mica.house.gov/about-john-mica/.

15. John Bresnahan and Jake Sherman, "White House Launches Charm Offensive with New Republican Chairs," *Politico*, December 13, 2010, RLP-Memoir, f. DOT. Transportation Reauthorization.

16. POTUS, "Address before a Joint Session of Congress on the State of the Union," January 25, 2011, *PPP*, RLP-Memoir, f. DOT. Transportation Reauthorization.

17. POTUS, "The Budget Message of the President," February 14, 2011, *PPP*, RLP-Memoir, f. DOT. Transportation Reauthorization.

18. Tanya Snyder, "Obama Proposes Infra Bank, Livability Grants, Doubling Transit Funds," *Streetsblog Capitol Hill*, February 14, 2011, RLP-Memoir, f. DOT. Transportation Reauthorization.

19. *AASHTO Journal*, Weekly Transportation Report, "Administration Proposes $556 Billion for Surface Transportation Over 6 Years," February 18, 2011, RLP-Memoir, f. DOT. Transportation Reauthorization.

20. *AASHTO Journal*, Weekly Transportation Report, "President's Signature Extends Highway & Transit Programs for 7 Months," March 4, 2011, RLP-Memoir, f. DOT. Transportation Reauthorization.

21. Jonathan Weisman, "Senate Passes 2-Year Transportation Bill," *NYT*, March 14, 2012, RLP-Memoir, f. DOT. Transportation Reauthorization.

22. *AASHTO Journal*, Weekly Transportation Report, "Senate EPW Leaders Unveil Bill Outline; Funding Remains Uncertain," July 22, 2011, RLP-Memoir, f. DOT. Transportation Reauthorization.

23. POTUS, "Remarks on Surface Transportation and Federal Aviation Administration Reauthorization Legislation," August 31, 2011, *PPP*, RLP-Memoir, f. DOT. Transportation Reauthorization.

24. POTUS, "Remarks on Transportation Infrastructure Improvement and Job Growth Legislation," November 2, 2011, *PPP*, RLP-Memoir, f. DOT. Transportation Reauthorization.

25. *AASHTO Journal*, Weekly Transportation Report, "Boehner: House Will Move Multiyear Bill by Year's End," November 4, 2011, RLP-Memoir, f. DOT. Transportation Reauthorization.

26. Weisman, "2-Year Transportation Bill."

27. *AASHTO Journal*, Weekly Transportation Report, "LaHood Urges House Passage of Transportation Bill During Appropriations Testimony," March 16, 2012, RLP-Memoir, f. DOT. Transportation Reauthorization.

28. *AASHTO Journal*, Weekly Transportation Report, "Senate Votes 74–22 to Pass MAP-21 Reauthorization Bill," March 16, 2012, RLP-Memoir, f. DOT. Transportation Reauthorization.

29. Jennifer Steinhauer, "Transportation Bill Faces a Wall of Opposition from Both Parties," *NYT*, February 24, 2012, RLP-Memoir, f. DOT. Transportation Reauthorization.

30. Burgess Everett and Adam Snider, "Transportation Bill Lurches Forward Despite Revenue Doubts," *Politico*, February 6, 2012, RLP-Memoir, f. DOT. Transportation Reauthorization.

31. Burgess Everett, "GOP Highway Spending Bill 'the Worst,' Ray LaHood Says," *Politico*, February 2, 2012, RLP-Memoir, f. DOT. Transportation Reauthorization.

32. Andrea Bernstein, "LaHood Heaps More Criticism on 'Lousy' House Transpo Bill," *Transportation Nation*, February 13, 2012, RLP-Memoir, f. DOT. Transportation Reauthorization.

33. The Keystone XL pipeline would carry oil from Alberta, Canada, through the western states, terminating at the Gulf of Mexico.

34. POTUS, "Statement of Administration Policy: H.R. 7—the American Energy and Infrastructure Jobs Act of 2012," February 14, 2012, *PPP*, RLP-Memoir, f. DOT. Transportation Reauthorization.

35. Burgess Everett, "W.H. threatens to veto House transportation bill," *Politico*, February 14, 2012, RLP-Memoir, f. DOT. Transportation Reauthorization.

36. Steinhauer, "Transportation Bill."

37. *AASHTO Journal*, Weekly Transportation Report, "LaHood Opens Washington Briefing with Call for Bipartisanship in Transportation Bills," March 2, 2012, RLP-Memoir, f. DOT. Transportation Reauthorization.

38. *AASHTO Journal*, Weekly Transportation Report, "LaHood Pitches President's Transportation Budget to House Appropriations Subcommittee," March 9, 2012, RLP-Memoir, f. DOT. Transportation Reauthorization.

39. Chrissy Mancini Nichols, "Your Guide to the New Federal Transportation Reauthorization," *Connector*, July 2, 2012, RLP-Memoir, f. DOT. Transportation Reauthorization.

40. POTUS, "Remarks on Signing the Moving Ahead for Progress in the 21st Century Act," July 6, 2012, *PPP*, RLP-Memoir, f. DOT. Transportation Reauthorization.

CHAPTER 14

LEADING THE DEPARTMENT OF TRANSPORTATION

February 12, 2009—my worst day on the job. Late that Thursday night, I received a phone call from the office. Colgan Air Flight 3407 had crashed near Buffalo, New York, at 10:17 p.m. EST, killing two pilots, two flight attendants, 45 passengers, and one person on the ground. In the flight's final minute from Newark Liberty International Airport, the pilot had apparently tried to abort the landing as the plane descended through light snow and icy mist, but the aircraft pitched violently and seconds later slammed into a house in Clarence Center, about six miles from the airport. The crash was the nation's deadliest since a Comair commuter jet went down in Lexington, Kentucky, on August 27, 2006, claiming 49 lives.

These tragedies are a transportation secretary's worst nightmare. Fourteen investigators from the National Transportation Safety Board (NTSB) were immediately dispatched to the site. They eventually determined that the pilot had reacted quickly enough but had done exactly the opposite of what he should have in order to land Flight 3407 safely. We also learned that both the pilot and co-pilot had flown across the country that day, likely without sufficient rest. NTSB's final report concluded that pilot error, the result of fatigue and action "inconsistent with his training and ... instead consistent with startle and confusion," had caused the crash.

Lynne Osmus, acting administrator of the Federal Aviation Administration (FAA), and I met the morning after the crash to begin the process of contacting families and developing measures to prevent another Colgan. Once Randy Babbitt was confirmed as FAA administrator, he and I decided to organize a series of 12 safety summits around the country. These sessions included representatives from all corners of the airline business, from company executives and pilots to air traffic controllers and maintenance personnel. "We must regain the public's trust," I said at the first summit, held on June 15 in Washington. "We must inspire confidence in every traveler every time he or she steps on a commercial aircraft of any size at any airport in our country."[1] The meetings addressed pilot flight time, rest and fatigue issues, and how to improve professionalism among pilots, as well as rules regarding pilot training and qualifications. The information the FAA gained from listening to these folks proved invaluable as we developed new safety regulations. Babbitt and I also met with the families of the victims many times in the weeks that followed. Their support and advocacy proved crucial as we went through the rule-making process.

In December 2011, we announced a "fatigue rule," the most sweeping change in pilot rules since the last major revision five decades before. The new decree provided that pilots have at least a 10-hour rest period before getting behind the controls—that rest period had to include eight hours of uninterrupted sleep, in contrast to looser provisions then in place. It further required that pilots have 30 consecutive hours of rest each week, a 25 percent increase over then-current standards. The Colgan crash prompted a second rule, too, one that required airlines to provide as much training for co-pilots as for pilots. The FAA had told me that 61 accidents over the past decade that killed more than 100 people could have been mitigated with better training for co-pilots.

SAFETY COMES FIRST

As the number one person in charge of transportation, I made safety in all modes of travel DOT's top priority. Thousands of people get up every day and get on a plane, a bus, a train or into their cars, and the one thing they don't think about is safety. They shouldn't have to, because that's what those at DOT think about every single day. The department's mission statement reads "[To] serve the United States by ensuring a fast, safe, efficient, accessible and convenient transportation system that meets our vital national interests and enhances the quality of life of the American people, today and into the future."[2] Had it been up to me, I would have listed *safe* first, ahead of *fast*. I can think of no more vital national interest or of anything more essential to quality of life than safe transport. The Colgan crash, only three weeks into my tenure, drove that point home in devastating fashion.

DOT had managed dozens of safety programs long before I came to the department. I believe, however, that my signature accomplishment as secretary was the renewed emphasis I placed on safety. By now, most Americans are familiar with our crusade against distracted driving. I have made what must be hundreds of speeches about the dangers of inattentive driving. During my travels, I heard countless stories of tragedy. Shelley Forney, of Fort Collins, Colorado, shared hers:

> Erica was riding her bike home from school on November 25, 2008. It was the last day of school before Thanksgiving break. A woman driving a Ford Expedition looked down at her cell phone and struck Erica. The accident occurred just a few houses from our home.
>
> Erica suffered a serious head injury and was airlifted to The Children's Hospital in Denver after first being rushed to Medical Center of the Rockies in Loveland. Erica's injuries were so severe the doctors couldn't do anything to save her.
>
> Two days later, on Thanksgiving Day, Erica died. She was just 9-years-old.[3]

At one time early in our campaign, we estimated that over 3,000 people had been killed and more than 400,000 injured in crashes that resulted from distractions such as talking or texting while behind the wheel. Eleven percent of all drivers under the age of 20 involved in fatal crashes were reported to have been distracted at the time of the crash. Among younger drivers, 15–19 years old, involved in fatal crashes, 21 percent were using cell phones. A quarter of teens respond to a text message once or more every time they drive. Sending or receiving a text takes a driver's eyes from the road for an average of 4.6 seconds, the equivalent— at 55 miles per hour—of driving the length of an entire football field, blind. At any given moment during daylight hours across America, about 660,000 drivers are using cell phones or other electronic devices when they should be paying attention to driving.[4] I used to be one of them, but I quit my own distracted driving in 2009.

In June 2012, we released "A Blueprint for Ending Distracted Driving." The plan encouraged the remaining 11 states without distracted driving laws to enact and enforce this critical legislation. We challenged the auto industry to adopt new guidelines for technology to reduce the potential for distraction in the features car makers put in their automobiles. We partnered with driver-education professionals to incorporate new curricular materials to educate novice drivers about the dangers of inattention. We also listed a variety of specific actions people could take to join the department's driver distraction campaign.

We complemented our programming with an aggressive public awareness offensive. The department commissioned a series of public-service announcements to raise awareness about the dangers of distracted driving based on the tag line "One Text or Call Could Wreck It All." The insurance industry stepped up to the plate, too—*American Idol* winner Jordin Sparks encouraged teens and their families to pledge to not text and drive as part of Allstate Insurance's "X the TXT" campaign. *The Oprah Winfrey Show* declared a national "No Phone Zone" day. United Nations secretary general Ban Ki-moon took DOT's call to end distracted driving global by banning UN employees from texting while driving. ESPN reminded sports fans to stay off the phone during its "On the Road to Camp" tour of 32 pro football training sites. The Ad Council targeted teens with a simple message: "Stop the Texts, Stop the Wrecks."

By 2014, 41 states had passed laws against distracted driving, up from 18 when I was sworn in. In late April 2013, the National Highway Traffic Safety Administration followed up one of the recommendations in our blueprint by issuing voluntary guidelines aimed at making it tougher for drivers to become distracted by the navigation and infotainment systems in new cars. The guidelines, which were developed with the Alliance of Automobile Manufacturers, urged car makers to restrict any system that lets drivers push buttons or manually input data while the car is moving. We wanted to ensure that drivers would not take their eyes off the road for more than two seconds at a time.

No one talked about distracted driving in 2009, but that changed under our leadership. If I had stayed for a second term at DOT, my goal would have been to get Congress to pass a national law to prevent distracted driving.

We did not restrict our safety initiatives to distracted driving, however. The National Highway Safety Administration unveiled a five-star rating program for cars, for example, that required manufacturers to put their automobiles through more rigorous crash tests. For the first time, consumers could choose the safest car based on one overall score.

We also cracked down on fatigue among truck drivers. The Federal Motor Carrier Safety Administration issued a final rule that required trucking companies to install electric onboard recorders in each of their fleet's vehicles if their operators violated hours-of-service regulations. These devices automatically register the hours that drivers spend behind the wheel and enable safety enforcers to identify serial violators more effectively. We put hundreds of unsafe motor-coach operators out of business, too, and we established a new office to oversee the safety of public transit systems nationwide.

In addition to these and other steps, we reorganized DOT to better coordinate our safety efforts by establishing a DOT Safety Council. We also developed www.distraction.gov, the "official US Government Website for Distracted Driving."

Our efforts produced results. As my tenure ended, the nation enjoyed its lowest traffic fatality and injury rates since the government started keeping statistics in 1950. Work to promote safety is never done, of course. I know that my successors will not rest until America's skies, roadways, railways, and waterways are the safest they can possibly be.

My Team at DOT

No one person, especially not a political appointee with relatively little hands-on transportation experience, can take credit for DOT's successes. By the time I left office, DOT employed over 55,000 people across the country, about twice the number as the Department of State, for example. Our budget for fiscal year 2014 was $77 billion, again about twice the amount allocated to State but only one-tenth the amount spent by the Department of Health and Human Services.

I headed the Office of the Secretary with overall responsibility for a dozen DOT agencies. They ranged from the familiar, such as the Federal Aviation Administration and the Federal Highway Administration, to the less well known, such as the Saint Lawrence Seaway Development Corporation and the Pipeline and Hazardous Materials Safety Administration. In my office, there were more than a dozen *modes*, the name DOT gives to divisions or departments. In addition to financial management and public affairs modes, the Office of the Secretary included a civil rights mode, a drug and alcohol mode, and an intelligence, security, and emergency-response mode.

DOT's work was guided by an annual performance plan, which we organized around five strategic goals: safety, state of good repair (referring to infrastructure), economic competitiveness, livable communities, and environmental sustainability. The 57-page document prepared for fiscal year 2014 proposed very specific objectives under each goal, accompanied by the measures we used to evaluate performance. It will come as no surprise that our mandate covered safety and infrastructure. DOT programs to promote livable communities and environmental sustainability are less well known. For example, two environmental-sustainability objectives targeted carbon emissions in aviation fuel and noise pollution in aviation. One of our livable-communities initiatives called for the Federal Transit Administration to increase the number of key rail-transit stations accessible to older adults and people with disabilities.[5]

When people asked me, "What does the Department of Transportation do?" it was hard to answer in a way that captured DOT's range of responsibilities. To this day, I haven't come up with a satisfactory 30-second answer.

A TRIUMPH: CAFE STANDARDS

When left to our own devices, and by that I mean without the interference of Congress (or of the White House, for that matter), we enjoyed some notable successes. DOT's work with Lisa Jackson and her Environmental Protection Agency (EPA) to set new fuel economy and emissions standards serves as a prime example.

Just a few days after his inauguration, President Obama issued a Presidential Memorandum, one of the first of his administration. Addressed to Jackson and me, he ordered our departments "to take all measures consistent with law ... to publish in the *Federal Register* by March 30, 2009, a final rule prescribing increased fuel economy for model year 2011." Further, we were directed to begin developing final rules for later model years that accounted for the relevant legal, technological, and scientific findings.[6] His instruction set in motion a very effective process that produced new CAFE (Corporate Average Fuel Economy) standards that improved the average fuel economy of cars and light trucks sold in the United States.

Fuel economy standards were first introduced in 1978 in the wake of the Arab oil embargo. They applied only to passenger vehicles and set 18 miles per gallon (mpg) as the standard. On March 31, 2009, we set the new standard at 27.3 mpg for cars, a 2.0 mpg increase over the 2010 model year average. This single-year standard, as it was called, would save about 887,000,000 gallons of fuel. At our announcement, I said that work on future year standards was well underway and that our review would include an evaluation of fuel-saving technologies, market conditions, and future product plans from the manufacturers.[7]

On May 19, the president proposed a new fuel economy program which adopted uniform federal standards to regulate both fuel economy and greenhouse gas emissions. He called it "a historic agreement to help America break its dependence on oil, reduce harmful pollution, and begin the transition to a clean energy economy."[8] This was a unified, national policy for all automakers and took the place of three possibly competing standards—a DOT standard for fuel economy, an EPA standard for emissions, and a California standard (which would have imposed even more restrictive regulations and would have applied to 13 other states).

This proposal represented a victory for DOT, EPA, the car companies, environmental advocates, and the United Automobile Workers (UAW). We rolled up our sleeves, got together, talked and listened to one another, and made government work in the public interest. The new fuel economy standards bumped the target up to 39 mpg for cars and 30 mpg for trucks by 2016 from the then-current average of 25 mpg for cars. The plan appealed to the industry by including provisions that reduced the cost of compliance and by proposing a uniform national standard. These measures provided some predictability over more than a single year, too. We appealed to consumers by saving them money through improved fuel efficiency and by preserving consumer choice—the rules did not dictate the size of vehicles, for example. "Now, in the past, an agreement such as this would have been considered impossible," the president said. "It's no secret these are folks who've been at odds for years, even decades." But, he said, "the status quo is no longer acceptable."

During the Rose Garden ceremony that day, the president held up our work as "the harbinger of change" in the way business was done in Washington. "No longer will we accept the notion that our politics are too small, our Nation too divided, our people too weary of broken promises and lost opportunities to take up a historic calling," he said. "No longer will we accept anything less than a common effort made in good faith to solve our toughest problems. And this is what this agreement seeks to achieve."[9]

EPA and DOT built upon these core principles articulated by the president and announced in September a historic national program to improve vehicle fuel economy and reduce greenhouse gases even more. Under the proposed program, which covered model years 2012 through 2016, automobile manufacturers would be able to build a single light-duty national fleet that satisfied all federal requirements, as well as the standards of California and other states. The proposed program included miles per gallon requirements under CAFE and the first-ever national emissions standards under EPA's greenhouse gas program. Our plan increased fuel economy by about 5 percent every year, reduced emissions by nearly 950 million metric tons, saved the average car buyer more than $3,000 in fuel costs, and conserved 1.8 billion barrels of oil.[10] We finalized those rules in April, as we continued to work on further improvements.

On July 29, 2011, the president announced an agreement with 13 large automobile manufacturers to increase fuel economy to 54.5 mpg for cars and light-duty trucks by model year 2025. He was joined by Ford, General Motors, Chrysler, BMW, Honda, Hyundai, Jaguar/Land Rover, Kia, Mazda, Mitsubishi, Nissan, Toyota, and Volvo—which together accounted for over 90 percent of all vehicles sold in this country—as well as by the UAW and the states. All partnered with us in the deal.

We accomplished this progressive improvement in CAFE standards over a relatively short period for a government bureaucracy. We put in a lot of hours working with our private sector partners to reach the president's goal. But the real key to success was this: we did not have to contend with Congress. We did not have to march to the Hill for 218 votes in the House and 60 votes in the Senate. The president acknowledged as much in his July remarks. "This agreement ought to serve as a valuable lesson for leaders in Washington," he said. "You are all demonstrating what can happen when people put aside differences. These folks are competitors, you've got labor and business, but they decided, we're going to work together to achieve something important and lasting for the country."[11] Relieved of the need to battle a divided Congress, Lisa Jackson and her staff and DOT and my staff worked it out. Once the president said, "I want this done," all it took was a little bit of leadership at EPA and DOT, and we made it happen.

Last Days

A few days before my tenure ended, I sent an e-mail message to all of the folks at DOT. "This truly has been the best job I have ever held, and for that I owe all of you a great deal of thanks," I wrote. "I have said before that DOT has some of the most professional and hardest working employees in the Federal Government, and I count myself lucky to have served with you." Among DOT's many accomplishments, I highlighted two dozen which I thought illustrated the breadth of the department's activity. Among them were the following:

> • DOT invested over $48 billion in stimulus funds in more than 15,000 infrastructure projects from coast to coast that put 65,000 people to work building and repairing roads, bridges, runways, railways, and shipyards. In sum, we built or improved more than 350,000 miles of road—enough to circle the globe more than 14

times. We upgraded more than 6,000 miles of rail—enough to go coast to coast and back. We repaired more than 20,000 bridges.

• Through our popular TIGER (Transportation Investment Generating Economic Recovery) grants program, we distributed over $3 billion to hundreds of innovative transportation projects.

• We banned long tarmac delays and deceptive advertising practices by airlines, imposed penalties for chronically late flights, required fee reimbursement for lost luggage, and increased compensation to passengers who were bumped from flights.

• We began to modernize our national airspace with satellite-based NextGen technologies, the largest investment ever made in our aviation system.

• We established IdeaHub, which generated more than 8,000 new ideas to improve DOT.[12]

I am particularly proud of the mentoring program we established for young women considering careers in transportation. I made a point of underscoring this initiative at DOT's retreats for the department's 100 or so political appointees. "All of you are here," I said, "because you were politically appointed, because you're talented, because you have expertise." I suspected, too, that all of us owed our success to someone who had mentored us, people like Tom Railsback and Bob Michel in my case. We needed people to carry on the mission, I explained. We were short-timers after all. So I charged each of them with the task of identifying someone in their mode to mentor.

When asked why I had a passion for mentoring, I told the story of my experience with a reading program called Everybody Wins. I had volunteered for the program when I was first elected to Congress. Beginning in 1995, on Tuesdays at noon I would visit John Tyler Elementary School at 1001 G Street Southeast to spend an hour reading a book and sharing lunch with a fourth-, fifth-, or sixth-grade student. I did that for 14 years. A few years ago, Mary Salander, the executive director of Everybody Wins, invited me to the organization's annual dinner to speak about my work with the students at Tyler. When I arrived, a little girl whom I had read to 14 years earlier was to be honored. Mary told me that Ashley Walton, then 21 years old, had asked me to present the award because I had read to Ashley when she was in fourth and fifth grade—I hadn't seen her since. My point to those at the DOT retreats was simple: you have no idea what influence mentoring can have. That is why mentoring is so important.

The payoff for me, personally, came in seeing Ashley again and in messages such as this handwritten note that I received near the end of my term:

> Mr. Secretary—
>
> When I arrived at DOT in 2009, at 22 years old—I had no idea where my journey would lead me. I can honestly say that you and your leadership team came into my life, and changed it forever. From the first briefing with you, until my last day here, your leadership, commitment to mentoring and kindness have opened doors for me. I truly believe that my success here, and my passion for transportation, has developed as a result of your unwavering support. Thank you for taking a chance, and giving me opportunities to learn and lead.
>
> With much appreciation,
> [Signed][13]

LEAVING THE CABINET

A week after the November 2012 elections, I told the president that I was ready to move on. He asked me to stay: "Do you want me to call Kathy? Give me her cell phone number." I said "That's not going to work. Lookit, I'm going to be 68 years old." The president wasn't buying it. Every reason I gave he threw back at me. He genuinely wanted me to continue. Truth is, I was conflicted. Even though there had been disappointments,

I loved working for the president. As much as I had enjoyed representing central Illinois in the House, working in a presidential administration meant that we got things done without having to find 218 votes to do so.

I had begun my four and a half years in the Cabinet with four expectations. All four proved to be unrealistic to some degree. The administration did not use my experience and network of relationships to build Republican support for the president's major policy initiatives. Even when they tried, which was not often, the results were mixed. Neither did the White House consult with me on strategy for obtaining such support before taking legislation to the Hill—too many times I came late to the game, or the inner circle didn't let anyone into the game at all. I had more influence on the substance of transportation policy but, as the episode with Jim Oberstar suggests, my words did not always carry weight. The White House did, however, give me the flexibility and independence to manage DOT, but the disconnect between the president's rhetoric about transforming transportation policy and the reality of getting it done never disappeared. Finally, I had hoped to play a larger role in the broad economic recovery efforts because DOT had such a direct and sizeable impact on job creation and economic development at the state and local levels. That proved not to be the case either.

On January 29, 2013, I announced my decision to leave the Cabinet formally:

> I have let President Obama know that I will not serve a second term as Secretary of the U.S. Department of Transportation. It has been an honor and a privilege to lead the Department, and I am grateful to President Obama for giving me such an extraordinary opportunity. I plan to stay on until my successor is confirmed to ensure a smooth transition for the Department and all the important work we still have to do.

When President Obama thanked me for my service, he said: "Years ago, we were drawn together by a shared belief that those of us in public service owe an allegiance not to party or faction, but to the people we were elected to represent. And Ray has never wavered in that belief."[14]

I followed the same principle that governed my decision to leave the House in 2008—as I said to reporters, "I've had a good run. I'm one of these people who believe you should go out while they're still applauding."[15]

I doubted that I could do much more to support the president's agenda, but I left on good terms. About three months after leaving DOT, during the October 2013 government shutdown, I decided to reach out to President Obama. I e-mailed Marvin Nicholson, the president's longtime aide, to see whether the president would meet with me to discuss a few ideas I had about dealing with congressional Republicans. "Let me check with the boss," Marvin e-mailed back. About half an hour later, he e-mailed again to say that President Obama would meet me at 5:00 that afternoon, Monday, October 7.

I arrived at the White House promptly and was ushered into the Oval Office at 5:20. For the next 30 minutes, the president and I enjoyed a warm, frank conversation—just the two of us, no staff. I advised him to push Congress to pass a clean continuing resolution and to offer to sit down with any member of Congress, including Senator Ted Cruz (R-TX), about any issue, even Obamacare. Cruz represented the tea party conservatives who had forced the shutdown in an ill-advised attempt to kill the president's health care reform. I did not expect the president to make any commitments that afternoon, and he did not, but the next day he held a press conference and said to Congress, in essence, "Send me a clean CR [Continuing Resolution], and I'm happy to talk to anyone."[16]

This single episode says something fundamental about Barack Obama. Even though I was not a close confidant, even though I was a Republican, and even though I had left government, the president agreed to see me, to listen to my ideas, and to act on them (although I certainly cannot take credit for his press conference remarks). From the very beginning, he and I struck up a strong, wonderful friendship grounded in mutual respect and a devotion to public service. Our relationship was bipartisanship writ small, and it worked.

NOTES

1. Lisa Stark and Kate Barrett, "FAA Holds Regional Airline Safety Summit," ABC News, June 15, 2009, RLP-Memoir, f. DOT. Leading DOT.
2. "U.S. Department of Transportation Mission," http://www.dot.gov/mission/about-us.
3. *FocusDriven* Business Plan, n.d., RLP-DOT, f. Cell-Free Driving.
4. "What Is Distracted Driving?" http://www.distraction.gov/content/get-the-facts/facts-and-statistics.html.
5. DOT, "Annual Performance Plan, Fiscal Year 2014," June 18, 2013, RLP-Memoir, f. DOT. Leading DOT.
6. "Presidential Memorandum—Fuel Economy," January 26, 2009, RLP-Memoir, f. DOT. CAFE Standards.
7. The new rules were challenged in court by the Center for Biological Diversity as not addressing inadequacies identified by courts in previous judicial rulings.
8. POTUS, "Remarks on Fuel Efficiency Standards," May 19, 2009, *PPP*, RL-Memoir, f. DOT. CAFE Standards.
9. Ibid.
10. Environmental Protection Agency, press release, "DOT Secretary Ray LaHood and EPA Administrator Lisa P. Jackson Propose National Program to Improve Fuel Economy and Reduce Greenhouse Gases/New Interagency Program to Address Climate Change and Energy Security," September 15, 2009, RLP-Memoir, f. DOT. CAFE Standards.
11. POTUS, "Remarks on Fuel Efficiency Standards," July 29, 2011, *PPP*, RLP-Memoir, f. DOT. CAFE Standards.
12. RL to "All DOT Employees and Contractors," July 2013, RLP-Memoir, f. DOT. Leading DOT.
13. [S.S.] to Mr. Secretary, March 2013, RLP-DOT, f. Retirement.
14. POTUS, "Statement on the Resignation of Raymond H. LaHood as Secretary of Transportation," January 29, 2013, *PPP*, RLP-Memoir, f. DOT. Leading DOT.
15. Ken Thomas, "Ray LaHood Leaving Obama Administration," Associated Press, January 29, 2013, RLP-Memoir, f. DOT. Leading DOT.
16. White House, Office of the Press Secretary, "Press Conference by the President," October 8, 2013, RLP-Memoir, f. DOT. Leading DOT.

Chapter 15

Reflections on a Career of Public Service

Those of us growing up in the working-class neighborhood on Peoria's East Bluff did not show much interest in politics or public service. Most of us lived day to day. We took on part-time jobs, hoped to graduate from high school and college, spent whatever leisure time we had playing sports or going to church, and planned to stay in our hometown, raise a family, and work, probably at Caterpillar, Peoria's largest employer. I lived the values of my upbringing—work hard, play by the rules, have faith in God. Yet no one who knew me then could have predicted the path I have traveled. I am as surprised by my good fortune as they are.

During my 35 years in politics and public service, often with a front-row seat on history, I did not ponder the meaning of passing events. Time slipped by too quickly, and I am not by nature a reflective person. As I move to the sidelines to write this account of my career, however, I am struck by two intertwined, principal qualities of politics that concern me today: pervasive partisan stridency and the absence of leadership.

THE CURSE OF PARTISAN STRIDENCY

I entered the House of Representatives just as the Bob Michels and Tom Foleys of the world were leaving center stage to be replaced by the Newt Gingriches and Nancy Pelosis. The trends were there long before, but the quality of leadership, of civil discourse, of mutual respect changed for the worse with the new leaders. I remember how Newt disparaged Bob by calling him an "accommodationist." But Gingrich was right. Leader Michel listened to Democrats (and to Republicans who disagreed with him), respected differences of opinion, upheld the virtue of thoughtful deliberation, refused to hold grudges, and sought the common ground, all with a sense of personal humility—that was the Michel version of accommodating.

We need more accommodating today. Instead, we have hyperpartisanship. The most obvious form shows up in the inability of Democrats and Republicans to negotiate, much less compromise. Both parties deserve blame. President Obama's early calculation that Democrats alone, led by Speaker Pelosi, could enact his legislative ambitions without cost proved mistaken. Republicans responded in kind by obstructing the president at almost every turn. The spiraling partisan arms race accelerated the tendencies toward incivility I had witnessed in the House—I regret that the decade-long civility initiative which I led there failed to reverse those trends. Today, Democrats and Republicans in both the House and the Senate sacrifice deliberation to engage in partisan brinksmanship.

What has happened to the forces of moderation? According to one recent report, only 11 House members in 2012 fell into that no-man's-land between the most liberal Republican and the most conservative Democrat. The political middle, which numbered 344 in 1982, has been reduced to fewer than a dozen. Taking stock of these numbers, the *Rothenberg Political Report* concluded, "There is no reason to expect the two parties will find more common ground in the months and years ahead."[1] Depressing news.

Partisan stridency has infected the Republican Party, too. Here the conflict is not between the two parties but within my party. A handful of senators and about 40 House Republicans, the tea party Republicans, inhabit a different world from mine. When I first campaigned for the House in 1994, I ran on the idea of using my position there to benefit the people who sent me to Washington. Congress could, and often did, play a positive role in public life. I never bad-mouthed the institution—I revered Congress. I respected the capacity of government programs, and the ability of people in government, to solve problems.

Newer members today are cut from a different cloth. Many of them do not want Congress to pass bills. Any government action is, by their definition, bad for the country. Their commitment to ideological purity prevents them from seeing the value of listening, bargaining, negotiating, or compromising—in a word, *accommodating*. Theirs is the language of battle, of take-no-prisoners, whether they are speaking about Democrats or "Republicans in name only." Every skirmish must be won, no matter how small the stakes. They regard those members who honor the institution with disdain. Their ideological rigidity translates into legislative obstructionism. Long-term solutions fall victim to short-term political calculations. They remind me of the Gingrich acolytes who wanted to turn the House upside down. I have no patience for these hard-edged partisans. I detest their Congress.

Together, these two forms of partisan stridency have caused respect for politics and for the institutions of government to fall to historic lows. Polls conducted during the 16-day government shutdown and potential debt default in October 2013 drove the point home. A *Washington Post*–ABC News poll showed that 70 percent of Americans disapproved of the way Republican lawmakers dealt with the budget negotiations. Democrats did not escape blame—61 percent of Americans disagreed with them.[2] Eight polls conducted during the first three weeks of October showed that an average of 73 percent of those surveyed thought the country was headed down the wrong track. Even more blamed Congress. During

the same period, 84.7 percent disapproved of Congress's performance.[3]
The ideological divide between the parties, enflamed by the sense of
partisan superiority claimed by both sides, produced legislative gridlock.
There were no winners. We need to get back to an America where
Congress solves problems, passes a farm bill, passes an immigration
bill, passes tax reform, passes a budget. It is possible. We proved it
during Bill Clinton's administration when a Republican Congress joined
a Democratic president to pass three budgets and welfare reform.

As I began serving in the president's Cabinet, I did not fully appreciate
the impact that partisan stridency would have on my personal effectiveness. Barack Obama had offered me the job, and I had accepted it, out of
a belief in the potential for bipartisan cooperation to address the nation's
problems. With the benefit of hindsight, I can say that I was the wrong
kind of Republican to reach out to the increasingly hostile members of
my party in the House. My brand of Republicanism—the pragmatic kind
practiced by Everett Dirksen, Bob Michel, Howard Baker, and Bob Dole—
has become marginalized. It's easy to assume that I was bound to fail, that
the promise of bipartisanship was an illusion—too far out of reach for a
single Republican in a Democratic Cabinet. Too formidable a challenge
for a new administration facing tremendous hardships. Too risky for a
young president beholden to a largely liberal constituency. Too much of
a stretch for the brand of Republicanism I represented. Too overmatched
by the partisan and parochial forces arrayed against bipartisanship. But
openings to change the culture of politics did present themselves. We
did not take the best advantage of them, however.

The Challenge to Leadership

Leadership offered one path out of the partisan thicket. Sadly, though,
our nation suffers from a shortage of leadership, both in the White House
and in Congress. As a presidential candidate, Barack Obama recognized
the issue:

What's stopped us is the failure of leadership, the smallness of our politics—the ease with which we're distracted by the petty and the trivial, our chronic avoidance of tough decisions, our preference for scoring cheap political points instead of rolling up our sleeves and building a working consensus to tackle big problems.[4]

I believe that Barack Obama felt a sense of destiny when he took the oath of office for the first time, a sense that he had arrived on the national scene with the unique and historic opportunity to change the terms and means of debate in Washington. His was a vision of a postpartisan world. And he was sincere—I am not cynical enough to believe otherwise. But his effectiveness has been hamstrung by the magnitude of the challenges he confronted when he entered office; by his tendency to rely on an inner circle of advisers, which isolated him; by his own lack of executive experience (and relatively little in the way of legislative experience); by failing to use some of the organizational tools at his disposal, such as the Cabinet, to plan strategy and to evaluate ideas; and by mistakes in judgment and political calculation that prevented cooperation between the political parties and sacrificed vision too easily for short-term gain. I leave it to historians to grapple with a question that still confounds me: Why did President Obama fail to impose his will on those around him and in his party, especially those on Capitol Hill? Surely he had the political capital and the personal skill to do so. Had he done so early on, I am convinced that we would have enjoyed more success.

On June 30, 2013, three days before I walked out the door, several newspapers published my last official op-ed. I used the forum to take stock of the Washington I saw that day, a town that was increasingly distracted by political sideshows and name-calling, rendering it virtually impossible to address our most pressing problems as a nation effectively. I suggested that one solution was to practice a different kind of leadership, one grounded in five qualities and reminiscent of the lessons I have drawn from my days in Congress.

Leaders listen. Bob Michel taught me that when you listen, really listen, you begin to see the issue from the other person's point of view. Their opinions deserve as much regard as mine. I don't get the impression that the White House or congressional Democrats listen to Republicans in the Senate and the House. Little listening occurs in the other direction, either.

Leaders judge honestly. They reach judgments about what people say and do without passing judgment on their character or motivation. Understanding this difference is a virtue. Members of both parties cross the line when they engage in hate-filled rhetoric. When my good friend Congressman Peter King, a Republican from New York, criticized Senator Ted Cruz (R-TX), Cruz's tea party supporters bombarded King's office with what King called "such vile, profane, obscene language."[5] That's crossing the line. Democratic representative Alan Grayson's (FL) reelection campaign sent an e-mail that compared the tea party to the Ku Klux Klan while depicting a burning cross. That's crossing the line. "The way we argue," Bob Michel reminded us at the memorial service for Tom Foley, "can be as important in the long run as the decisions we reach."[6]

Leaders are prudent. By that I mean they are practical and use common sense. These skills are not necessarily the essence of personal charisma or thrilling oratory. Prudence is a quiet quality and demands long periods of considered judgment. Regrettably, the pace and tenor of politics today make it nearly impossible to think, speak, or act prudently.

Leaders conduct themselves with civility—in victory or defeat. Successful public service in a democracy does not require the destruction of one's adversaries. As Abraham Lincoln told a postelection serenade on November 10, 1864, "So long as I have been here I have not willingly planted a thorn in any man's bosom." He added: "May I ask those who have not differed with me, to join with me, in this same spirit towards those who have?"[7]

Finally, leaders—good leaders—take responsibility for how they conduct themselves and for the decisions they make. People want leaders who answer for their actions.[8]

I leave public service not without hope. Our nation has survived greater challenges than those we face today. And we will prevail again. Along the way, we have a duty to fight for those things we believe in. But as we champion our causes, we should remember that we can accommodate differences without abandoning principles. Members of both parties should recognize that they are joined in a partnership—a partnership to govern in the interests of us all. Our challenge today calls for leaders who believe in give and take, with all sides doing some of each. Those leaders will emerge—I am sure of it.

Notes

1. "The Political Middle Has Disappeared," *Rothenberg Political Report*, October 25, 2013, RLP-Memoir, f. DOT. Reflections.

2. Dan Balz, "Shutdown Shines Spotlight on Rift in Republican Party," *Washington Post*, October 7, 2013, RLP-Memoir, f. DOT.

3. Poll results posted on Real Clear Politics (www.realclearpolitics.com) and reproduced in RLP-Memoir, f. DOT. Reflections.

4. Associated Press, "Illinois Sen. Barack Obama's Announcement Speech," February 10, 2007, RLP-Memoir, f. DOT. Bipartisanship.

5. Tal Kopan, "Peter King: 'Vile' Phone Calls by Ted Cruz Allies," *Politico*, September 26, 2013, RLP-Memoir, f. DOT. Reflections.

6. "Remarks by Bob Michel at Memorial Services for Speaker Tom Foley," October 29, 2013, RHMP, Accession 2013/11/11–1, f. Foley.

7. Lincoln Institute, *Mr. Lincoln & Friends*, "Opponents and Enemies," http://www.mrlincolnandfriends.org/inside.asp?pageID=26, RLP-Memoir, f. DOT. Reflections.

8. RL, "Nation's Problem-Solvers: Strong Leaders Need to Overcome Partisan Debate," *Chicago Tribune*, June 30, 2013, RLP-Memoir, f. DOT. Reflections.

Afterword

A person gets only one chance to write a memoir. Although I finished the 15-chapter manuscript in June 2014, I thought it best to delay publication until nearer the end of the Obama administration to see if events, particularly the 2014 congressional elections and the approach of the 2016 presidential election, would change my evaluation of his presidency and the state of play in Congress. My verdict: the fundamentals remain mostly the same—too many cases of excessive partisanship and inconsistent leadership at both ends of Pennsylvania Avenue. In recent events, however, I see evidence for guarded optimism.

Since I left public service more than two years ago, Republicans have won majorities in both the Senate and the House transforming the political landscape. Would the long-promised bipartisanship approach to governing result? Would conditions force the Democratic president and the Republican Congress to join in tackling the formidable public policy challenges facing the nation? It seemed possible. On the day after the November 2014 elections, the president claimed he had heard the voters' message and stood ready to work with the new congressional majority.[1] Republican leaders in the House and Senate replied cautiously. Speaker of the House John Boehner admitted that "finding common ground is going to be hard work."[2] Incoming Senate Majority Leader Mitch McConnell pledged to cooperate with the Obama, noting that both Presidents Reagan and Clinton had worked with the opposition majority party in Congress to pass meaningful legislation.[3]

For the next few months, however, Congress and the president walked a well-traveled path. McConnell chastised the president only days after the midterm elections for threatening to use executive orders to bypass Congress, particularly on immigration. "I had maybe naively hoped the president would look at the results of the election and decide to come to the political center and do some business with us," McConnell said. "I still hope he does that at some point, but the early signs are not good." The Speaker sounded the same note in blunter language: "We're going to fight the president tooth and nail if he continues down this path. This is the wrong way to govern."[4] That partisan testiness has persisted throughout 2015 in battles on issues ranging from approving a federal budget to recognizing Cuba to reauthorizing the Patriot Act and far beyond.

Granted substantial majorities by the voters, Republican leaders vowed to make the 114th Congress a showcase for their governing ability. Their record is mixed. Congress saw only two bills become law in the first three months of the new Congress—a terrorism insurance measure and a veterans' suicide prevention bill, both holdovers from the previous Congress. On at least three occasions, Republican leaders in the House had to pull bills off the floor because they lacked enough GOP votes to pass. To top it off, hyper-conservative House Republicans threatened to withhold funding for the Department of Homeland Security (DHS) in an ill-fated ploy to reverse the president's executive order ending the deportation of five million illegal immigrants. To what end? The House eventually voted to fund the department, yet every provision sought by Republicans to halt the president's executive actions on immigration fell by the wayside.

Then the calculus apparently shifted when, in the immediate aftermath of the DHS debacle, Republicans in Congress adopted a different strategy. The Speaker permitted votes on six budget alternatives in late March, for example—three authored by Republicans, three by Democrats. Further, Boehner and Democratic leader Nancy Pelosi reached agreement on Medicare doctors' payments—the so-called "doctor fix," which permanently eased scheduled cuts and partially funded the change by means testing.[5] In the other chamber, senators acted in bipartisan fashion to overhaul the No Child Left Behind education law, to provide for limited congressional review of negotiations with Iran over its nuclear weapons program, to pass an anti-sex trafficking bill, and to approve attorney general nominee Loretta Lynch. On May 5, the Senate cleared a House-passed agreement that promised a balanced budget within a decade. In McConnell's words: "It's a reminder that the new Republican majority is getting Congress back to work."[6]

At the end of June, the president and Congress passed landmark trade legislation—it was, according to one source, the first time the president and GOP leaders successfully negotiated to pass a major bill.[7] At stake was trade promotion authority, which would make it easier for the administration to conclude trade deals by preventing Congress from amending them. The president sought this fast-track legislation in order to negotiate an agreement with 11 Latin American and Asian nations known as the Trans-Pacific Partnership. The bill followed the tug-of-war that usually characterizes the passage of substantive legislation: behind-the-scenes negotiations among key members of Congress, followed by an announcement of a deal in mid-April, resulting in outcries from the wounded parties (primarily liberal Democrats in the Senate), generating more compromises, and, after a series of votes in the House and Senate, passing Trade Promotion Authority and the Trade Preferences Extension Act, which the president signed into law on June 29.

"Now, I think it's fair to say that getting these bills through Congress has not been easy," the president said to laughter at the signing ceremony. "They've been declared dead more than once. ... We're supposed to make sure that we air our differences and then, ultimately, Congress works its will—especially on issues that inspire strongly held feelings on all sides." He thanked Republican leaders in the House and Senate before concluding: "This was a true bipartisan effort. And it's a reminder of what we can get done—even on the toughest issues—when we work together in a spirit of compromise."[8]

I count the law a success for bipartisanship and leadership. In this memoir I have faulted President Obama for falling short of his vow to govern in a new, more productive, and bipartisan way. But in this case, the president employed his formidable skills to advance the trade legislation. He made the calls. He took the meetings. He made it a personal mission. It reminded me of the early months of his administration when the president went to bat for the economic stimulus package and health care reform. His engagement on the trade issue was refreshing and encouraging to see. When Barack Obama employs the full power of the presidency, it's hard to beat him.

Whether or not the trend continues remains to be seen, of course. Congressional Republicans, if they are sincere in their vow to show they can govern, have a stake in continued cooperation with a Democratic president who, after all, has the power to veto what Congress passes without much fear of an override. For his part, the president has his legacy to consider.

The chief obstacle to sustained legislative progress remains, in my opinion, obstructionist Republicans. I don't intend to paint all members of my party with the same brush—my gripe is with the 50 or so in the House and the handful in the Senate who have given up the ability to produce legislation for the sake of uncompromising principle. They tell their colleagues that defeat is better than victory so long as no concession is involved. They treasure a loss more than a measure of progress. They see a slight deviation from some ideological abstraction as the first step on the road to political ruination. That's nonsense. When the normal disagreements inherent in a healthy democracy cease to be differences and become dogmas instead, then neither side will abandon their fixed positions.[9] Paralysis supplants action. The bargaining that produced the trade law provides a better model.

Congress returned from its summer recess on September 8. Will the members revert to form and turn every policy debate into a pitched ideological battle? Or will cooler heads prevail? As I write these concluding words, it is clear that the president's Iran nuclear deal will provide the first test. Although the final outcome awaits House action, the Senate chapter of the story seems settled. As with the trade bill, the president combined his personal skill and the power of the office to marshal support from enough Democrats in the Senate to prevent Republicans from torpedoing the agreement. Barack Obama won that historic achievement one-on-one, wooing each senator in turn, up close and personal. Count the Iran vote in the Senate a huge victory for the president but a loss for bipartisanship—all Republican senators pledged to vote against the agreement. The House is another matter entirely. Conservative Republicans, chiefly members of the House Freedom Caucus, threw a wrench into Speaker Boehner's plans to vote on the agreement on September 9—yet another example of their obstructionist tactics in what is most likely another empty gesture.

Other tests of leadership and bipartisanship will come in quick succession—passing a spending bill by September 30 (which conservative Republicans have threatened to hold hostage to their plan to defund Planned Parenthood), or acting on a stop-gap measure to keep the government running, or, failing that, shutting down the government—again; raising the debt ceiling limit by the end of November or risking default; and replenishing the highway trust fund on a long-term basis (the current extension ends on October 29) or resorting to a short-term solution for the umpteenth time.[10] And how will the dynamics of Senate action change when there are five sitting senators—one Democrat and four Republicans—who have declared for their party's presidential nomination?

Even in the best of times, politics would color the debates on these consequential issues. But the 2016 presidential election adds a wild card. The candidacies of Donald Trump and Bernie Sanders have tapped into popular anger and exasperation with all of our political institutions and with the people who serve in them. The last time more Americans thought the country was headed in the right direction rather than the wrong one was more than 10 years ago in January 2004.[11] Neither party escapes blame. Regrettably, the overheated rhetoric that accompanies our campaigns obscures legitimate differences of opinion over public policy. But the nation needs to hear those honest differences expressed in respectful, civil terms. I am, at heart, an optimist. I do believe that our political leaders will see eventually that bipartisanship holds the key to overcoming our challenges. It will take time, I know. But it will be worth the wait.

Finally, on a more personal note. On March 17, 2015, Aaron Schock, my successor in Congress, announced his resignation following allegations that he misspent taxpayer money. The special election to select the new representative from Illinois's 18th congressional district took place yesterday. Kathy and I are proud that our son, Darin, won that election with nearly 70 percent of the vote. He will occupy the seat I once held. I take comfort in the fact that he sees the same opportunity as I did 20 years ago to represent central Illinois and his country. Darin now inherits the mantle of responsibility once borne by Abraham Lincoln, Everett McKinley Dirksen, and Robert H. Michel—a legacy he will honor.

Ray LaHood
September 11, 2015

NOTES

1. Barack Obama, "The President's News Conference," November 5, 2014, *PPP*, RL-Memoir, f. Afterword.
2. "House Speaker Weekly Briefing, November 6, 2014, C-SPAN, http://www.c-span.org/video/?322595-1/house-speaker-john-boehner-roh-briefing. Accessed February 23, 2015.
3. "Senate Minority Leader McConnell on Midterm Elections," C-SPAN, http://www.c-span.org/video/?322580-1/senate-minority-leader-mitch-mcconnell-news-conference. Accessed February 23, 2015.
4. Michael McAuliff, "Mitch McConnell Is 'Very Disturbed' By President Obama," *The Huffington Post*, November 13, 2014, RL-Memoir, f. Afterword.
5. Michael Gerson, "The Pelosi-Boehner Compromise on Medicare is a Rare Bird," *The Washington Post*, March 31, 2015, RL-Memoir, f. Afterword.
6. Rachel Blade, "Republicans Finally Get Their Budget," *Politico*, May 5, 2015, RL-Memoir, f. Afterword.
7. Colleen McCain Nelson and Siobhan Hughes, "Pragmatic Alliance Got Bill Through," *The Wall Street Journal*, June 24, 2015, RL-Memoir, f. Afterword.
8. Barack Obama, "Remarks by the President at Signing of the Defending Public Safety Employees' Retirement Act and the Trade Preferences Extension Act of 2015," June 29, 2015, RL-Memoir, f. Afterword.
9. These sentiments echo those of my dear friend and mentor Bob Michel. See Robert H. Michel, "In Praise of Compromise," American Bar Association Leadership Institute, March 19, 1987, RHMP, Speech and Trip Files.
10. Kelsey Snell, "Congress's Awful Autumn," *Washington Post's* Power Post, August 17, 2015.
11. Patrick O'Conner and Janet Hook, "Splits Plague Parties as Fall Campaign Starts," *The Wall Street Journal*, September 8, 2015, RL-Memoir, f. Afterword.

ACKNOWLEDGMENTS BY RAY LaHOOD

Public service requires a fair amount of sacrifice. I count myself so blessed that Kathy LaHood, my wife of 47 years, supported me without reservation while she raised our four wonderful children so that I could pursue my dreams and ambitions. Whatever success I have enjoyed, I share with her enthusiastically.

As you will have discovered in reading this memoir, I began my career not as a politician but as a teacher. I had the good fortune to spend six years teaching social studies in classrooms at St. Joseph School, Pekin; Holy Family School, Peoria; and Oak Grove West, near Bartonville. Working with those students stimulated my own curiosity and interest in government and politics. Without knowing it, they helped chart the course for my 35-year career in Washington, DC.

I owe a profound debt of gratitude to two mentors and lifelong friends. Former congressman Tom Railsback gave me my first job as a congressional staffer when he selected me as his district representative in Illinois's 17th congressional district. Among the many lessons he taught me was the importance of taking care of constituents. Bob Michel—I cannot overstate the impact Bob had on me and on my career. He represented my hometown in Congress for 38 years and served as Republican leader in the House for 14. Bob hired me first as his district assistant and then as his chief of staff; in all, I worked for him for 12 years. He gave me a rare opportunity to see the best that a member of Congress can offer to constituents, to colleagues on both sides of the aisle, and to the nation. No one could ask for a better teacher than Bob Michel. His example, his wisdom, and his friendship prepared me to succeed him when he chose to retire.

The people of central Illinois's 18th congressional district placed their faith in me to serve as their voice and their vote in the House of Representatives for 14 years. I am grateful for their trust. And I could not have carried out my responsibilities to them without a talented, hardworking, and dedicated staff. I was privileged to share my time in public service with an outstanding staff—in my campaigns, in Congress, and in the Cabinet. A heartfelt thank you to them.

My time in public life came to an end in July 2013 when I stepped down as secretary of the U.S. Department of Transportation. I knew Barack Obama as a fellow Illinoisan and colleague in the state's congressional delegation before his election to the White House. When he invited me to join his Cabinet, I knew it was a historic opportunity. And I was not disappointed. He and I did not always agree on policy or on specific decisions, of course. We sometimes brought different perspectives to the issues of the day. But I continue to admire him as a person and as the leader of our country. It was the highlight of my life to serve in his Cabinet.

I hesitate to single out others among my many, many friends in politics and public service who have given me their sage advice and unstinting support. As much credit as they deserve, listing them risks leaving someone out, something I do not want to do. But I make an exception for Rahm Emanuel. As I have explained, he and I are a study in contrasts, but our friendship has endured for many years. I treasure that. We are proof that bipartisanship can work. And I have no doubt that Rahm, by his endorsement, made it possible for me to serve in the president's Cabinet.

I appreciate the expertise that Toni Tan, director of Cambria Press, and her staff brought to this project. A memoir by its nature is a personal story, and the telling of it has been much improved by their editorial contributions.

Finally, my thanks to Frank Mackaman for his guidance, writing skill, friendship, and encouragement in assisting with the writing of this book. Frank directs the work of The Dirksen Congressional Center in Pekin, Illinois. In addition to a variety of research and educational programs, the center houses my congressional collection, along with the papers of Everett McKinley Dirksen and Bob Michel, two central Illinois Republicans who represented the best traditions of bipartisanship, of civil political discourse, of effective lawmaking. I am reminded of something Senator Dirksen proclaimed during the tense Senate negotiations over the Civil Rights Act of 1964: "I am a legislator, not a moralist." We need fewer moralists and more legislators.

Appendix A

Republican Contract with America

As Republican Members of the House of Representatives and as citizens seeking to join that body we propose not just to change its policies, but even more important, to restore the bonds of trust between the people and their elected representatives.

That is why, in this era of official evasion and posturing, we offer instead a detailed agenda for national renewal, a written commitment with no fine print.

This year's election offers the chance, after four decades of one-party control, to bring to the House a new majority that will transform the way Congress works. That historic change would be the end of government that is too big, too intrusive, and too easy with the public's money. It can be the beginning of a Congress that respects the values and shares the faith of the American family.

Like Lincoln, our first Republican president, we intend to act "with firmness in the right, as God gives us to see the right." To restore accountability to Congress. To end its cycle of scandal and disgrace. To make us all proud again of the way free people govern themselves.

On the first day of the 104th Congress, the new Republican majority will immediately pass the following major reforms, aimed at restoring the faith and trust of the American people in their government:

> **FIRST,** require all laws that apply to the rest of the country also apply equally to the Congress;
> **SECOND,** select a major, independent auditing firm to conduct a comprehensive audit of Congress for waste, fraud or abuse;

THIRD, cut the number of House committees, and cut committee staff by one-third;

FOURTH, limit the terms of all committee chairs;

FIFTH, ban the casting of proxy votes in committee;

SIXTH, require committee meetings to be open to the public;

SEVENTH, require a three-fifths majority vote to pass a tax increase;

EIGHTH, guarantee an honest accounting of our Federal Budget by implementing zero base-line budgeting.

Thereafter, within the first 100 days of the 104th Congress, we shall bring to the House Floor the following bills, each to be given full and open debate, each to be given a clear and fair vote and each to be immediately available this day for public inspection and scrutiny.

1. THE FISCAL RESPONSIBILITY ACT: A balanced budget/tax limitation amendment and a legislative line-item veto to restore fiscal responsibility to an out-of-control Congress, requiring them to live under the same budget constraints as families and businesses.

2. THE TAKING BACK OUR STREETS ACT: An anti-crime package including stronger truth-in-sentencing, "good faith" exclusionary rule exemptions, effective death penalty provisions, and cuts in social spending from this summer's "crime" bill to fund prison construction and additional law enforcement to keep people secure in their neighborhoods and kids safe in their schools.

3. THE PERSONAL RESPONSIBILITY ACT: Discourage illegitimacy and teen pregnancy by prohibiting welfare to minor mothers and denying increased AFDC for additional children while on welfare, cut spending for welfare programs, and enact a tough two-years-and-out provision with work requirements to promote individual responsibility.

4. THE FAMILY REINFORCEMENT ACT: Child support enforcement, tax incentives for adoption, strengthening rights of parents in their children's education, stronger child pornography laws, and an elderly dependent care tax credit to reinforce the central role of families in American society.

5. THE AMERICAN DREAM RESTORATION ACT: A $500 per child tax credit, begin repeal of the marriage tax penalty, and creation of American Dream Savings Accounts to provide middle class tax relief.

6. THE NATIONAL SECURITY RESTORATION ACT: No U.S. troops under U.N. command and restoration of the essential parts of our national security funding to strengthen our national defense and maintain our credibility around the world.

7. THE SENIOR CITIZENS FAIRNESS ACT: Raise the Social Security earnings limit which currently forces seniors out of the work force, repeal the 1993 tax hikes on Social Security benefits and provide tax incentives for private long-term care insurance to let Older Americans keep more of what they have earned over the years.

8. THE JOB CREATION AND WAGE ENHANCEMENT ACT: Small business incentives, capital gains cut and indexation, neutral cost recovery, risk assessment/cost-benefit analysis, strengthening the Regulatory Flexibility Act and unfunded mandate reform to create jobs and raise worker wages.

9. THE COMMON SENSE LEGAL REFORM ACT: "Loser pays" laws, reasonable limits on punitive damages and reform of product liability laws to stem the endless tide of litigation.

10. THE CITIZEN LEGISLATURE ACT: A first-ever vote on term limits to replace career politicians with citizen legislators.

Further, we will instruct the House Budget Committee to report to the floor and we will work to enact additional budget savings, beyond the budget cuts specifically included in the legislation described above, to ensure that the Federal budget deficit will be less than it would have been without the enactment of these bills.

Respecting the judgment of our fellow citizens as we seek their mandate for reform, we hereby pledge our names to this Contract with America.

Source. http://www.house.gov/house/Contract/CONTRACT.html. Accessed January 6, 2009.

Appendix B

Proposed Follow-Up Activities for the Retreat Planning Committee, March 1997

One-minute day about the retreat

Periodic joint caucus/conference meetings

Person-to-person follow-up between those attending and those who did not

Party self-policing of floor behavior

Distribution of opening video to all members

Special Order by Planning Committee to explain what happened in Hershey

Monthly co-Team Leader meetings

Arrange for all Members to see the opening video and speeches

Wednesday sandwich night in the Members' dining room for Members and families

Hershey kisses in the cloakroom

Wear retreat name tags on the floor

Hold shorter retreats on a monthly or quarterly basis

Make the Speaker Pro Tempore more active in stopping bad behavior before it gets out of control

Establish a goal of having no words taken down this year

Hold another bipartisan congressional retreat next year

Establish a monthly lecture series around the topics of civility and the factors affecting House debate

More use of the family room

Combine the cloakrooms on a periodic basis

Move one-minutes to the end of the day

Write a "Hershey Accords" memorializing the agreements coming out of the retreat

Retreat with the media

Congressional staff retreat

Committee retreats

Regular bipartisan leadership meetings

Bipartisan freshmen orientation

Make the ethics process less subject to abuse

Work on making the schedule more family friendly

More bipartisan social events

Ongoing facilitation coaching

More foreign travel for Members and family

Source. Charles to Diane, March 12, 1997, RLP-DC-S, f. Civility Retreats. 1997. Correspondence.

Appendix C

H12038 CONGRESSIONAL RECORD —HOUSE December 19, 1998

The SPEAKER pro tempore. The Chair is prepared to rule.

Knowing that the House may wish to express its will on this question, the Chair nevertheless will follow the course set by presiding officers for at least the past 150 years by rendering a decision from the Chair.

The gentleman from New York has made the point of order that the amendment in the motion to recommit offered by the gentleman from Virginia is not germane to House Resolution 611.

The rule of germaneness derives directly from the authority of the House under section 5 in article I of the Constitution to determine its own rules. It has governed the proceedings of the House for all of its 210-year history. Its applicability to a motion to recommit is well established. As reflected in the Deschler-Brown Precedents in volume 10, chapter 28, both at section 1 and at section 17.2, then-Majority Leader Carl Albert made these general observations about the rule in 1965, and I quote:

> It is a rule which has been insisted upon by Democrats and Republicans alike ever since the Democratic and Republican parties have been in existence. It is a rule without which this House could never complete its legislative program if there happened to be a substantial minority in opposition.

> One of the great things about the House of Representatives and one of the things that distinguish[es] it from other legislative bodies is that we do operate on the rule of germaneness. No legislative body of this size could ever operate unless it did comply with the rule of germaneness.

At the outset the Chair will state two guiding principles. First, an otherwise privileged resolution is rendered nonprivileged by the inclusion of nonprivileged matter. This principle is exemplified in the ruling of Speaker Clark on January 11, 1916, which is recorded in Cannon's Precedents at volume 6, section 468. Accordingly, to a resolution pending as privileged, an amendment proposing to broach nonprivileged matter is not germane.

Second, to be germane, an amendment must share a common fundamental purpose with the pending proposition. This principle is annotated in section 798b of the House Rules and Manual. Accordingly, to a pending resolution addressing one matter, an amendment proposing to broach an intrinsically different matter is not germane.

As the excellent arguments in debate on this point of order have made clear, these two principles are closely intertwined in any analysis of the relationship between the amendment proposed in the motion to recommit and the pending resolution. The Chair thanks those who have brought their arguments to the attention of the Chair.

The pending resolution proposes to impeach the President of the United States. As such, it invokes an exclusive constitutional prerogative of the House. The final clause of section 2 in Article I of the Constitution mandates that the House, "shall have the sole power of impeachment." For this reason, the pending proposal constitutes a question of the privileges of the House within the meaning of rule IX. Ample precedent is annotated in the House Rules and Manual at section 604.

The amendment in the motion to recommit offered by the gentleman from Virginia proposes instead to censure the President. It has no comparable nexus to an exclusive constitutional prerogative of the House. Indeed, clause 7 of section 3 in article I of the Constitution prescribes that "judgment in cases of impeachment shall not extend further than to removal from office and disqualification to hold and enjoy any office of honor, trust or profit under the United States."

An instructive contrast appears in clause 2 of section 5 in article I of the Constitution, which establishes a range of alternative disciplinary sanctions for Members of Congress by stating that each House may, "punish its Members for disorderly behavior, and with the concurrence of two-thirds, expel a Member." This contrast demonstrates that, while the constitutional power of either body in Congress to punish one of its Members extends through a range of alternatives, the constitutional power of the Congress to remove the President, consistent with the separation of powers, is confined to the impeachment process.

Thus, a proposal to discipline a Member may admit as germane an amendment to increase or decrease the punishment (except expulsion, which the Chair will address presently), in significant part because the Constitution contemplates that the House may impose alternative punishments. But a resolution of impeachment, being a question of privileges of the House because it invokes an exclusive constitutional prerogative of the House, cannot admit as germane an amendment to convert the remedial sanction of potential removal to a punitive sanction of censure, as that would broach nonprivileged matter. For this conclusion the Chair finds support in Hinds' Precedents at volume 5, section 5810, as cited in Deschler's Precedents at volume 3, chapter 14, section 1.3, footnote 8.

The qualitative difference between these two contrasting sources of disciplinary authority in the Constitution signifies an intrinsic parliamentary difference between impeachment and an alternative sanction against the President. The Chair believes that this distinction is supported in the cited precedents and is specifically discussed in the parliamentary notes on pages 400 and 401 of the cited volume. An analogous case emphasizing an intrinsic difference is recorded in Cannon's Precedents at volume 6, section 236, reflecting that on October 27, 1921, Speaker Gillett held that an amendment proposing to censure a Members [sic] of the House was not germane to a resolution proposing that the Member be expelled from the House. [Time: 12:45]

The cited precedent reveals several occasions when the Committee on the Judiciary, having been referred a question of impeachment against a civil officer of the United States, reported a recommendation that impeachment was not warranted and, thereafter, called upon the report as a question of privilege.

The occasional inclusion in an accompanying report of the Committee on the Judiciary of language recommending that an official be censured has not been held to destroy the privilege of an accompanying resolution that does not, itself, convey the language of censure.

The Chair is aware that, in the consideration of a resolution proposing to impeach Judge James Peck in 1830, the House considered an amendment proposing instead to express disapproval while refraining from impeachment. In that instance no Member rose to a point of order, and no parliamentary decision was entered from the Chair or by the House. The amendment was considered by common sufferance. That no Member sought to enforce the rule of germaneness on that occasion does not establish a precedent of the House that such an amendment would be germane.

Where the pending resolution addresses impeachment as a question of the privileges of the House, the rule of germaneness requires that any amendment confine itself to impeachment, whether addressing it in a positive or a negative way. Although it may be possible by germane amendment to convert a reported resolution of impeachment to resolve that impeachment is not warranted, an alternative sanction having no equivalent constitutional footing may not be broached as a question of privilege and, correspondingly, is not germane.

The Chair acknowledges that the language of House Resolution 611 articulates its proposition for impeachment in language that, itself, tends to convey opprobrium. The Chair must remain cognizant, however, that the resolution does so entirely in the framework of the articles of impeachment. Rather than inveighing any separate censure, the resolution only effects [sic] the constitutional prayer for judgment by the Senate.

The Chair is not passing on the ultimate constitutionality of a separate resolution of censure. Indeed, the Chair does not judge the constitutionality of measures before the House. Rather, the Chair holds today only that the instant proposal to censure or otherwise admonish the President of the United States—as it does not constitute a question of the privileges of the House—is not germane to the pending resolution of impeachment—an intrinsically separate question of the privileges of the House.

The gentleman from Missouri (Mr. GEPHARDT), the minority leader, is recognized.

APPENDIX D

PHOTO GALLERY

Figure 1. Ray LaHood, aged five.

Source. Ray LaHood Papers.
Note. This was taken in Peoria, Illinois.

Figure 2. Parents Mary and Ed LaHood, ca. 1978.

Source. Ray LaHood Papers.

Figure 3. Chief of staff to House Republican Leader Robert H. Michel, 1989.

Source. Ray LaHood Papers.
Note. March 14, 1989.

Figure 4. Ray LaHood's first election to the House of Representatives, 1994.

Source. Ray LaHood Papers.
Date: November 8, 1994.

Figure 5. With Republican Leader Michel at the State of the Union Address, 1995.

Source. Ray LaHood Papers.
Date: January 24, 1995.

Figure 6. President George W. Bush visits Peoria, Illinois, 2007.

Source. White House Photo Office, Ray LaHood Papers.
Date: January 30, 2007.

Figure 7. Vice President Joe Biden conducts ceremonial swearing-in, 2009.

Source. White House Photo Office, Ray LaHood Papers.
Date: January 27, 2009.

Figure 8. First Lady Michelle Obama visits the Department of Transportation, 2009.

Source. White House Photo Office, Ray LaHood Papers.
Date: February 9, 2009.

Figure 9. With Vice President Joe Biden on Air Force Two, 2009.

Source. White House Photo Office, Ray LaHood Papers.
Date: June 2009.

Figure 10. The president visits the Department of Transportation, 2009.

Source. White House Photo Office, Ray LaHood Papers.
Date: June 25, 2009.

Figure 11. Notes from the first Cabinet meeting, 2009.

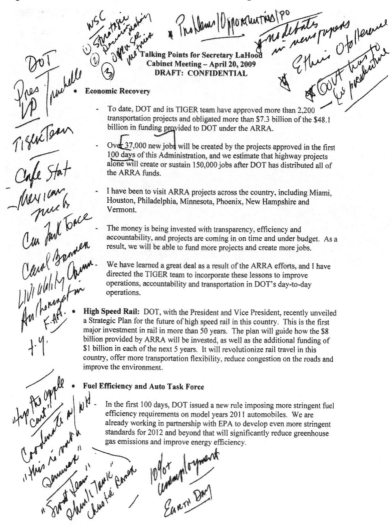

Source. RLP-DOT, f. Cabinet Meetings, 2009.
Date: April 20, 2009.

Figure 12. Ray LaHood blocks for the president, 2010.

Source. White House Photo Office, Ray LaHood Papers.
Date: House Republican Conference meeting, Baltimore MD, January 29, 2010.

Figure 13. Advisers meet about Hurricane Irene, White House Situation Room, 2011.

Source. White House Photo Office, Ray LaHood Papers.
Date: August 28, 2011.

Figure 14. Aboard Marine One, the presidential helicopter, 2011.

Source. White House Photo Office, Ray LaHood Papers.
Date: September 22, 2011.

Figure 15. Signing ceremony, Moving Ahead for Progress in the 21st Century Act, 2012.

Source. White House Photo Office, Ray LaHood Papers.
Date: July 6, 2012.

Figure 16. Golf with the president, 2013.

Source. White House Photo Office, Ray LaHood Papers.
Date: May 18, 2013.

Figure 17. Viewing the 2013 Inaugural Parade.

Source. White House Photo Office, Ray LaHood Papers.
Date: January 21, 2013.

Figure 18. Kathy and Ray LaHood, 2010.

Source. Unknown.
Date: October 3, 2010, Camp David, Maryland.

Authors' Note on Sources

In writing this account, Frank Mackaman and I have relied on archival collections housed at the Dirksen Congressional Center, Pekin, Illinois. Documents from the following collections are cited in the endnotes (short titles for frequently cited sources are listed at the end of this note):

> Ray LaHood Information File, The Dirksen Congressional Center
> Ray LaHood Papers, The Dirksen Congressional Center
>> Campaign Subject File
>> Department of Transportation Files
>> Friends of Ray LaHood Files
>> Memoir Reference File
>> Peoria Office Files
>> Personal Files
>> Tim Butler Subject Files
>> Washington, DC, Office Files, Subject File
> Robert H. Michel Information File
> Robert H. Michel Papers, The Dirksen Congressional Center
>> Campaigns and Elections Series

This account has made extensive use of news clippings saved by my office staff and collected in preparation for writing the memoir. The endnotes contain references to stories published by the following newspapers and periodicals: *AASHTO Journal* (American Association of State Highway and Transportation Officials), ABC News *The Note*, *AllPolitics*, the *American Editor*, the Associated Press, *Between the Lines*, *Blueprint America*, the *Boston Globe*, *CQ Researcher*, *Chicago Magazine*, the *Chicago Sun-Times*, the *Chicago Tribune*, CNN's *State of the Union with Candy Crowley*, *Congress Daily*, the *Connector*, the *Decatur Herald and Review* (Decatur, IL), the *Dirksen Congressional Center Report*, the *Dispatch and the Rock Island Argus* (Rock Island, IL), *The Hill*, the *Journal-Courier* (Jacksonville, IL), *Logistics Management*, the *Los Angeles Times*, the *National Journal*, the *New York Times*, the *Omaha World-Herald*, the *Patriot-News* (Harrisburg, PA), the *Pekin Daily Times* (Pekin, IL), the *Peoria Journal Star*, *Politico*, *PR Newswire*, Reuters, *Roll Call*, the *Rothenberg Political Report*, the *Spokesman-Review* (Spokane, WA), the *Springfield State Journal* (Springfield, IL), the *State Journal-Register* (Springfield, IL), the *Tampa Bay Times* (Tampa, FL), the *Times-Picayune* (New Orleans, LA), *USA Today*, *U.S. News and World Report*, *Time* magazine, *Transportation Nation*, *Vanity Fair*, the *Washington Post*, the *Washington Times*, and the *Wilson Quarterly*.

The following published sources are cited in the book: Peter Baker, *Breach: Inside the Impeachment and Trial of William Jefferson Clinton* (New York: Scribner, 2000), Kindle edition; Daniel J. Balz and Ronald Brownstein, *Storming the Gates: Protest Politics and the Republican Revival* (Boston: Little, Brown, & Co., 1996); Steven Carter, "Toward an Integral Politics," in *Integrity* (New York: HarperCollins, 1996); Congressional Quarterly, *Congress and the Nation*, vol. 10, 1997–2001 (Washington, DC: CQ Press, 2002); Congressional Quarterly, *Congress and the Nation, 2001–2004*, vol. 11 (Washington, DC: CQ Press, 2006); Congressional Quarterly, *Congress and the Nation, 2001–2002* (online edition by subscription); Jackie Koszczuk and Martha Angle, eds., *Congressional Quarterly's Politics in America 2008: The 100th Congress* (Washington, DC: Congressional Quarterly, 2007); Philip D. Duncan and Christine C. Lawrence, *Congressional Quarterly's Politics in America 1998: The 105th Congress* (Washington, DC: Congressional Quarterly, 1997); and Lisa Young, "Freshman Congressman Once a Freshman Here," *Spoon River College Anthology* (Winter 1995).

We have cited the following websites in the manuscript:

- the Biography Channel (http://www.biography.com/tv)
- the Heritage Foundation (http://www.heritage.org)
- Democrats.com Unity (http://www.democrats.com)
- the Lincoln Institute (http://www.abrahamlincoln.org/)
- PollingReport.com (http://www.pollingreport.com/)

- Politico.com (http://www.politico.com/)
- Real Clear Politics (www.realclearpolitics.com)
- *Streetsblog USA* (http://dc.streetsblog.org/)
- *Transportation for America Blog* (http://t4america.org/blog/)
- U.S. Congressman John Mica (http://mica.house.gov/about-john-mica/)
- U.S. Department of Transportation (http://www.dot.gov/)
- YouTube (http://www.youtube.com).

Among the government records cited: U.S. Senate Committee on Intelligence and U.S. House Permanent Select Committee on Intelligence, "Joint Inquiry into Intelligence Community Activities Before and After the Terrorist Attacks of September 11, 2001," H.R. Rep. No. 107-792 (December 2002).

SHORT TITLES

Archival Collections

RHMP Robert H. Michel Papers

RHMIF Robert H. Michel Information File

RLP-Campaign Ray LaHood Papers, Campaign Subject File

RLP-DC-S Ray LaHood Papers, Washington DC Office Files, Subject File

RLP-DOT Ray LaHood Papers, U.S. Department of Transportation

RLP-FORL Ray LaHood Papers, Friends of Ray LaHood

RLP-Memoir Ray LaHood Papers, Memoir Reference File

RLP-Peoria Ray LaHood Papers, Peoria Office

RLP-Peoria-TBS Ray LaHood Papers, Peoria Office, Tim Butler Subject Files

Other

CQ *Congressional* Quarterly

Cong. Rec. *Congressional Record*

DCC The Dirksen Congressional Center

DOT U.S. Department of Transportation

NYT New York Times

PPP Public Papers of the President, the American Presidency Project (www.presidency.ucsb.edu/index.php)

POTUS Barack Obama, President of the United States

About the Authors

Ray LaHood joined Barack Obama's Cabinet as U.S. secretary of transportation in January 2009, retiring in July 2013. In the president's words: "Years ago, we were drawn together by a shared belief that those of us in public service owe an allegiance not to party or faction, but to the people we were elected to represent. And Ray has never wavered in that belief." Previously, LaHood served in the Illinois House of Representatives, as a staff member to U.S. representative Thomas F. Railsback (R-IL) and to House Republican leader Robert H. Michel (R-IL). LaHood won the first of seven elections as a Republican from central Illinois to the U.S. House of Representatives in 1994 (He did not run in 2008). He holds a BS in education and sociology from Bradley University. In January 2014, LaHood joined DLA Piper, a global business law firm, as a senior policy advisor.

Frank H. Mackaman directs the work of The Dirksen Congressional Center (Pekin, Illinois), a nonpartisan, nonprofit organization. Previously director of the Gerald R. Ford Library and Museum, he holds a PhD and an MA in American history from the University of Missouri and a BA from Drake University. Mackaman's publications include *Understanding Congressional Leadership, Gerald R. Ford: Presidential Perspectives from the National Archives* and *The Education of a Senator: Everett McKinley Dirksen.* He has taught courses on the presidency and Congress at the University of Michigan and Bradley University. Mackaman is past president of the Association of Centers for the Study of Congress.

PRAISE FOR *SEEKING BIPARTISANSHIP*

"Bipartisanship can work, and it should work better. Ray and I did it in Congress. My relationship with Ray is proof of that. He is a Republican; I am a Democrat. He came from downstate; I represented Chicago. He is a Lebanese American; I am a Jewish American. He supported John McCain in 2008; I supported Barack Obama. Despite all of this, we did not let what separated us prevent us from developing a great friendship. If we could work together, and we did, anything is possible. This much-needed book—not only for American politics but also for the American people and all who believe in democracy—is a brilliant account of how we can and should seek bipartisanship. It presents an important part of American history—when Democrats and Republicans reached across the aisle."

– Rahm Emanuel,
Mayor, City of Chicago

* * *

"Ray LaHood succeeded me in the House, and I could not be prouder. As his book makes clear, Ray earned the respect of Democrats and Republicans by the way he conducted himself and by his efforts to foster good will among members, particularly in the House. I found his account of the four "civility retreats" he helped to organize compelling and disheartening at the same time. I can only wish that his approach to politics and public service could be emulated throughout Congress today. He did one whale of a job for his district and for the country."

– Robert H. Michel,
U.S House of Representatives, 1957–1995

* * *

"There is something about the Peoria/Pekin area of Illinois that produces great statesmen: Everett Dirksen, Bob Michel, and Ray LaHood. LaHood's public service, as a key staff member to Michel, a longtime member of the House himself, and as Secretary of Transportation, reflected a fierce commitment to bipartisanship and a desire to make policy and solve problems for his constituents and the nation. His new book, written with Frank Mackaman, underscores those commitments and reflects on the seminal events that characterized and shaped a model career in public service. If we had more Ray LaHoods, we would not be so concerned about the deep, tribal dysfunction that now characterizes our politics."
– Norman J. Ornstein,
Resident Scholar, American Enterprise Institute
for Public Policy Research

* * *

"No one is better positioned than Ray LaHood to tell the story of why relationships within Congress have broken down in these last decades and what needs to be done to fix the system. A veteran political moderate who fought the good fight throughout his career, LaHood is a skilled storyteller, making the reader feel as if he is in the midst of the battles on the floor and in the cloakroom. This is a thoroughly entertaining memoir as well as an important one."
– Doris Kearns Goodwin,
Historian